Canada, the GATT and the International Trade System

Canada, the GATT and the International Trade System

FRANK STONE

Second Edition

Institute for Research on Public Policy/
Institut de recherche en politiques publiques

Canadian Cataloguing in Publication Data

Stone, Frank, 1923-1989.

Canada, the GATT and the international trade system
(second edition)

(Essays in international economics, ISSN 0826-4384)

Prefatory material in English and French.
Includes bibliographical references.
ISBN 0-88645-145-0

1. General Agreement on Tariffs and Trade (1947)
2. General Agreement on Tariffs and Trade
(Organization)   3. International economic relations.
4. Canada — Foreign economic relations.
I. Institute for Research on Public Policy.
II. Title.   III. Series.

HF1479.S67   1992   382′.92   C92-098626-9
74922

Production management and camera-ready copy by:
PDS Research Publishing Services Limited
P.O. Box 3296
Halifax, Nova Scotia
B3J 3H7

Published by:
The Institute for Research on Public Policy
1470 Peel Street, Suite 200
Montreal, Quebec
H3A 1T1

Contents

Foreword

The first edition of *Canada, the GATT and the International Trade System* by Frank Stone became an Institute classic. The preparation of this second edition, which Frank Stone had initiated, was interrupted by his death in December 1989.

Today the negotiation of trade agreements or the handling of trade disputes have become matters of broad public concern, and the community of Canadian scholars, policy makers, practitioners, and opinion leaders with an interest in international trade issues has expanded substantially during the last decade. This book is intended for them and for all those who knew and respected Frank Stone.

The second edition reproduces the first edition and includes three new chapters. The first of these chapters examines the pressures on the GATT-based trading system in the 1980s that shaped the agenda for the Uruguay Round of GATT negotiations and which will shape the trading system that emerges. The second chapter considers the relationship between the GATT and the Canada-U.S. Free Trade Agreement. The third chapter explores the linkages and interaction between international trading rules and environmental policies which constitute an important new set of challenges.

The book provides a comprehensive review throughout the post-war period of Canada's participation in the GATT-based trading system, as well as other organizations created to promote multilateral economic co-operation including the International Monetary Fund, the World Bank and the Organisation for Economic Co-operation and Development.

Beyond the historical contribution, the book provides many useful insights into the challenges faced in completing the Uruguay Round of GATT negotiations. Whatever the specific outcome of the Uruguay Round or the current North American Free Trade Negotiations, Frank Stone's book will continue to provide a valuable reference work for understanding the evolution of the international trading arrangements, which has such important implications for the Canadian economy and the formulation of public policy.

Monique Jérôme-Forget
President
March 1992

Avant-propos

L a première édition de *Canada, the GATT and the International Trade System*, de Frank Stone, est devenue l'un des classiques de l'Institut. La préparation de cette seconde édition, qui avait été commencée par Frank Stone, s'est trouvé interrompue par sa mort, en décembre 1989.

Aujourd'hui, la négociation des accords commerciaux et le règlement des différends qui surgissent en ce domaine sont devenus des sujets qui préoccupent le public dans son ensemble. Par ailleurs, le nombre de chercheurs, de responsables de l'élaboration des politiques, de professionnels et de chefs de file de l'opinion qui, au Canada, s'intéressent aux problèmes de commerce international, s'est prodigieusement accru durant la dernière décennie. Ce livre est publié à leur intention et à celle de ceux qui ont connu et estimé Frank Stone.

La seconde édition reproduit la première et y ajoute trois nouveaux chapitres. Le premier de ceux-ci est consacré à l'examen des pressions auxquelles se trouve soumis le système commercial basé sur le GATT, problèmes qui constituent l'ordre du jour des négociations de l'Uruguay Round et qui influenceront le nouvel ordre commercial en train d'émerger. Le second chapitre traite des relations entre le GATT et l'Accord de libre-échange américano-canadien. Le troisième examine les liens et l'interaction existant entre les règlements de commerce internationaux et les politiques environnementales, ce qui suscite un nouveau type de défis d'une grande importance.

Le livre présente un examen approfondi de la participation du Canada au

GATT, pour la période de l'après-guerre, de même qu'à d'autres organismes créés afin de promouvoir la coopération économique multilatérale, tels que le Fonds monétaire international, la Banque mondiale et l'Organisation de coopération et de développement économique.

Outre les renseignements d'ordre historique qu'il fournit, ce livre offre également des aperçus très utiles sur les défis rencontrés dans la conduite des négociations du GATT, à l'occasion de l'Uruguay Round. Quelle que soit l'issue particulière de l'Uruguay Round, ou celle des négociations actuelles concernant l'Accord de libre-échange nord-américain, le livre de Frank Stone demeurera un ouvrage de référence de valeur, facilitant la compréhension de l'évolution des mécanismes du commerce international, ce qui est d'une telle importance pour l'économie canadienne et pour l'élaboration des mesures de politique générale.

Monique Jérôme-Forget
Présidente
Mars 1992

The Author

Frank Stone graduated in 1949 from Queen's University, Kingston, Ontario, with a degree in Economics and History. During the Second World War he was a pilot in the Royal Air Force, and served in Britain, Western Europe and North Africa. After retiring from the Department of External Affairs, he began to teach and undertake research in international economics at The Norman Paterson School of International Affairs, Carleton University, Ottawa. He joined the International Economics Program of the Institute for Research on Public Policy in 1981 and continued as a Senior Research Associate in the Ottawa office until his death in 1989.

During his career with the Canadian Department of External Affairs, Mr. Stone acquired extensive experience in international trade and economic affairs. His foreign assignments included two tours of duty at the Permanent Mission to the United Nations in Geneva, Switzerland. From 1958 to 1961, as First Secretary at the Permanent Mission, he worked mainly on GATT affairs. From 1973 until 1977, as Minister at the Canadian Mission, he was responsible for Canadian interests in GATT, UNCTAD, and other international organizations in Geneva that are concerned with economic and trade issues. During 1963–69 he was Economic Counsellor at the Canadian Embassy in Washington. In the early 1970s, he was seconded to the Department of the Environment, where he coordinated the negotiations which led to the 1972 Canada-United States Agreement on Great Lakes Water Quality. He retired from the Department of External Affairs in 1979, after serving as Canada's Ambassador to Pakistan and Afghanistan.

In addition to having written the first edition of the present work, Mr. Stone is the author of a study entitled *The Consumer Interest in Canadian Trade Policy*, published by the Department of Consumer and Corporate Affairs, Ottawa, and was co-editor of *Building a Canadian-American Free Trade Area* and *Assessing the Canada-U.S. Free Trade Agreement* and was also co-author of *The Canadian Import File: Trade, Protection and Adjustment*.

Preface

Preparation of the second edition of *Canada, the GATT and the International Trade System* was complicated enormously by the untimely death of Frank Stone in December 1989. Frank had envisaged several chapters to substantially update and extend the first edition. Drafts of the three new chapters were completed by Frank, but these drafts required editing and annotation for publication. In addition, some of the factual material has been updated to take account of recent developments. Philip Rourke and Cai Wenguo have worked diligently and with care to provide these annotations and updates without altering the substantive aspects of Frank's work. Lynda Lennon orchestrated the preparation of the manuscript.

I hope that we have succeeded in preserving the essential spirit of Frank's work. From my association with him, I found Frank to be a keen scholar of the GATT, but he was also a thoughtful critic and a quiet yet firm advocate of institutional reform in the trading system.

Murray G. Smith

Préface

L a préparation de cette seconde édition de *Canada, the GATT and the International Trade System* a été énormément compliquée par le décès infortuné de Frank Stone, en décembre 1989. Frank avait envisagé de créer plusieurs chapitres, afin de procéder à une mise à jour importante et de compléter la première édition. Le brouillon de trois nouveaux chapitres a pu être réalisé par Frank, mais ces brouillons avaient besoin d'être révisés et annotés pour pouvoir être publiés. Par ailleurs, il a fallu remettre à jour certains renseignements concernant des faits, pour tenir compte d'éléments nouveaux. Philip Rourke et Cai Wenguo ont travaillé diligemment et avec soin pour apporter les annotations et les mises à jour nécessaires sans altérer le fond de l'œuvre de Frank. Lynda Lennon a coordonné la préparation du manuscrit.

J'espère que nous avons réussi à préserver l'essentiel de l'esprit qui animait l'ouvrage de Frank. Je sais d'expérience, pour avoir travaillé avec lui, que Frank était un spécialiste du GATT particulièrement averti. Il était également un critique éclairé de cet organisme et un partisan paisiblement déterminé d'une réforme institutionnelle du système commercial.

Murray G. Smith

1

Introduction

This study examines, from a Canadian perspective, the international agreements and institutions, largely within the United Nations (UN) framework, that represent the multilateral trade system.[1] The study focuses on the origins, structure and operation of the General Agreement on Tariffs and Trade (GATT),[2] which is the central element of that system. It also covers the trade-policy activities of the Organisation for Economic Co-operation and Development (OECD), the trade activities of the United Nations Conference on Trade and Development (UNCTAD), the international commodity agreements that have been concluded to deal with the special problems of trade in a number of primary products, and the trade-related functions of several other international agreements and institutions.

The institutions that made up the multilateral trade system represent the outcome of a succession of international negotiations over the post-Second World War period. The system constitutes a great advance in international co-operation over the anarchical conditions that characterized world-trade relationships during the inter-war period and, indeed, represents one of the most successful efforts in international co-operation of the post-war period. Canada has played a leading role in the creation and evolution of the system, especially in GATT and, in doing so, has demonstrated its very great interests in world trade; most of this trade it conducts with much larger trading countries. Chapter 2, which presents the background material for this study, examines Canada's trade relationships over the period before the Second

World War, and the final chapter includes an assessment of Canada's special interests in GATT.

The agreements and institutions that make up the multilateral trade system are complex, and they are becoming more so. There are available a number of excellent studies of the separate components of the system, but few treat these components together under one cover, and few examine these components from the perspective of Canada's role and interests in them. This study represents an attempt to provide such a comprehensive treatment. It is explanatory rather than judgemental; it does not pretend to be exhaustive or definitive, but rather to offer a guide through the system that will be of interest to the general reader, rather than to the trade-policy specialist. Throughout this work, there are references to more detailed and authoritative studies in the field.

Four distinct but closely related processes are evident in the operation of the multilateral trade system. One process comprises the continuous international discussion and consultation that take place, not only on world-trade-policy developments and issues, but also on the trade policies and practices of member countries. This process takes place in all elements of the system, among different groups of countries and in a variety of contexts. And Canada usually has a seat at the head table at all such international discussions of trade-policy matters.

A second process is represented by the progress that has been made, although very unevenly, in creating an open and liberal order for world trade. Since the Second World War, tariffs and other barriers to trade have been greatly reduced, especially by the industrialized countries; this has happened most recently as an outcome of the Kennedy Round in the mid-1960s and the Tokyo Round in the 1970s. Canada has benefited greatly from this process of world-trade liberalization and has made an appropriate contribution to it. But many barriers remain, some of which continue to affect adversely Canadian economic and trade interests.

A third process has been the maintenance and progressive enlargement of a common body of rules that govern the trade policies of member countries and their trade relations with one another. These rules have been put in place mainly, but not entirely, within the GATT framework. Although they have all too often been ignored or side-stepped, nevertheless they have provided valuable restraints and disciplines over the policies and practices of the member countries, especially the larger countries, which are more capable than smaller ones of following policies narrowly designed to serve their own interests.

A fourth process is the growing use of international facilities and procedures for the resolution of trade disputes. These procedures are most highly developed within the GATT system, where it is routine for the member countries to issue collective recommendations for the settlement of particular disputes, on the advice of independent panels appointed to assist them.

Effective international procedures for the settlement of trade disputes are of special interest to middle-sized and smaller countries, which are commonly at a disadvantage in negotiating their differences bilaterally with larger countries. The multilateral trade system is not presented in this study as offering an alternative approach to the pursuit of trade-policy objectives on a bilateral basis, but rather as providing a complementary approach. Essentially, the multilateral trade system, and especially GATT, provides an internationally accepted framework and set of common rules within which individual countries conduct their trade with one another. The multilateral rules do not preclude the development of special bilateral or regional, trading arrangements, but impose internationally accepted conditions on the form and operation of such arrangements.[3]

The multilateral trade system has come under severe strains during recent years of particularly adverse conditions in the world economy. New elements of protectionism have emerged, which, in some cases, involve a reversion to bilateral arrangements, outside the rules of GATT, to restrict trade. For the present, these elements stand in the way of further progress towards trade liberalization and of other efforts to achieve a more efficient and equitable world-trade system. Moreover, the increasing involvement of governments almost everywhere in domestic economic affairs has reinforced pressures on those governments to treat their international trade policies simply as extensions of domestic economic strategies, which are often narrowly defined. One general conclusion of this study is that Canada should regard the maintenance and progressive improvement of the multilateral trade system, in itself, as a major objective of Canadian trade policy. This suggestion was also one of the chief conclusions reached in the government's recently issued review of Canadian trade policy.[4]

Notes

1. The use of the term 'multilateral trade system' involves certain difficulties, partly of a semantic nature. The international agreements and institutions involved are, in fact, more concerned with trade policy than with the flow of actual trade; and it is questionable whether, collectively, they represent a 'system.' For the purposes of this study, however, the term is serviceable enough.

2. This study follows the usual practice of reserving the term 'GATT' to refer to the General Agreement as an institution. The accord itself is referred to as the 'General Agreement.'

3. For an insight into the conduct of Canada-United States (USA) trade relations within the multilateral trade system, see M.G. Clark "Canada-United States Trade Relations." A rather different, but not necessarily conflicting, assessment of opportunities for pursuing Canada-USA trade negotiations on a bilateral basis is in R. de C. Grey, *Trade Policy in the 1980s: An Agenda for Canadian-U.S. Relations*. Grey argues that in the future, bilateral, rather than multilateral,

negotiations may be a more successful way of dealing with remaining US tariff, and especially non-tariff, barriers to Canadian exports (pp. 6-8).

4. Canada, Department of External Affairs, *Canadian Trade Policy for the 1980s: A Discussion Paper*, pp. 35-40; Department of External Affairs, *A Review of Canadian Trade Policy: A Background Document to Canadian Trade Policy for the 1980s*, Chapter 7 and p. 239.

2

The Pre-War Background

E ven today, the collapse of world trade and the disintegration of the
world-trade framework that took place in the 1930s are often cited to warn
against weakening the multilateral trade system that has been constructed over
the post-war years. The GATT Director General, Mr. Arthur Dunkel, reminded
a Toronto audience in April 1981 that the architects of the General Agreement
on Tariffs and Trade "were determined that precisely the kind of stresses we
are experiencing today should not result in the panic-stricken run for cover
which led to the disasters of the 1930s."[1] The lessons and experience of the
inter-war years were, of course, fresh in the memories of the participants at the
post-war trade negotiations in 1947–48 from which GATT emerged, and they
shaped, in large measure, the structures and rules of the post-war multilateral
trade system. In the light of the severe trade problems Canada had experienced
during the depression years and a long history of difficulties in maintaining
satisfactory bilateral trade relationships with its main trade partners, particularly the United States (USA), Canada had good reason to join in efforts to
establish the new system.

The trading world that existed before the Second World War was particularly precarious for Canada. When the Great Depression struck, Canada was
more exposed than most countries. Then, even more than now, large areas of
its economy depended heavily on exports of a narrow range of agricultural and
other resource-based products. In the late 1920s, the world price of wheat and
other agricultural products collapsed in the face of import restrictions imposed

by most European countries. With the onset of the Depression, prices and world demand for industrial raw materials declined steeply. Between 1928 and 1932, the annual value of Canada's exports fell by more than half. Across the country, but particularly in export-oriented areas, the results were catastrophic in terms of unemployment and loss of income.[2]

The trade policies followed by Canada's two main trading partners, the United States and Britain, historically exerted fundamental influences on the nature and rate of Canada's economic development. Within bilateral relationships with these two major economic powers, however, the balance was severely tilted. While Canada made continuing attempts to influence the course of trade policy in London and Washington, its trade policies were largely adaptive and were pursued in response to external conditions and policies over which it had little control.[3] From the middle of the nineteenth century until the mid-1930s, Canada made continuing efforts to broaden its exports and improve access for them to the United States (US) market. Until the mid-1930s, however, except for a brief period before the First World War, the US market was surrounded by a wall of high protective tariffs, with some 'holes' for those primary products and raw materials in short supply or not produced in the USA. Britain, on the other hand, followed opposite policies of free trade until the early 1930s; and Canada made continuing and largely unsuccessful efforts for several generations, to induce Britain to change course and provide preferential access for Canadian exports by imposing tariff and other barriers to competing imports from non-Empire sources. To encourage Britain to change its trade policies, Canada, from the beginning of the twentieth century, granted lower preferential customs duties on British goods and extended somewhat similar preferential arrangements to other Empire countries. These preferential arrangements created further obstacles to the development of more open, bilateral, trade relationships with the United States. On the import side, partly in response to continuing high US tariffs, Canada raised its own customs duties in order to shelter its infant manufacturing sector from import competition. These higher tariffs were a prominent feature of Sir John A. Macdonald's 'National Policy' of the 1870s, on the basis of which nation building was to proceed. Even the lower preferential duties on British and other Empire goods were generally high enough to give a good measure of protection to Canada's manufacturing sector. Looking back from the present time, Canada's pre-war trade policies appear to have been not only largely defensive, but also complex and contradictory. This may explain why earlier trade policies and strategies, in contrast to those of the post-war period, gave rise to continuing domestic conflict and political controversy.

Canada-United States Trade Relations

Between 1854 and 1866, a 'Reciprocity Treaty' was in effect between the United States and the British provinces in North America, providing tariff-free bilateral trade for most agricultural and other 'natural' products, but not for manufactured goods. In 1866 the USA terminated this treaty for several reasons, including frictions arising from the American Civil War and resentment over an increase in protective tariffs which the Province of Canada imposed on manufactured goods just prior to Confederation. The main reason for the collapse of tariff-free bilateral trade, however, was that this arrangement ran counter to new, and more severe, protectionist, trade policies that were introduced by the US government at the beginning of the 1860s, and that remained in place until the mid-1930s.[4] Thus, for about seventy years, the two countries imposed their highest tariff rates against each other's imports, and these rates were usually very high indeed, especially on the US side. Repeated efforts were made by one country or the other to correct this unneighbourly state of affairs, but these attempts were unsuccessful, chiefly because of the opposition of Congress to breaching the wall of US import protection. In 1911, however, it was opposition in Canada that blocked the conclusion of a Canada-United States 'reciprocal' trade agreement that would have lowered barriers to bilateral trade.[5]

On both sides there were some gaps in the barriers to bilateral trade. US tariffs were removed or reduced to low levels for a range of needed, industrial, raw and semi-processed goods such as newsprint and other forest products, non-ferrous metals and asbestos; and these goods comprised most of Canada's exports to the United States. On the Canadian side, free entry or low rates of duty were extended for industrial machinery and equipment used by industry or by farmers under a system of 'duty remissions.' On the other hand, both countries used various administrative measures to increase the protective effects of their tariffs. Early in the twentieth century, Canada invented a system of special 'dumping' duties on goods that were exported at prices lower than those charged in the country of export, and refined a system for increasing the declared value of imported goods, which could be used to give additional protection by increasing the amount of the customs duty; these features of Canada's customs tariff were aimed primarily at the United States.[6] For its part, the USA also employed a variety of administrative measures, deployed by its customs service, to create additional obstacles to imports; and these were the subject of continuing objections by Canada.[7]

During most of the inter-war period, the United States followed import policies that were especially damaging to Canadian trade interests. Legislation passed by Congress in the early 1920s and in 1930 raised US tariffs to unprecedented heights: after the increases in 1930, the average rate on dutiable imports stood at almost 50 per cent. To quote a leading authority on Canada-USA trade relations during this period:

> On the southern front developments during the twenties were most unfavourable to Canadian trade. The United States was undergoing one of those periods of high protection, which always have had severe

repercussions on Canada. Under the Underwood Tariff of 1913, Canada enjoyed relatively favourable tariff treatment for its goods imported into the United States, especially in respect of agricultural products. The situation changed drastically with the coming into force of the Emergency Tariff of 1921 and the Fordney-McCumber Tariff a year later. These restored the level of protection existing before 1913. They were, however, only a prelude. High-tariff sentiment continued to be dominant in the United States and eventually found expression in the enactment of the Hawley-Smoot Tariff of 1930, which raised American rates of Duty to the highest level in history. Together with the introduction of certain revenue duties in 1932, the new tariff barriers effectively shut off Canadian exports to the United States of live cattle, lumber, copper, dairy products, potatoes and a number of fish products.[8]

The historic reversal of US trade policies which took place in 1934 will be discussed below. But the Hawley-Smoot tariff increases, imposed by the USA in 1930, provoked many other countries, including Canada, to raise new barriers to their imports, partly in retaliation and partly in efforts to protect domestic markets and employment after the onset of the Great Depression. In 1931 and 1932, Canadian tariffs were substantially increased; the average rate on dutiable imports rose from about 23 per cent to about 28 per cent.[9]

British Preferences

Beginning about 1900, Canada introduced a system of lower preferential tariffs on goods from Britain and the British colonies, partly in order to encourage Britain to introduce a system of customs duties from which Canadian exports would be exempt, and partly in order to counter protests in Canada, especially by Western farmers, against high Canadian duties on imports of manufactured goods.[10] These (British Preferential) 'BP rates' initially involved an across-the-board reduction of the general tariff rates for imports from Britain, but this system was soon changed to differential reductions for individual products. Canada exerted continuing pressure for recipro- cal preferences in the British market and was supported by influential groups in Britain, which favoured a comprehensive system of imperial preferences; but Britain continued its free-trade policies generally until the 1930s, and Canada meanwhile gained few advantages for its exports to Britain in ex- change for the preferences it extended on British goods. From early in the twentieth century, Canada extended its BP rates to other countries of the Empire, and gradually, most of these countries introduced preferential tariff systems of their own that applied to their imports from Canada.

In 1907 Canada introduced an 'intermediate' tariff schedule, with rates set, for the most part, between the higher 'general' rates and the lower BP rates, as a basis for the negotiation of trade agreements with non-British countries.

These intermediate rates were extended to a number of European and other countries with which Canada progressively concluded trade agreements over the pre-war period; these agreements were generally based on the most-favoured-nation (MFN) principle.[11] As noted below, the intermediate rates were accorded to imports from the United States as a result of the Canada-USA trade agreement of 1935, in exchange for MFN treatment and certain other concessions on the US side. The intermediate rates thus evolved into the MFN schedule in Canada's present tariff structure.

The Ottawa Agreements of 1932

Canada took the lead in organizing a conference of Commonwealth governments in Ottawa in 1932, primarily with the objective of helping the recovery of Canada's exports by obtaining greater preferential access to Commonwealth markets, especially in Britain.[12] In 1931 Britain had abandoned its traditional policy of free trade and imposed a duty, of 10 per cent on all imports except wheat, meat and a few raw materials. Imports from Commonwealth sources, however, were exempted from this duty, pending the outcome of the Ottawa Conference. The series of agreements concluded among Commonwealth countries at Ottawa represented a substantial extension and consolidation of the British preferential system, although the results fell far short of anything resembling a Commonwealth free-trade area, and there were no undertakings to move closer to free trade within the Commonwealth. Britain continued to give duty-free treatment to most imports from Canada and other Commonwealth sources, although quantitative limits were imposed on a few agricultural products. Elsewhere within the BP system, tariff preferences were broadened and enlarged for products on agreed lists, which were not uniform.

The British preferential system was enlarged in the early 1930s more by increasing the tariffs of the participants on imports from outside sources than by liberalizing trade among the participants. Accordingly, the existing level of protection for domestic Canadian industries was hardly decreased and was probably increased overall. The British preferential system was thus highly 'trade diverting' rather than 'trade creating.' Much of the increase in inter-Commonwealth trade that followed was at the expense of outside countries.

The Ottawa agreements represented a further erosion of the MFN principle in international trade and were criticized on these grounds by outside countries, although the United States accepted these preferences as a legitimate exception to the MFN rule.[13] In any event, most countries disregarded the MFN principle during the 1930s. The Ottawa agreements had an adverse effect on broader international efforts, within the League of Nations framework, to arrest the spread of protectionism and discrimination; indeed, at a later stage, during the Second World War, they became a main target of US policies which led to the establishment of the GATT system. One feature of the Ottawa agreements created particular difficulties in the negotiation of trade agreements with outside countries and in the later GATT negotiations; this was the 'binding' of the degree of preference conferred. Where preferential margins were bound, MFN and other higher rates could not be decreased without a corresponding decrease in the preferential rate, made to preserve the 'margin of preference.'

The Ottawa agreements were also criticized in Canada. Mackenzie King, then Leader of the Opposition, whose government would later join in the war-time and post-war efforts to establish a multilateral trade system, charged that the Ottawa agreements

> . . . have increased restrictions; they have raised barriers; they have made trade more difficult in this country than it was before, more difficult as between parts of the British Empire, more difficult as between the different countries of the world . . . . [I]nstead of freedom and peace, their action was more in the direction of economic war.[14]

The British (UK) preferential tariff system was an established feature of world trade, despite strong US efforts to dismantle it, when the multilateral trade system was being designed and put into place at the end of the Second World War. In the post-war years, Canada's preferential access to British and other Commonwealth markets provided a valuable basis for the restoration of Canadian exports to those markets and the diversification of those exports into a broader range of processed and manufactured products. The existence of preferences also provided additional bargaining leverage in post-war GATT negotiations when Canada and other Commonwealth countries tried to secure reductions in US tariffs and in those of other countries; even so, the results often took the form of reductions in the MFN tariffs of Commonwealth countries rather than that of a reduction of preferential margins, and thus the preferences were left largely intact. However, the United States succeeded in writing into the GATT rules provisions that no new preferences could be introduced, and that existing preferences could not be increased.[15]

The US Reciprocal Trade Agreements Act of 1934

President Roosevelt's Administration came to power in 1933, with a pledge to fight the Depression by increasing US exports rather than by restricting imports, and generally to pursue a policy of world-trade liberalization. The Reciprocal Trade Agreements Act of 1934 was the legislative basis for this historic reversal of US trade policy and the basis, also, for the later initiatives that led to the creation of the post-war multilateral trade system.[16]

The new legislation reflected a growing recognition in the United States that the excessively high US tariffs damaged not only the interests of other countries, but also the interests of its own industry and agriculture; and that it would serve US interests to seek a general reduction of tariff and other trade barriers throughout the trading world. Departing from traditional practice, the Act made the US tariff negotiable. Congress delegated to the President the authority to reduce US tariffs and enter into other commitments, for specified short periods of time and within limits set out in the legislation, in return for 'reciprocal' tariff reductions and concessions by other countries that would benefit US exports. Under new trade agreements with foreign countries, the President could reduce US tariffs by up to 50 per cent without further reference to Congress. With certain exceptions, trade agreements concluded under the Act were required to be on the basis of unconditional MFN treatment. Under the 1934 legislation or its extensions, the United States negotiated or renegotiated a series of bilateral trade agreements with over twenty countries for the reduction of tariffs and other trade barriers, including two agreements it made with Canada in 1935 and in 1938.[17]

Canadian Negotiations with the USA and Britain, 1934–1938

Canada was among the first countries to respond to the new US trade legislation. After some delays, Mackenzie King's incoming government concluded a bilateral trade agreement with the United States in 1935. The striking of this agreement—the first such since 1866—opened a new era of co-operation in trade between the two countries. Canada granted its lower 'intermediate' (that is, MFN) tariff rates to imports from the USA, rather than the higher 'general' rates that it had previously imposed. In return, Canada obtained MFN treatment by the United States, as well as useful reductions in certain US tariffs on Canadian export products, although quantitative quota limits were imposed on a few products. Thus, for the first time, the two countries exchanged MFN treatment, even though, in this respect, the agreement was somewhat one-sided, since the USA accepted that the British preferences in the Canadian tariff system were a legitimate exception to the MFN rule. The United States, for its part, continued for a period to give certain tariff preferences to Cuba.

The rather limited 1935 agreement was further extended by a second round of more comprehensive negotiations in 1938. Meanwhile Canada had renegotiated its 1932 trade agreement with Britain, in part to obtain releases from commitments to preserve bound margins of preference, and had thus gained greater scope to negotiate with the United States.[18] The 1938 negotiations were 'triangular,' in that the Canada-USA negotiations took place simultaneously with US-UK trade negotiations. These 1938 negotiations not only further liberalized trade among the three countries, but also set a pattern for future negotiations under GATT, since they involved a rudimentary 'multilateralization' of bilateral negotiations. Thus, for example, Canada agreed to a reduction of British preferences for Canadian lumber exports to Britain, in exchange for US agreement to reduce its own duties on lumber, which benefited Canadian exports. Nevertheless, the Canadian and British negotiations with the United

States were complicated and made more difficult by the existence of the preferences exchanged among Commonwealth countries at the 1932 Ottawa Conference, although the USA accepted these preferences as an exception to the MFN rule.

League of Nations Efforts in Trade Areas

The series of US bilateral agreements under the 1934 Trade Act led to a significant liberalization of trade among the countries concerned, but these changes came too late to repair an overall record of failure to preserve a liberal trade system during the inter-war period. Within the League of Nations framework, a series of international conferences was held, beginning in the early 1920s. These conferences were aimed at dismantling the trade barriers put in place by many countries during the First World War, at holding back the trend toward greater trade protection during the 1920s, and at preventing the collapse of the trade system during the early 1930s.[19] While some useful conventions on administrative trade controls were concluded among certain groups of countries, it was not possible to achieve co-operative action in broader and more fundamental trade and monetary areas.

In 1927 the League convened a World Economic Conference in an effort to replace systems of quantitative trade controls, maintained by many European countries since the First World War, with import systems based on customs tariffs, combined with concerted action to reduce excessive tariffs and prevent further tariff increases. This Conference adopted a series of recommendations to reduce tariffs and control the use of non-tariff measures within a framework of long-term, bilateral, trade agreements based on unconditional and unrestricted MFN treatment. Some liberalization of trade within western Europe resulted, and for several years world trade generally expanded. Further progress in trade liberalization was soon blocked, however, by a depression of world agriculture and by the prospect of further and formidable increases in US tariffs. By early 1930, the Great Depression had set in, resulting in a global escalation of protectionist trade measures.

In the early 1930s, efforts within the League to restrain the spread of trade protection were largely unsuccessful. In 1933 the League convened a major world Monetary and Economic Conference in London, with an agenda covering the linked problems of international debt, monetary stabilization, and tariff and trade barriers. This Conference broke down, however, on the central issue of monetary stabilization, and the League reported: "The breakdown of the negotiations confirmed the trend towards economic nationalism and discouraged further attempts to salvage the world trading system through general multilateral agreement."[20]

Canada played a minor and generally unhelpful role in League of Nations efforts during the inter-war period to improve and advance international co-operation in trade and economic areas.[21] In the Canadian view, the trade and economic work of the League was of secondary importance. Further, Canada regarded tariffs and other trade measures as internal matters that were outside the mandate of the League; it considered that problems in these areas should be dealt with primarily through bilateral negotiations between the countries concerned, outside the League framework. Canada's approach to this aspect of the League's work was doubtless shaped, in part, by the fact that its largest trading partner and the world's foremost economic power, the USA, was not a League member.

Thus Canada opposed several initiatives in the League during the 1920s to deal with widespread controls and taxes on exports of raw materials. At the 1927 World Economic Conference, the Canadian delegate informed his colleagues that many Members of Parliament at Ottawa had been asking, "Who are these people at Geneva who are presuming to give us advice on our own tariffs?"[22] Prime Minister Bennett attended the 1933 Monetary and Economic Conference in London, but his comments on trade matters were directed mainly at justifying preferential arrangements within the British Commonwealth and questioning the validity of the MFN rule. After the mid-1930s, however, Canada's approach to international co-operation in trade and economic matters became more positive. Prime Minister King, at the League Assembly in 1936, applauded efforts within the League "to combat the economic nationalism and the endless devices of control which are strangling international trade."

In 1933 Canada also played a more constructive role—indeed a leading role—in the negotiation within the League framework of the first International Wheat Agreement. This agreement was concluded by the main exporting countries (United States, Canada, Australia and Argentina) together with thirteen importing countries; its objective was to raise world wheat prices through quota arrangements which were designed to reduce existing levels of production and stocks. The 1933 agreement was in some respects, the 'grandfather' of future international commodity agreements involving both exporting and importing countries that were concluded after the Second World War within the framework of United Nations and of UNCTAD.[23]

The outbreak of the Second World War in 1939 introduced a whole new set of controls and distortions within the world-trade system. With leadership from Washington, however, new concepts were discussed in the early 1940s, among the United States, Britain and Canada, for post-war co-operation in world trade, within a broader United Nations system for international co-operation in political, social and economic areas. These post-war efforts to create a multilateral trade system proceeded on the basis of the experience and lessons of the inter-war period. Moreover, despite the relative lack of success of the League of Nations in trade areas, precedents had been established for trying to deal with trade-policy issues within a framework of multilateral negotiations; and the body of analysis of trade-policy issues that emerged from successive trade conferences and from the League Secretariat made an essential contribution to the successful creation of a post-war multilateral framework for trade co-operation within GATT.[24]

Notes

1. Address by Mr. Arthur Dunkel, Director-General of GATT, at the World Trade Centre, Toronto, 3 April 1981; reprinted in *Import-week* 71 (8 April 1981).

2. An historical analysis of Canadian economic problems, issues and policies before the Second World War is in W.A. Mackintosh, *The Economic Background of Dominion-Provincial Relations*. Chapter 6 contains an account of the consequences of the Depression for Canadian trade and the Canadian economy.

3. For a detailed account of Canada's pre-war commercial relations, see O.J. McDiarmid, *Commercial Policy in the Canadian Economy*. Mackintosh, in Chapter 7, *Economic Background*, examines Canada's pre-war tariff policy with particular attention to its effects on the various regions of Canada. An historical account of Canadian tariff policy before 1939 is in J.H. Young, *Canadian Commercial Policy*, Chapters 3 and 4.

4. A detailed study of this treaty is in D.C. Masters, *The Reciprocity Treaty of 1854*.

5. For an account of the efforts made in 1911 to conclude a reciprocal Canada-USA trade agreement, see McDiarmid, *Commercial Policy*, pp. 228-38; a detailed study is in L.E. Ellis, *Reciprocity, 1911: A Study in Canadian-American Relations*.

6. Detailed historical studies of the Canadian customs system, although somewhat out of date, are in G.A. Elliott, *Tariff Procedures and Trade Barriers: A Study of Indirect Protection in Canada and the United States*; and G. Blake, *Customs Administration in Canada: An Essay in Tariff Technology*.

7. Some of these administrative obstacles in the US customs system, as they existed in the 1940s, were noted in W. Plumptre, "Exports to the United States" in J.D. Gibson (ed.), *Canada's Economy in a Changing World*, pp. 208-43.

8. L.D. Wilgress, *Canada's Approach to Trade Negotiations*, p. 7.

9. See Economic Council of Canada, *Looking Outward: A New Trade Strategy for Canada*, p. 4, for a chart comparing average nominal rates of duty imposed by Canada and the United States, 1869–1973.

10. A detailed study, from a Canadian perspective, of the origins, structure and operation of the British preferential system is in D.R. Annett, *British Preference in Canadian Commercial Policy*.

11. For an account of the introduction of the intermediate tariff, see McDiarmid, *Commercial Policy*, pp. 221-24. For Canadian pre-war trade agreements with non-British countries other than the United States, see McDiarmid, *Commercial Policy*, pp. 268-70.

12. See Annett, *British Preference*, pp. 57-71, for an account of the Imperial Eco-

nomic Conference held in Ottawa in 1932. See also Wilgress, *Canada's Approach*, pp. 7-8 and D. Wilgress, *Memoirs*, pp. 94-96.

13. The MFN clause has a long history in trade agreements, and is a basic principle of the General Agreement on Tariffs and Trade, as among its members. (See Chapter 4, below.) In general, this clause requires that the country assuming the obligation shall not treat other parties to the agreement less generously than it treats any third country, with respect to the measures covered by the clause. For an analysis of the principles and issues involved, see H.C. Hawkins, *Commercial Treaties and Agreements; Principles and Practice*, pp. 60-87. The application of the MFN principle in Canada's pre-war bilateral trade agreements was complicated by the tariff preferences exchanged with other British Commonwealth countries: see, for example, McDiarmid, *Commercial Policy*, Chapters 9 and 12; and Wilgress, *Canada's Approach*, Chapter 2.

14. Annett, *British Preference*, p. 69.

15. See Wilgress, *Canada's Approach*, p. 17.

16. For a study of the Reciprocal Trade Agreements Act of 1934 and its operation until the late 1940s, see J.M. Letiche, *Reciprocal Trade Agreements in the World Economy*.

17. It was under an extension of the Reciprocal Trade Agreements Act, in 1945, that the USA launched and joined in the post-war multilateral negotiations that led to the conclusion of the General Agreement on Tariffs and Trade. Under subsequent extensions of the basic legislation, as amended in one way or another, the USA participated in follow-up GATT rounds of tariff negotiations until 1962. A pattern was established, which has continued to be a feature of the GATT system, by which the timing, and also the scope, of GATT tariff and trade negotiations is largely determined by the timing and scope of US trade legislation. On several occasions, Congress has overridden US undertakings entered into by the Administration under the authority of the Reciprocal Trade Agreements Act, as well as successor legislation, by subsequently adopting conflicting trade legislation.

18. Wilgress, *Canada's Approach*, pp. 8-13, contains brief accounts of the Canada-USA trade agreement of 1935, the 1937 revision of the Canada-United Kingdom (UK) trade agreement, and the 1938 trade agreements between Canada and the USA, and between the USA and the UK. A more detailed account of the 1938 Canada-USA negotiations is in J.L. Granatstein, *A Man of Influence: Norman A. Robertson and Canadian Statecraft 1929–1968*, Chapter 3.

19. An historical survey by the League of Nations Secretariat of commercial policy problems in the inter-war years, and of international efforts within and outside the League to deal with these issues is in League of Nations, *Commercial Policy in the Inter-war Period: International Proposals and National Policies*. An analytical study of these issues, with prescriptions for dealing with them in the post-war period, is in League of Nations, *Commercial Policy in the Post-War World: Report of the Economic and Financial Committees*.

20. League of Nations, *Commercial Policy in the Post-War World*, p. 17.

21. For an account of Canadian participation in the League of Nations, see R. Veatch, *Canada and the League of Nations*; also S.M. Eastman, *Canada at Geneva: An Historical Survey and its Lessons*.

22. Eastman, *Canada at Geneva*, p. 32.

23. See C.F. Wilson, *Grain Marketing in Canada*, for an account of the International Wheat Agreement of 1933. See also C. Nappi, *Commodity Market Controls: A Historical Review*, pp. 36-37.

24. The contribution made by the League of Nations to the development of the post-war trade system is evident in the 1945 report of its Economic and Financial Committees, published in League of Nations, *Commercial Policy in the Post-War World*. These committees finished their report at a meeting in Princeton, New Jersey, in 1945; the members included W.C. Clark and Louis Rasminsky of Canada, who both played prominent roles in the post-war creation of the International Monetary Fund, the International Bank for Reconstruction and Development (World Bank) and GATT. Dr. Clark was Deputy Minister of Finance during the early post-war period. Mr. Rasminsky served at a later date as Governor of the Bank of Canada.

3

The Post-War Multilateral Trade System: Origins and Main Elements

During 1946–48 a set of international negotiations took place within the new United Nations (UN) framework for the purpose of putting into place a new order for international co-operation in world trade. This order was intended to replace the pre-war network of bilateral trade agreements, reduce or prohibit the high tariffs, quantitative restrictions and other barriers that had blocked world trade during the Depression years, and eliminate or reduce discriminatory trade arrangements. These negotiations led to the drawing up, in early 1948, of the Havana Charter, which contained a comprehensive set of rules for international trade and would have established a formal International Trade Organization (ITO) as a companion to the already established International Monetary Fund (IMF) and the International Bank for Reconstruction and Development (World Bank). As a result of these negotiations, in late 1947, a smaller group of twenty-three of of the world's leading trading countries, including Canada, adopted the General Agreement on Tariffs and Trade as an interim arrangement, pending the coming into force of the Havana Charter and the establishment of the ITO. The General Agreement represented a truncated version of the Havana Charter, but it contained the central provisions covering the conduct of trade. The adoption of the General Agreement also involved negotiations among the twenty-three countries for the reduction of their tariffs on a most-favoured-nation (MFN) basis—the first of the seven rounds of multilateral trade negotiations that have been held under GATT over the preceding thirty-five years.

The Havana Charter never came into force, and the ITO was not established, largely because of opposition within the United States (US) Congress; and GATT, which was designed as an interim arrangement, has served as the central element of the multilateral trade system. Over the years, the trade rules in the General Agreement that were carried over from the Havana Charter have been extended and strengthened in various ways, and GATT, as an institution, has come to resemble the proposed ITO, although the General Agreement still lacks a number of major provisions that appeared in the Havana Charter, and GATT still lacks the solid institutional base that the ITO would have enjoyed.

Over the following years, other international institutions and agreements were put into place, both inside and outside the United Nations framework, to fill some of the gaps in the world-trade system as it had been originally designed, or to respond to new developments and issues in world trade. These include the United Nations Conference on Trade and Development (UNCTAD); a number of international commodity agreements among groups of producer and consumer countries (for wheat, tin, coffee, sugar, cocoa, natural rubber and jute); and the activities relating to trade policy of the Organisation for Economic Co-operation and Development (OECD). In addition, a variety of organizations within the United Nations system make important contributions to the operating of the world-trade system; these organizations include the International Monetary Fund (IMF), the World Bank, the Food and Agriculture Organization (FAO), and the UN regional economic commissions.

Within this array of international institutions and agreements concerned with trade matters, GATT remains the central and strongest element. The focus of this chapter is, accordingly, on the origins of GATT, its underlying concepts and principles, its basic structure, and its operation. The following chapter will review the main rules for world trade provided by GATT, and other elements of the GATT system. Other chapters will examine the origins, purposes and operations of other institutions and agreements which form part of the multilateral trade system.

Origins of GATT

The concept of a 'multilateral' trade system emerged in Washington during the Second World War, where it was recognized by the Administration that the United States (USA), as the world's foremost economic power, carried primary responsibility for planning the post-war international trade system. The Administration also recognized that post-war US trade interests would be advanced by a general reduction of tariffs and other barriers to world trade, and by the reduction of preferential trade arrangements that discriminated against US exports, such as those existing among Canada and other Commonwealth countries within the British Preferential (BP) system. A post-war trade system that would lessen the risk of trade conflicts was also regarded as essential to broader efforts within the United Nations to maintain world peace in the future. On the initiative of the USA, general undertakings to create a multilateral, liberal and non-discriminatory trade system were written into the Atlantic Charter as early as 1941, and were also inserted into lend-lease agreements with Britain ad other countries.[1]

More specific proposals for a post-war trade system were developed in war-time discussions with Britain and Canada, and were issued by the USA in 1946 as "Proposals for Expansion of World Trade and Employment."[2] These Proposals called for the convening of a United Nations Conference on Trade and Employment, for the purposes of negotiating an international trade agreement and establishing an international trade organization.

In February 1946 the UN Economic and Social Council, at its first session, set up a Preparatory Committee of eighteen countries, including Canada, to draft an agenda and to make other preparations for the planned UN Conference on Trade and Employment. Over the following months, the USA elaborated and circulated a "Suggested Charter" for an International Trade Organization. This Charter was adopted as a basis for discussion by the Preparatory Committee, now enlarged to include twenty-three countries, when it met for its first session, in London, in October–November 1946. The Preparatory Committee debated the draft Charter in detail and convened for a second session in Geneva during April–August 1947. From this session, a further revision of the draft Charter emerged for presentation to the UN Conference, which was scheduled to open in Havana in November.

The US "Proposals" had also called for separate and prior tariff negotiations among a smaller group of countries, as a contribution to the success of the UN Conference. These prior negotiations would carry out "negotiations on trade barriers . . . [and] get down to cases, seeking to reduce tariffs, to eliminate preferences, and to lighten or remove other barriers to trade" (p. 7). Concurrently with the second session of the Preparatory Committee in Geneva, negotiations among the same group of twenty-three countries took place for the reduction of tariffs, as well as the preparation of the more limited "General Agreement on Tariffs and Trade," which would include as annexes the results of the tariff negotiations. Canada carried out tariff negotiations with seven of the participating countries, but is main negotiations were with the United States.

The General Agreement not only covered the results of the tariff negotiations, but also contained a truncated version of the draft Charter for the proposed ITO. Its articles were drawn chiefly from the central chapter of the draft Charter, titled "Commercial Policy"; they set out the basic commitments to the most-favoured-nation principle, as well as rules governing the use of trade-policy measures such as national treatment of internal taxation, the valuation of goods for customs purposes, quantitative restrictions, subsidies, anti-dumping and countervailing duties, and state trading. The General Agreement did not contain other provisions in the draft Charter, which dealt with employment, international investment, restrictive business practices, international commodity agreements, and the establishment of the International Trade Organization. In selecting the provisions of the draft Charter for inclusion in the General Agreement, the US delegation tried to limit the choice to those that the Administration could implement under existing trade legislation, and that would not require further approval by Congress.

On 30 October 1947, the General Agreement on Tariffs and Trade was signed by all the participants at the Geneva negotiations, it came into effect at the beginning of January 1948. While the General Agreement contains no expiry date, it was considered at the time as an interim document that would be superseded by the Charter that was to be adopted at the Havana Conference and would come into force following ratification by its signatories.

As noted above, during the spring and summer of 1947, while the Geneva tariff negotiations were under way, and while the General Agreement on Tariffs and Trade was being concluded, the same delegations were putting the finishing touches on the more comprehensive draft Charter for the proposed ITO; it was this Charter that was to be presented at the United Nations Conference on Trade and Employment when it opened in Havana later in the year. This Havana Conference was attended by most of the sixty-one members of the United Nations, although the Soviet Union was absent. It finished its work in March 1948, having produced the completed Charter.[3]

The Havana Charter required separate approval by the US Congress, but various groups in the United States combined to oppose it. Protectionists protested that under the Charter, the United States would lose control over its trade policies. Advocates of a liberal system objected that there were too many loopholes and exceptions in the new trade rules. Defenders of free enterprise protested that the Charter would lead to state control over the economy and to socialism. In Congress there were objections that responsibility for trade policy would be transferred to the Administration. Officials in the Administration, having achieved most of their objectives in the form of the General Agreement and in the recently concluded Geneva tariff negotiations, progressively backed away from a confrontation with opposing elements in Congress; and in 1950 the Administration quietly withdrew the Charter from its legislative program.[4] Other countries, including Canada, took no action to ratify the Charter when it failed to obtain ratification by the United States.

Thus the GATT, rather than the proposed ITO, has served as the central element in the multilateral trade system. Several attempts were made in subsequent years to establish a more comprehensive international trade organization along the lines planned for the ITO, but these did not succeed, partly because of US opposition. The multilateral trade system has been enlarged over the years in less structured ways, partly by extending the GATT system, and partly by creating new trade bodies outside GATT.

Canada's Interests

The US design for a post-war multilateral trade system was well in line with Canadian trade-policy objectives, as well as with broader Canadian concepts of international co-operation within the new United Nations framework. The US "Proposals" represented a confirmation of the liberal trade policies adopted by the United States during the mid-1930s and embodied in the 1934 Reciprocal Trade Agreements Act; on the basis of this Act, Canada had concluded trade agreements with the USA in 1935 and 1938. In negotiations under the new multilateral rules, Canada could expect further tariff and other concessions by the United States, as well as by other countries, which would be all the greater because of the combined leverage of the participating countries. Any losses Canada suffered in preferential access to British and other Commonwealth markets would be compensated by concessions made by the USA and other countries. The new trade rules, moreover, would allow the continuation of traditional policies of tariff protection, especially for Canada's secondary manufacturing industries, although some tariff cuts would have to be made. The new multilateral trade rules, while limiting Canada's freedom of action, were generally in line with Canadian practices and would serve as valuable constraints on the United States and other larger countries. Canada could expect to play an important role in the new system, on the basis of its important place in the post-war world economy; and the new multilateral system would give Canada greater influence in world trade than would a system based on bilateral agreements.

Thus Canada gave positive support from the beginning to the US initiatives for a post-war multilateral trade system and for an early round of tariff negotiations, pending the entry into force of the ITO Charter.[5] In the 1947 Geneva tariff negotiations, those between Canada and the United States were the most important of any that took place. The outcome of the Geneva tariff negotiations and the conclusion of the General Agreement on Tariffs and Trade were regarded by the Canadian government as highly satisfactory. On 17 November 1947, Prime Minister King, in a radio broadcast from London, stated:

> I can think of no recent event more encouraging for the future than the successful conclusion of the General Agreement . . . . In the Agreement . . . there are incorporated the results of the most comprehensive, significant and far-reaching negotiations ever undertaken in the history of the world trade . . . . The Agreement clearly charts out long-run course.[6]

The new General Agreement superseded Canada's 1938 trade agreement with the United States. On the day the General Agreement was signed, Canada and the USA signed a supplementary agreement to the effect that the 1938 trade agreement would "remain inoperative" and would come back into effect only in the event that either country should withdraw from the General Agreement.[7] Thus, for thirty-five years, the General Agreement has served as Canada's main trade agreement with the United States.

When the General Agreement was signed, Canada and Britain also exchanged notes that released each other from any contractual obligations with respect to existing margins of tariff preferences; this arrangement allowed both countries to implement reductions in their MFN tariff rates for products covered by these tariff preferences.[8] This release from commitments to maintain particular margins of preferences, in itself, represented a significant contribution towards trade liberalization and the success of the Geneva negotiations.

Main Elements of GATT

GATT is not merely an international treaty containing a set of rules for trade; it has also evolved to serve many of the institutional and other functions that would have been given to the ITO, if it had come into being. The General Agreement has now attracted a membership of eighty-nine countries; one other has acceded provisionally, and a further twenty-nine countries apply GATT rules to the conduct of their trade on a *de facto* basis. Together these countries account for about four-fifths of world trade. All of the industrialized countries and most of the developing countries, as well as five East European state-trading countries are members of GATT. Non-members include the Soviet Union, China, East Germany, Venezuela, Mexico and most Middle East oil-producing countries; but indirectly, the GATT rules also influence, in one way or another, the conduct of the international trade of non-members.

The GATT system, like the proposed Havana Charter/ITO system, rests on the underlying body of economic theory which holds that international trade serves to increase global prosperity, as well as the prosperity of individual trading countries. It rests, too, on the concept that an orderly trade system governed by widely accepted rules for world trade lessens the risks of trade wars and thus is an essential part of broader efforts to maintain durable world peace and stability.

The GATT system can be considered as serving the following five distinct functions:

- GATT provides a permanent framework for continuing international consultations on world-trade-policy developments and problems, and the evolving trade policies and practices of individual member countries.

- The General Agreement provides a common set of rules for the conduct of trade, which constrain and discipline the trade policies and practices of individual member countries. The several supplementary codes and agreements that have been adopted within the GATT framework provide further rules and disciplines for those countries that have signed them.

- GATT provides a framework for the liberalization of world trade, through negotiations aimed at lowering the tariffs of member countries and exchanging commitments not to increase these tariffs, as well as by the application of rules that prohibit or control the use of non-tariff measures.

- GATT provides facilities and agreed procedures for the resolution of trade disputes among its member countries.

- GATT provides facilities for collecting and disseminating information about developments in world trade and the trade policies and measures of member countries, as well as for independent research and analysis of trade-policy issues.

The member countries meet as "Contracting Parties," usually once a year, in late November. Periodically these meetings take place at Ministerial level, as in November 1982. Ongoing GATT business is dealt with by a Council of Representatives, comprising all members, which meets nine to twelve times a year, as required. A complex of committees exists to deal with specified trade measures (for example, the Balance of Payments Committee) and with the supplementary agreements and codes within the GATT framework (for example, the Multifibre Arrangement and the Anti-dumping Code). A Consultative Group of Eighteen, composed of senior trade-policy officials from the capitals of a broadly representative group of countries, including Canada, meets four times a year, as a rule, to review trade-policy developments of special interest, to give broad direction to the management of the GATT system, and to help co-ordinate GATT and IMF activities. Working parties and panels are established as needed to deal with specific issues, such as the admission of new members, and to facilitate the settlement of disputes. The operation of the GATT system is assisted by an international Secretariat located in Geneva, where many member countries, including Canada, maintain permanent missions to deal with their interests in GATT.

The General Agreement is commonly regarded as providing a balanced and multilateral exchange of rights and obligations among its members. The willingness of one member to accept the disciplines of GATT and conduct its trade policy in accordance with GATT rules is thus conditional on a parallel acceptance of these disciplines and rules by all other member countries; and the readiness of one member country to open its economy to international trade is conditional on the readiness of other members similarly to open theirs.

While GATT has served its several functions with varying degrees of effectiveness, it has provided the main framework for co-operation in trade areas among most countries of the world over the post-war period. Its rules, as they have evolved, have given a relatively high degree of stability and predictability to the trade policies and practices of the member countries. Largely as a result of seven successive, multilateral, trade-negotiating conferences within GATT, the tariffs of the industrialized countries, in particular, have been substantially reduced, and other trade barriers have been reduced or at least brought under varying degrees of international control. Moreover the dispute-settlement procedures of GATT have served to resolve a great many trade disputes that might otherwise have disrupted the world-trade system. GATT can be credited with making a large contribution to the very great expansion of international trade, which has taken place over the past thirty-five years, and which exceeds the expansion of production of goods that has taken place in the same period.

While the GATT system must rank as one of the most successful efforts in post-war international co-operation, it retains serious gaps and weaknesses, partly because of the inability of member countries to shore up or extend the GATT rules, and partly because members have pursued policies and practices that are inconsistent with the GATT principles and rules. GATT has not been used very effectively as framework for consultations on trade policy among member countries and for the broad management of the trade system, although its role in these areas has been strengthened by the creation, in the mid-1970s, of the Consultative Group of Eighteen. Consultative and management functions have been dispersed, on the one hand, into broader and more highly politicized United nations bodies and, on the other hand, into the more narrowly based OECD framework, meetings of the Summit group, and even more severely restricted bodies. The GATT system has been confined to international trade in goods, and it remains to be seen whether it can be extended successfully to cover the large and growing area of trade in services. GATT rules for trade in agricultural products have been weak from the start and have often been ignored or side-stepped. The less-developed countries have not been fully integrated into the system: on the one hand, important sectors of their exports, such as textiles and clothing, have been subjected to discriminatory restrictions and, on the other hand, their own trade regimes are subject to somewhat more relaxed rules and disciplines than those accepted by the industrialized countries. GATT rules for customs unions and free-trade areas have not proved to be effective in preventing or controlling a number of arrangements in western Europe and elsewhere that are simply extensions of trade preferences among the countries concerned. During recent years of adverse world economic conditions, recession and high unemployment, the GATT rules have been unable to prevent many members from adopting new and severe trade measures designed to protect domestic producers against international competition and to promote domestic economic strategies and programs. In some important trade areas, these measures have taken the form of restrictive bilateral arrangements, imposed outside the GATT framework, or they have been imposed unilaterally, inflicting new and serious strains on the GATT system.

Despite these and other flaws and weaknesses, the GATT system is widely considered to have special advantages for middle-sized and smaller countries with substantial trade interests. Within a multilateral system, these countries are able to influence the evolving world-trade-policy agenda more effectively than they could within a network of bilateral agreements. The GATT rules have exercised a valuable constraint over the trade policies and practices of the larger countries, and in all countries have helped governments to turn back pressures for special measures of protection, applied by domestic producer interests. Multilateral techniques for tariff negotiations generally help smaller countries to gain better export access to larger markets than they could gain through bilateral negotiations. And GATT procedures and facilities for dispute settlement help smaller countries to resolve trade disputes with larger countries more equitably than would be possible through bargaining between countries of unequal negotiating strength.

While the multilateral system may favour middle-sized and smaller countries in the ways just noted, the effective operation of the system depends, in large measure, on continued support and positive participation by the major trading countries. The leadership role in GATT, which was exercised from the start by the United States, has come to be shared to a degree, in recent years, with the European Community (EC) and Japan: the 'Big Three.' But while the USA has generally continued to give strong and positive support to the GATT system, the European Community has tended to favour a more limited and a diminished role for GATT, and Japanese participation in GATT has tended to be neutral and responsive. The dispersal of leadership in GATT among the 'Big Three,' and the emergence of a more highly organized grouping of developing countries, have altered, but not necessarily diminished, the role in GATT of middle-sized countries such as Canada. Canada has continued to participate actively, and generally positively, in the whole range of GATT activities, as in the trade activities of the other institutions that comprise the broader multilateral trade system.

Notes

1. A good account of planning for a post-war trade and economic system is in R.N. Gardner, *Sterling-Dollar Diplomacy: The Origins and Prospects for Our International Economic Order.*

2. The US "Proposals for Expansion of World Trade and Employment" were transmitted in December 1945 to a number of governments, including the Canadian Government, and issued in Department of State *Publication 2411* (Washington, D.C., 1945); the "Proposals" were published, along with certain related documents, by the Department of External Affairs in *Conference Series, 1945, No. 3* (Ottawa: King's Printer, 1946).

3. There are several detailed accounts available of the negotiations for the Havana Charter and the General Agreement on Tariffs and Trade; these include C. Wilcox, *A Charter for World Trade*; W.A. Brown, *The United States and the Restoration of World Trade*; G. Curzon, *Multilateral Commercial Diplomacy*; and K. Kock, *International Trade Policy and the GATT 1947–1967*. L.D. Wilgress, *Canada's Approach to Trade Negotiations* contains a brief account of Canadian participation in the negotiations for the General Agreement and the Havana Charter. The original text of the General Agreement was published by the United Nations in 1947 as the *Final Act Adopted at the Conclusion of the Second Session of the Preparatory Committee of the United Nations Conference on Trade and Employment: General Clauses of the General Agreement on Tariffs and Trade*, Volume 1. The schedules of tariff concessions agreed to by the participating countries were issued in Volumes 2, 3 and 4. It should be noted that the articles of the General Agreement were based on the draft Charter for the proposed ITO, as it was drawn up by the Preparatory Committee during the summer of 1947 in Geneva; during the Havana Conference, numerous amendments were made to this text, and after the Havana Conference, the GATT Articles were changed to bring them into line with the revised text of the Charter. The text of the original General Agreement was published, along with related material, in *Canada Treaty Series 1947*, No. 27 (Ottawa: King's Printer, 1947); the text of the General Agreement, as amended following the Havana Conference, was published in *Canada Treaty Series 1948*, No. 31 (Ottawa: King's Printer, 1949), along with related documents.

4. For a full account of the fate of the Havana Charter in Congress, see W. Diebold, *The End of the ITO*.

5. Canada, Department of External Affairs, *Documents on Canadian External Relations, Vol. 12 (1946)*, pp. 1032-54. This work contains a number of memoranda and other documents relating to discussions of plans for the ITO, which took place in Ottawa in 1946.

6. The full text is in Canada, Department of External Affairs, *Statements and Speeches, No. 47/20*.

7. Agreement between Canada and the United States Supplementary to the General Agreement on Tariffs and Trade of October 30, 1947, signed at Geneva, October 30, 1947. *Canada Treaty Series, 1947*, No. 27.

8. The texts of this exchange of notes are also in *Canada Treaty Series, 1947*, No. 27.

4

GATT: The Main Rules and Other Features

As we noted earlier, the General Agreement on Tariffs and Trade is, first and foremost, a multilateral treaty among most of the world's trading countries, and it contains a set of rules which govern the trade policies and practices of its members and their trade relations with one another. The original trade rules have remained essentially intact since the Agreement was drawn up in 1947, but have been strengthened and extended over the years by the adoption of a number of supplementary codes and agreements, especially as an outcome of the Tokyo Round of multilateral trade negotiations in the 1970s.

The GATT system is largely concerned with the producers and traders of goods, and with the laws and policies of governments in support of these enterprises. On the one hand, the GATT rules are designed to establish the rights of producers in one country to sell their products in other member countries. On the other hand, the rules define and limit the freedom of governments to restrict the importation of goods and otherwise to protect their domestic producers against international competition. There is little in the GATT rules which is concerned with broader aspects of domestic economic policy or with the interests of consumers. Nevertheless, the existence and operation of the GATT system is, or should be, highly relevant from the perspective of a member country's overall economic interests and from a consumer perspective. The broader public interest is served by the opportunities provided under GATT for domestic producers and traders to extend their markets beyond national boundaries, to earn foreign currency, to enlarge their profits, and to offer greater opportunities for employment. The interests of consumers are served by the constraints which limit the freedom of their governments to reserve home markets for domestic producers, to block imports of cheaper or better products, and to restrict freedom of choice.

These rights and these obligations of producers and governments, which are embodied in the GATT system, are founded on sound economic doctrines, however often these doctrines are side-stepped by governments in response to domestic pressures of one kind or another. Economists have long demonstrated that less restricted international trade raises real income for the world as a whole and usually for all individual countries as well, and results in a more efficient use of the world's resources. They have also demonstrated that tariffs and other barriers to trade represent taxes on domestic consumers or on foreign producers, and have the effect of shifting income within a country to the protected sectors and away from consumers, as well as from non-protected and export-oriented sectors of production. For a smaller country, the trade barriers of larger trading partners commonly have the effect of worsening its terms of trade, while its own import barriers often simply raise prices for consumers and users of imported goods and many domestic products.[1]

The GATT Rules

The General Agreement itself consists of thirty-eight Articles, divided into four Parts. Part I contains the first two Articles, which set out the basic most-favoured-nation (MFN) rules and govern the application of the tariff rates established under GATT negotiations; these Articles can only be amended by unanimous agreement of all members. Part II contains twenty-one Articles governing the use of particular trade-policy measures and practices. The Part-II Articles can be amended by a two-thirds vote, but amendments are effective only to members that accept them. Part III, with thirteen Articles, deals mainly with procedural matters. Part IV contains three new Articles which were added in the mid-1960s to deal with the special trade interests of developing countries.[2]

Membership in GATT imposes on each participant a variety of general obligations, some of which are implied, but nevertheless impelling. These include obligations to apply trade policies and measures to all other member countries on a non-discriminatory basis, except as otherwise agreed; not to impose restrictions other than customs duties on imports, except as provided by the GATT rules or under waivers; to enter, on request, into negotiations with other member countries, for reductions in tariffs and other barriers to trade; to publish promptly trade statistics and information about trade laws and regulations; and to enter into consultations with other members in the event of trade disputes, with the object of resolving those disputes by conciliation, rather than by the threat of retaliatory measures. The General Agreement also incorporates a general, but rarely observed, obligation on member countries to observe "to the fullest extent of their executive authority" the principles of all the substantive provisions of the Havana Charter.

Complaints are often made that the GATT rules are weakly enforced, easily avoided, and widely abused. This is far from the truth. It is true that the concept of 'illegality' in GATT is elusive, and that the process of enforcement is complex. GATT is not a policing operation, nor has it any enforcement powers of its own. But underlying the General Agreement is the concept of an exchange of 'rights and obligations' among the member countries, based on some measure of reciprocity. An infringement of GATT rules is, therefore, not necessarily an act to be exposed and punished, but rather an act that can lead to withdrawal of equivalent concessions by other countries whose interests are adversely affected, unless acceptable compensation is offered for the injury.

Non-Discrimination and MFN

Article I of the General Agreement obliges a member country to extend unconditional MFN treatment in tariff and other trade-policy areas to all other contracting parties; if more favourable treatment is granted to any other country whatsoever, it must also be extended at once to all members of the General Agreement. There are, however, several exceptions to this general rule, including the following:

- An exception was written into Article I to permit the continuation of tariff preferences that existed in 1939, such as those among Commonwealth countries and within the French colonial system. However, the 'margins' of such preferences (that is, the gap between the MFN rate and the preferential rate) could not be increased.

- An exception was written into a separate Article XXIV for countries which form customs unions or free-trade areas, enabling them to eliminate tariffs and "other restrictive regulations of commerce" among themselves, without extending the same advantage to outside countries. The formation and operation of customs unions and free-trade areas, however, is subject to the specified and detailed conditions set out in Article XXIV. (See Chapter 7, below.)

- Article XIV provides that countries which apply import restrictions for balance-of-payments reasons may, under certain circumstances, discriminate among sources of their imports.

- In the early 1970s, the Contracting Parties granted special waivers from the MFN rules to permit developed countries to extend tariff preferences to imports from developing countries, and also to enable developing countries to exchange preferential tariff treatment among themselves.

Developing countries were given further freedom to exchange tariff and trade preferences among themselves as an outcome of the Tokyo Round. (See Chapters 10 and 11, below.)

- A limited number of waivers from the MFN rules have been granted to individual countries to enable them to give preferential tariff treatment to particular imports from particular countries. One such waiver, granted in the mid-1950s, covers the operation of the European Coal and Steel Community; another was granted to the United States (USA) in the mid-1960s to cover its participation in the Canada-USA Automotive Agreement, permitting the removal, on a preferential basis, of customs duties on imports of automotive products from Canada.

- A further departure from MFN rules was made by the several special arrangements relating to trade in textile products, which have been concluded since the early 1960s, and which are now contained in the Multifibre Arrangement (MFA). This arrangement permits the imposition of quantitative controls on trade in textile products, on a discriminatory basis, under specified conditions. (See Chapter 9, below.)

- Certain of the supplementary codes and arrangements concluded within the GATT framework as an outcome of the Tokyo Round contain elements of 'conditional' MFN treatment. Signatories are obligated to extend certain benefits under these codes only to other signatories, rather than to all other GATT members. (See Chapter 15, below.)

Tariff Bindings

Despite these exceptions, the principle of unconditional MFN treatment, especially in tariff matters, remains a cornerstone of the GATT system. The basic MFN rule is reinforced by Article II, which is concerned with the status of tariffs that have been reduced and/or 'bound' (that is, guaranteed against increase) as a result of negotiations under GATT, and thereby entered in tariff schedules which are an integral part of the General Agreement. The obligation under this Article is as follows:

> Each contracting party shall accord to the commerce of the other contracting parties treatment no less favourable than that provided for in the . . . Schedule annexed to this Agreement. (P. 3.)

This Article has the important additional function of preventing member countries from increasing tariff rates that have been agreed upon in prior negotiations, except under rather strict rules set out elsewhere in the Agreement. No similar constraints are imposed on tariff rates that are not 'bound,' but Canada and most of its trading partners have bound most of their tariff rates as a result of successive GATT negotiations. This Article thus provides strong protection for the trade liberalization that has been achieved over the years within the GATT system. While the tariffs of the leading trading countries have been greatly reduced by a series of negotiations within GATT, there are relatively few instances where tariffs have been increased.

The obstacles to increasing tariffs that have been bound as a result of GATT negotiations are formidable. One avenue is provided under Article XXVIII (Renegotiation of Schedules). This involves reaching agreement with the exporting countries "primarily concerned"; it usually involves, too, the payment of compensation by reducing other tariffs, and compliance with other specified procedures. Another avenue is provided under the so-called 'safeguard' provisions of Article XIX, which are further discussed below, and which are also difficult to use in GATT.

As we noted above, the provisions relating to non-discrimination, MFN-tariff treatment and tariff bindings constitute Part I of the General Agreement. Some of the main trade rules in the Part-II Articles are reviewed in the following sections.

National Treatment

Article III of the General Agreement requires that once a product has been imported, it

> ... shall be accorded treatment no less favourable than that accorded to like products of national origin in respect of all laws, regulations and requirements affecting their internal sale, offering for sale, purchase, transportation, distribution or use.

For example, this Article prevents a government from taxing an imported product more heavily than it taxes a similar product produced at home. The Article does not apply to the procurement by government agencies of goods for their own use; and during the Tokyo Round, a new code of rules governing certain government-procurement policies was adopted by the industrialized countries, including Canada. (See Chapter 15, below.)

Customs Valuation

Customs duties are most often imposed, especially in recent periods, as an *ad valorem* basis: that is, as a percentage of the value of an imported product. The method of assigning a value to the product for customs purposes can therefore be important, since an increase in the assigned value will automatically increase the amount of the duty to be paid and, thus, that duty's protective effect. The cost of the product shown on the invoice and the amount actually paid by the importer are not necessarily accepted by customs officials as representing the value of the product for duty purposes, and the practices of countries in valuing goods for duty purposes have varied considerably. Canada's system, and the United States' (US) system as well, have traditionally incorporated practices that have sometimes been used to offer domestic producers an added measure of tariff protection by valuing certain imports at prices higher than those actually paid.

Rules aimed at achieving a common system for the valuation of goods for customs purposes were written into the General Agreement. Article VII calls on contracting parties to base the calculation of customs duties on the "actual value" of an imported product, which is defined as "the price at which ... such or like merchandise is sold or offered for sale in the ordinary course of trade under fully competitive conditions" (p. 12). This rule has not corresponded to traditional Canadian practice, which has been generally to value imports for customs purposes at their 'fair market value' in the exporting country. This 'fair market value' is, essentially, the price at which like goods are sold freely under comparable conditions and circumstances in the country of export, and this domestic price may often be higher than the price quoted to foreign buyers. As we shall discuss further in Chapter 15, below, one result of the Tokyo Round was the adoption of modified GATT rules for customs valuation, based, generally, on the use of the 'transaction value' of an imported product (that is, usually, the invoice price of a shipment). Canada has undertaken to use the new GATT rules after 1985, and this will involve making significant changes in the Canadian system.[3]

Quantitative Restrictions

As we noted earlier, the General Agreement prohibits, in principle, the use of quantitative restrictions to limit imports (or exports), and where exceptions are permitted, their use is governed by specified conditions and circumstances. The general prohibition is set out in forthright terms in the opening paragraph of Article XI ("General Elimination of Quantitative Restrictions"). However, a number of important exceptions to this rule were written into the General Agreement; these include the following:

- *Agricultural products.* Quantitative restrictions are permitted on imports of agricultural and fisheries products, where these are subject to government-support programs which also restrict the production or sale of the product concerned, or involve free or subsidized distribution of the product to certain groups of domestic consumers. Such restrictions, however, may not be used to decrease the proportion of imports to domestic production. (Article XI, paragraph 2.)[4]

- *Balance-of-Payments Restrictions.* Quantitative restrictions may be used by countries in serious balance-of-payments difficulties, but only under specific conditions and subject to supervision by the Contracting Parties (Article XII for developed countries; Article XVIII for developing countries). The International Monetary Fund (IMF) must be consulted with respect to such restrictions. (Article XV).[5]

- *Safeguards.* As discussed below, quantitative restrictions are among the measures that countries may impose, under the conditions specified in Article XIX, as 'safeguard' measures to prevent serious injury to domestic producers from an increase of imports of like or directly competitive products. Any such restrictions must be imposed on a non-discriminatory basis, against all sources of imports.

- *Textiles and Clothing.* Under the Multifibre Arrangement quantitative restrictions may be imposed by an importing country on imports from a particular exporting country, or by an exporting country on its exports to a particular importing country, under circumstances and conditions set out in the MFA.

- *Other.* Quantitative restrictions or prohibitions may be placed on imports for health, safety, security and other special reasons (Articles XX and XXI). Under this exception, many countries, including Canada, impose a variety of restrictions on trade. Canada and the United States, for example, prohibit, on health grounds, the import of fresh meat from many sources.

Subsidies and Countervailing Duties

The use by contracting parties of government subsidies which affect trade is limited by Article XVI of the General Agreement. The Article describes a subsidy by a contracting party as including "any form of income or price support, which operates directly or indirectly to increase exports of any product from, or to reduce imports of any product into, its territory." A distinction is made between 'domestic' subsidies and 'export' subsidies. Domestic subsidies are tolerated, but GATT must be notified of their use; moreover, if their use seriously prejudices the interests of other countries, the country employing them must, on request, consult with the affected countries or with GATT. Export subsidies, however, are prohibited, but only on manufactured and industrial products; the use of subsidies to assist exports of agricultural or primary products is permitted. Even so, export subsidies on these products must not give the country concerned "more than an equitable share of world export trade in that product" (Section B of Article XVI). Export subsidies have not been defined in GATT, because of the difficulties involved; but illustrative lists of prohibited export subsidies have been drawn up, most recently during the Tokyo Round.

An imported product that has benefited from a subsidy in the exporting country may be subjected to a special 'countervailing duty' by the importing country. Rules that limit the use of such countervailing duties are contained in Article VI of the General Agreement. A countervailing duty must not exceed the amount of the subsidy in the country of export. Moreover, such a duty may not be imposed unless it has been determined that the effect of the subsidization "is such as to cause or threaten material injury to an established domestic industry, or is such as to retard materially the establishment of a domestic industry." As we shall see below, in Chapter 15, the rules governing the use of countervailing duties, and of subsidies, were strengthened as a result of the Tokyo Round.

Anti-dumping Duties

'Dumping' is the sale of goods in a foreign market at prices that are lower than those at which the producer sells the same goods in the home market. Goods are not considered to be 'dumped,' therefore, simply because they are imported at prices below those of comparable goods produced in the importing country. The General Agreement does not condemn or seek to control exports at dumped prices, which may often be welcomed by an importing country, and especially by consumers of the dumped products unless the dumped exports injure producers in the importing country. Rather, the GATT rules are designed to discipline the use of 'anti-dumping duties' by importing countries.

Article VI of the General Agreement governs the use of anti-dumping duties. It permits an importing country to impose an anti-dumping duty, in addition to any normal customs duty, if the imported product is sold by the exporting firm at less than its 'normal value,' as defined in the Article. However, like a countervailing duty, an anti-dumping duty may be imposed only if the dumped import is causing or threatening 'material injury' to a domestic industry in the importing country or retarding the establishment of an industry; and the amount of the extra duty imposed in those circumstances cannot be greater than the margin of dumping. The basic GATT rules on anti-dumping were strengthened by the adoption of a supplementary Anti-dumping Code; this code was adopted in the mid-1960s by a group of GATT members, including Canada, and was modified in certain respects during the Tokyo Round.[6]

Safeguards

The General Agreement contains special 'safeguard' provisions that are set out in Article XIX. Under that Article, an importing country may increase tariffs or impose quantitative restrictions on an imported product, or take other appropriate measures to control imports, in circumstances where the imports are causing or threatening "serious injury" to domestic producers of similar goods. Other conditions for imposing such safeguard measures are spelled out in Article XIX, and they are quite restrictive. Among other Article XIX stipulations, safeguard measures must be applied on a non-discriminatory basis to imports of a given product from all sources. Exporting countries affected by the safeguard measure may request compensation, in the form, for example, of tariff reductions by the importing country on some other products; where agreement cannot be reached on compensation, exporting countries may take retaliatory measures, for instance, by raising tariffs on imports from the country concerned. Any retaliatory measures that are challenged, however, are subject to disapproval by GATT.

Because of various difficulties associated with the use of Article XIX provisions, an attempt was made during the Tokyo Round to conclude a supplementary agreement to clarify, and possibly modify, the safeguard rules. To date, however, it has not been possible to reach agreement on any modification of the existing rules. Canada, as well as several other countries, especially the United States, has used the Article XIX safeguard provisions on several occasions to limit 'injurious' imports. Since 1977, for example, under the safeguard provisions of Article XIX, Canada has restricted imports of footwear of various types. During the period from 1976 to 1979, Canada also restricted imports of clothing, under Article XIX rules, but generally has used the provisions of the Multifibre Arrangement to control imports of clothing, as well as of certain textile products from 'low-cost' sources.[7]

State Trading

The General Agreement contains rules, in Article XVII, which govern the foreign-trade operations of state-owned or -controlled enterprises. These enterprises are required to conduct their foreign purchases and sales "in accordance with commercial considerations" and otherwise to operate much like private interests. The Article XVII rules apply to state monopolies, such as those maintained by a number of countries for tobacco products; they apply to bodies in Canada such as the Canadian Wheat Board, the Canadian Dairy Commission and the provincial liquor-control authorities. The provisions of Article XVII have not been very helpful, however, in dealing with the participation in GATT of countries with totally state-controlled economic and trade systems, such as the Eastern European countries. The participation of these countries in GATT has been accommodated by the special terms of their accession to the General Agreement. The subject of state trading and GATT is dealt with in more detail in Chapter 14, below.

Customs Unions and Free-Trade Areas

As we noted above, the General Agreement incorporates a special exemption from the basic MFN rules for countries which form customs unions and free-trade areas. The formation and operation of such arrangements are governed by special rules laid down in Article XXIV. A prime requirement is that members of such regional groups must eliminate internal tariffs and "other restrictive regulations of commerce" on "substantially all" the trade among themselves. Another is that the formation and operation of such regional groups shall not result in an increase in barriers to trade with outside countries. The subject of customs unions, free-trade areas, and other regional trade groups is dealt with in more detail in Chapter 7, below.

Dispute Resolution

The GATT system embodies the concept that trade disputes should be settled, if possible, through a process of bilateral consultations and conciliation, rather than by retaliation and counter-retaliation, which can reverse progress towards trade liberalization and erect new barriers to international trade. Thus the General Agreement provides special procedures for arranging bilateral consultations within the GATT framework to deal with trade disputes and, if these are not successful, for calling on the assistance of the Contracting Parties collectively. The Contracting Parties may make their own recommendations and rulings on the matter, and if these are not adopted, they may authorize a retaliatory measure by the injured party.

These procedures are set out in Article XXII ("Consultation"), and Article XXIII ("Nullification and Impairment"). Article XXII simply sets out the general commitment to consult with another member "with respect to any matter affecting the operation of this Agreement" (p. 39), and asserts the competence of the Contracting Parties to intervene in any such issues, but only on request. Article XXIII goes much further. First, it covers a very wide range of disputes, not merely those where specific trade injury is involved, but also situations where a member country considers that "any benefit accruing to it directly or indirectly under this Agreement is being nullified or impaired or that the attainment of any objective of the Agreement is being impeded" (p. 39). Secondly, it covers not only disputes involving violations of the GATT rules, but also those where no violation is involved, and even disputes arising from "the existence of any other situation" (p. 39). Thirdly, where bilateral consultations fail to resolve the issue, the Contracting Parties, on request, are required to investigate the dispute promptly and to "make appropriate recommendations to the contracting parties which they consider to be concerned, or give a ruling on the matter, as appropriate" (p. 40). Fourthly, they may authorize the injured party to retaliate, by suspending "such concessions or other obligations under this Agreement as they determine to be appropriate in the circumstances" (p. 40).

There is a long and somewhat erratic history of dispute settlement in GATT, involving both Article XXII and Article XXIII procedures, as well as the setting up of special working parties and dispute-settlement panels to investigate and prepare recommendations and rulings on behalf of the Contracting Parties. The earliest procedures involved the submission of complaints under Article XXIII, and the establishment of working parties during annual sessions to consider them. Such working parties are composed of representatives of the countries directly concerned, along with others, and their object is to obtain a negotiated solution acceptable to the two sides. The system of 'dispute panels' was invented after 1952, when a particularly large number of complaints appeared on the GATT agenda. These panels are composed of named experts, drawn from countries that are not directly interested, who meet privately, hear presentations from the two sides, as well as from other interested parties, and present their findings and recommendations to the Contracting Parties; their recommendations are generally accepted. These experts are commonly government officials, but serve on panels in a private capacity.

In practice, the distinction in GATT dispute settlement between a working party and a panel is somewhat blurred, and the reasons for choosing one procedure over another are often obscure. However, the working party route tends to lead to negotiated solutions to disputes, while the use of an independent panel tends to lead to quasi-judicial rulings. In 1975, for example, the United States requested a working party to consider whether the Canadian import regime for eggs under the new supply-management system conformed to the GATT, and the deliberations of this working party led to a solution acceptable to both sides.

The list of disputes that have been dealt with in GATT by independent dispute panels is very long. Between 1952 and 1963, almost thirty such panels were established. The acrimony that surrounded several cases in the early 1960s contributed to a trend, maintained for several years after 1965, for contracting parties to avoid using the GATT dispute-resolution procedures or to pursue the less controversial route of employing working parties under Article XXII procedures. Recourse to Article XXIII, involving requests for examination of complaints by panels, even tended for a period to be considered a hostile act. However, the USA continued to file complaints under Article XXIII that involved panels, and submitted a growing number of these complaints after 1972. In 1973 the European Community (EC) submitted a complaint about the subsidy effects of the DISC (Domestic International Sales Corporations) system introduced by the United States in 1972. The USA, in turn, filed counter-complaints against the subsidy effects of certain Belgian, Dutch and French tax practices. Difficulties arose over the composition of panels to consider these cases that delayed matters for several years, and the findings of the panels, when finally presented, led to further complications, which are still not completely resolved.

Other Article XXIII dispute-settlement cases involving panels have included a complaint by the European Community, in 1976, about Canada's announced intention to withdraw tariff concessions in retaliation for an increase in Community tariffs on lead and zinc, and a United States (US) complaint in 1976 about an EC system of minimum import prices for processed fruits and vegetables. During the early 1980s, Canada obtained a favourable ruling from an Article XXIII panel, regarding the operation of a tariff quota established by the European Community for high quality beef. At Canada's request, a panel examined the compatibility with GATT rules of a US restriction on imports of tuna fish products; the result was the removal of this restriction. Another panel examined a Canadian complaint about Japanese restrictions on imports of leather, and this dispute, too, was satisfactorily resolved. In March 1982, the United States requested the establishment of a panel to examine the compatibility with GATT rules of various elements of Canada's Foreign Investment Review Act (FIRA). This panel found that certain, but not all, of the disputed elements of FIRA were inconsistent with GATT rules.

As noted in Chapter 15 of this study, one outcome of the Tokyo Round was the adoption of more effective procedures for the operation of GATT panels. These procedures were further strengthened as a result of decisions reached at the 1982 GATT Ministerial Meeting.[8] (See Chapter 17, below.)

Protocol of Provisional Application

A legal peculiarity of the General Agreement is that the founding countries brought it into force on 1 January 1948, not by signing the Agreement itself, but rather by signing a "Protocol of Provisional Application," reflecting the expectation that the Agreement would shortly be superseded by the proposed Havana Charter. This 'provisional' application of the General Agreement has continued in use ever since, and by itself, it has given rise to few substantive problems. However, the Protocol contains a 'grandfather' clause which has created a number of difficulties. This grandfather clause allows that the Articles in Part II of the Agreement, which cover a broad range of trade-policy measures, need only be applied "to the fullest extent not inconsistent with existing legislation." The clause was inserted into the Protocol because it was recognized that many countries would be unable to implement the provisions of the Part II Articles immediately, without changing existing legislation that conflicted with these Articles. As it turned out, a number of countries, including Canada, continued to maintain legislation and trade measures that were inconsistent in certain respects with the GATT rules, under the loophole provided by the Protocol of Provisional Application. For example, Canada's continued prohibition on imports of most used cars and aircraft, under Schedule 'C' of the Customs Tariff, could be defended under the 'existing legislation' clause, as could, presumably, certain operations of the Canadian Wheat Board.

It is difficult to assess the practical effect of this 'existing legislation' loophole in the General Agreement. No agreed upon list has ever been prepared of trade measures that such legislation might cover. The clause has been applied only with respect to measures falling under the Part II articles, and not to the basic commitments in Part I that cover MFN treatment. Moreover, the clause has long been interpreted as covering only legislation that by its terms or expressed intent, is of a mandatory nature, and not as covering legislation that would simply permit (but not require) inconsistent measures to be maintained. Over time, the clause has become increasingly regarded as a weak defence for measures that conflict with the Part II rules. The clause does not apply to the various supplementary codes and arrangements that have been developed within GATT during recent years, including those that emerged from the Tokyo Round.[9]

Compliance with GATT Rules

The main responsibility for the enforcement of GATT rules rests with individual contracting parties, rather than with the Contracting Parties collectively, or with the GATT Secretariat. In the absence of complaints by individual contracting parties, infractions of the GATT rules can pass unnoticed and without protest. But when infractions are identified and protested by a member country, the Contracting Parties, supported by the Secretariat, can play an important and quasi-judicial role in the enforcement process.

Departures from GATT rules may be condoned by the Contracting Parties, especially if they are acceptable to the countries mainly concerned, and if they are 'legitimized' under waiver procedures that are set out in Article XXV. This Article provides that a two-thirds majority vote, "In exceptional circumstances not elsewhere provided for in this Agreement, the Contracting Parties may waive an obligation imposed upon a contracting party by this Agreement" (p. 44). Not many such waivers involving significant departures from GATT rules have been granted. Canada has found it necessary to obtain only one minor Article XXV release from its GATT obligations.[10] A waiver of historic significance that was particularly damaging to the GATT system was granted to the United States in 1955; it permitted the United States to enlarge its system of restrictions on imports of agricultural products in ways that otherwise would violate the General Agreement.[11]

A country which departs from the GATT obligations and is unable to obtain the agreement of a two-thirds majority may nevertheless decide to proceed, often advancing its own interpretation of the GATT rule involved. Other countries in these circumstances commonly reserve their 'GATT rights,' and may or may not proceed to exercise those rights by retaliating against the other member. Since 1980 the Canadian government has had certain authority to retaliate against countries which impose trade measures that impair Canadian rights under GATT or other trade agreements, or that adversely affect Canadian trade interests.[12]

The Canadian approach in GATT has tended to be somewhat 'legalistic,' in the sense of emphasizing its functions as a body of trade law, favouring a minimum of exceptions, and emphasizing the need for conformity with GATT provisions. This approach is in line with Canada's large interests in international trade, most of which is conducted with more powerful countries that have greater bargaining strength on particular trade issues and greater influence within the GATT system generally. For Canada, the General Agreement has the same status as other treaties and international agreements entered into formally by the Canadian government; so have the supplementary codes and other arrangements concluded and accepted by Canada within the GATT framework, including those entered into as an outcome of the Tokyo Round. In the United States the legal status of the General Agreement is more complex. The US Administration has participated in GATT under successive pieces of legislation adopted by Congress, but the Agreement itself has never been approved by Congress, and its provisions can be, and have been several times, overridden by conflicting US domestic legislation. The codes and arrangements that emerged from the Tokyo Round are being implemented by the USA under the Trade Agreements Act of 1979. Thus neither the General Agreement nor the supplementary GATT codes have undergone the formal, and usually difficult, treaty-ratification process in the US Congress.[13]

Canada's international obligations under GATT are not necessarily binding on provincial governments, unless under particular federal-provincial arrangements. The situation of countries with federal systems is covered in the General Agreement by paragraph 12 of Article XXIV as follows:

> Each contracting party shall take such reasonable measures as may be
> available to it to ensure observance of the provisions of this Agreement
> by the regional and local governments and authorities within its
> territory. (P. 44.)

On a number of occasions, Canada's federal government has carried out negotiations in GATT on matters falling within provincial jurisdiction, in agreement with the provinces concerned; on several occasions, the federal government has also intervened with provincial authorities to persuade them to adjust particular programs and measures and to bring them into line with GATT rules.

GATT as an Institution

GATT is not only a multilateral trade agreement embodying a set of trade rules, but it is also an international organization for trade policy, which has developed an elaborate set of institutional arrangements and procedures aimed at its effective operation. Among its members, few have been consistently more zealous than Canada in the general management of GATT activities.

Because it was expected that the International Trade Organization (ITO) would come into being, the General Agreement, when it was drawn up in 1947, did not include provisions dealing with institutional and organizational matters such as were contained in the Havana Charter, beyond providing (in Article XXV) that the Contracting Parties

> . . . shall meet from time to time for the purpose of giving effect to those provisions of this Agreement which involve joint action and, generally, with a view to facilitating the operation and furthering the objectives of this Agreement. (P. 44.)

On this basis, the original signatories met as the GATT 'Contracting Parties' at the end of the Havana Conference and again, in Geneva, later in 1948. A Secretariat was provided by the United Nations (UN) in the form of the Interim Commission for the International Trade Organization (ICITO), which had been established by the Havana Conference to prepare a work program for the ITO. ICITO developed into the present permanent GATT Secretariat.[14]

Although GATT is not, strictly speaking, one of the specialized agencies of the United Nations, it has developed the main features of such bodies: it has a headquarters in Geneva, a permanent Secretariat, an annual budget with assessed contributions, an elaborate committee structure, and an imposing schedule of annual meetings. Switzerland has granted GATT the same privileges and immunities as other UN bodies located there. Secretariat personnel serve, for all practical purposes, under standard UN conditions and rules.

The original membership of twenty-three countries that negotiated and signed the General Agreement in October 1947 or shortly thereafter grew larger. Twelve more countries, including the Federal Republic of Germany, acceded to the General Agreement during tariff conferences in 1949 and 1951–52; Japan acceded in 1955; in the 1950s and 1960s a large number of newly-independent developing countries joined GATT; and in the 1960s and 1970s, four East European countries became members. As we noted earlier, there are now eighty-nine signatories; one other country is a provisional member, and another twenty-nine countries apply the General Agreement on a *de facto* basis. In addition, a number of non-members have participated in GATT rounds of tariff negotiations and have signed at least some of the supplementary codes and agreements that have been concluded within the

GATT framework. For Canada, the General Agreement provides its only, or its main, trade agreement with most trading countries of the world.

The members of the General Agreement, when they meet as the Contracting Parties, have a broad mandate, including authority to approve or disapprove trade measures of particular countries in specified circumstances; to make recommendations to member countries regarding particular policies or measures; to interpret the provisions of the Agreement; to waive obligations of individual member countries under the Agreement; and to help settle trade disputes. However, decisions of the Contracting Parties are not binding on an individual member country, nor can the Parties add to a member's GATT obligations, without that member's consent. Each member country has a single vote, but decisions are almost always taken by consensus, except in the rare circumstances where the Agreement calls for voting. GATT differs from most other international bodies in that issues of an essentially political nature are almost never raised at its meetings.

In earlier years, the Contracting Parties met regularly for lengthy annual sessions for the purpose of managing and administering the Agreement. In the late 1950s, a Council of Representatives was created, composed of all member countries. This Council meets several times a year and serves as a kind of executive committee for GATT. Annual sessions of the Contracting Parties have become correspondingly shorter and more formal, serving mainly to ratify the activities and decisions of the Council during the year. From time to time, the Contracting Parties meet at the level of Ministers, to deal with broader policy issues of special importance. The autumn 1982 session was held at the Ministerial level. (See Chapter 17, below.) The Chairman of the Contracting Parties and the Chairman of the Council are chosen annually; together with the GATT Director-General, they play key roles in the management of GATT affairs.[15]

Apart from the Council of Representatives, the GATT committee structure includes the following:

- The Balance-of-Payments Committee, which holds annual consultations with developed countries that maintain quantitative restrictions under the provisions of Article XII. It normally holds consultations every two years with less-developed countries that maintain quantitative restrictions under Article XVIII.

- The Trade and Development Committee, which is concerned with the special trade interests of developing countries

- The Textiles Committee, which exercises general supervision over the operation of the Multifibre Arrangement and serves as a forum for negotiations for extensions of the MFA

- A Consultative Group of Eighteen, which was created in 1975 and is

composed of key GATT countries, including Canada, chosen by a negotiating process. This body serves as a forum for regular consultations on
broad trade-policy developments and provides general direction to the
GATT program of work; senior trade-policy officials from capitals
usually attend.

- The Committee on Safeguards, which was established after the Tokyo
  Round to pursue proposals to establish a new Safeguards Code designed
  to elaborate and clarify the provisions of Article XIX.

Other committees include those established to exercise general supervision
over the operation of the supplementary codes and agreements that resulted
from the Tokyo Round. As noted earlier, working parties are set up from time
to time, as the need arises, to deal with particular issues: for example, to
examine proposals for waivers and applications for accession; and working
parties and independent panels are set up as the need arises, for the purpose of
resolving trade disputes.

The GATT Secretariat has grown from the small group of UN employees
assembled in 1947 to service the Havana Conference to number some three
hundred and fifty persons at the present time. It is still, however, one of the
smaller secretariats of its kind in the UN family. The Secretariat's main
functions are to assist and advise member countries in regard to GATT work,
to service conferences and meetings, to assemble and present information, to
undertake research and analysis of significant developments in world trade,
and generally to assist in the operation of the GATT system.[16] A feature of
that system is the unusual degree to which member countries participate
directly, although often informally, in its management and operation.

Among the various international organizations within the United Nations
family, GATT has long been regarded as one of the most successful, although
a number of important elements in the ITO system have still not been put in
place as originally planned. While its underpinning as an organization is
slender, GATT has steadily grown in membership and in its operations to
resemble the kind of world-trade body designed in the early post-war years.
One American authority on GATT has referred to it approvingly as follows:

> In legal and institutional patrimony, the GATT is one of the most
> humble, if not deprived, of the multitude of international bodies on the
> current world scene. But in positive accomplishments, the GATT must
> surely rank near the top.[17]

Notes

1. Full discussions of international trade theory are in the standard textbook by R.E.
   Caves and R.W. Jones, *World Trade and Payments: An Introduction.*

2. The current text of the General Agreement on Tariffs and Trade is in GATT, *Basic Instruments and Selected Documents*, Volume 4. Supplements in this *BISD* series are issued annually; these contain the texts of important GATT documents, reports, and decisions made by the GATT Contracting Parties during the year. An exhaustive analysis of GATT principles, rules and procedures is in J.H. Jackson, *World Trade and the Law of GATT*; other authoritative studies of GATT include G. Curzon, *Multilateral Commercial Diplomacy*; K. Kock, *International Trade Policy and the GATT 1947–1967*; K.W. Dam, *The GATT: Law and International Economic Organization*. A shorter and more recent analysis of GATT is in J.A. Finlayson and M.W. Zacker, "The GATT and the Regulation of Trade Barriers: Regime Dynamics and Functions." GATT, *Analytical Index* (3d revision) contains "Notes on the Drafting, Interpretation and Application of the Articles of the General Agreement." The GATT Secretariat has also issued a useful pamphlet titled *GATT: What It Is, What It Does*; it also publishes a newsletter, *GATT Focus*.

3. Canada's system of valuing goods for duty purposes is set out as in ss. 35–50 of the Customs Act. A recent review of the Canadian system is contained in Canada, Tariff Board, *A Report of an Inquiry by the Tariff Board Respecting the GATT Agreement on Customs Valuation, Part I: Proposed Amendments to the Customs Act*, pp. 6-9.

4. This 'agricultural exception' was inserted at the insistence of the United States to protect its domestic agricultural-support programs that had been introduced during the 1930s; it represented an important contradiction to broader post-war US policies for trade liberalization. This exception continues to provide a basis for US restrictions on imports of a number of agricultural products; it is also the basis for Canadian import restrictions on products covered by federal agricultural-support programs, including dairy products, certain poultry, and eggs. See Chapter 13, below, for a fuller discussion of problems of trade in agricultural products.

5. Until the end of the 1950s, most Western European countries and Japan maintained quantitative restrictions on many imports that were defended on grounds of balance-of-payments difficulties. Canada, in the early 1960s, and the United States, in the early 1970s, imposed tariff surcharges on imports for short periods for balance-of-payments reasons. During the Tokyo Round, it was agreed that the GATT rules and procedures would be extended to permit explicitly the use of import surcharges for balance-of-payments purposes, as an alternative to quantitative import restrictions.

6. An analysis of the GATT rules governing anti-dumping duties, the Canadian anti-dumping system, and the 1968 Anti-dumping Code is in R. de C. Grey, *The Development of the Canadian Anti-dumping System*.

7. In recent years, there has emerged a concept of 'fair' and 'unfair' import competition. The subsidization and dumping of exports have come to be called 'unfair' trade practices, especially in the United States, as distinct from normal import competition which is regarded as a 'fair' trade practice. Both fair and unfair import competition can cause problems for domestic producers. As discussed in the text, 'fair' import competition which causes or threatens 'serious injury' to domestic producers may, under the trade legislation of many countries, lead to the imposition of special 'safeguard' import measures, as permitted by GATT Article XIX. 'Unfair' subsidization or dumping of exports which causes or threatens 'material injury' to an industry in the importing country may lead to the imposition of countervailing duties or anti-dumping duties, as provided in Article

VI. For a discussion of US legislation governing 'fair' and 'unfair' import competition, see R. de C. Grey, *United States Trade Policy Legislation: A Canadian View*, Chapters 3 and 4.

8. For a detailed account of GATT dispute-settlement procedures, see R.E. Hudek, *The GATT Legal System and World Trade Diplomacy*. J.H. Jackson, "The Crumbling Institutions of the Liberal Trading System," contains a relatively pessimistic view of the success of GATT in dispute settlement during the late 1960s and early 1970s. The various codes that were adopted as a result of the Tokyo Round have their own separate procedures for the settlement of disputes arising from the operation of the codes. Under the Multifibre Arrangement, the Textiles Surveillance Body (TSB) serves as a kind of standing panel of quasi-independent experts to consider disputes over textiles-trade issues arising from the operation of the MFA.

9. The text of the Protocol of Provisional Application is in GATT, *Basic Instruments and Selected Documents, (BISD)*, 4, pp. 77-78. For a discussion of the Protocol, see Dam, *The GATT*, pp. 341-44.

10. In 1968 Canada obtained a temporary waiver to permit a short delay in implementing certain tariff concessions on chemicals and plastics products that had been agreed to during the Kennedy Round because the dissolution of Parliament had delayed the enactment of the required changes to the Customs Tariff. See GATT, *Basic Instruments and Selected Documents Sixteenth Supplement*, pp. 20-22.

11. Canada and other agricultural exporting countries vigorously opposed granting this waiver to the United States, but the United States was nevertheless able to muster the required two-thirds majority approval. For an account of its adoption and implications, see Jackson, *World Trade*, pp. 733-37.

12. In 1980 the Canadian Customs Act was revised to authorize the government to impose a surtax or other penalties on imports in order to retaliate against measures by other countries that adversely affect Canadian trade interests. On this basis, at the beginning of 1984, the government raised duties on certain stainless steel imports from the USA after that country had increased its duties and imposed quotas on certain steel imports, including those from Canada. This authority to retaliate will be further extended by proposed new legislation, set out and discussed in Canada, Department of Finance, *Proposals on Import Policy: A Discussion Paper Proposing Changes to Canadian Import Legislation*. See also Canada, House of Commons Standing Committee on Finance, Trade and Economic Affairs, Subcommittee on Import Policy, *Report on the Special Import Measures Act*.

13. For the status of the General Agreement under US law, see Jackson, *World Trade*, pp. 49-53; for the legal status in the USA of the Tokyo Round codes and agreements, see C.R. Johnston, "Introductory Note: United States Trade Agreements Act of 1979."

14. The Executive Secretary of ICITO was Eric (later Sir Eric) Wyndham White, a former British public servant, who remained as Executive Secretary of GATT until his retirement in 1968. Dana Wilgress of Canada, who had led the Canadian delegations at the Geneva and Havana Conferences, was elected as the first Chairman of the Contracting Parties and continued to serve in this capacity at successive annual sessions until 1951. Wilgress, along with Wyndham White, contributed largely to guiding GATT through its formative years. Wilgress had a

long and distinguished career in the Canadian public service; during the war years, he was Canadian Minister in Moscow, and in the late 1940s, while Canadian Minister in Berne, Switzerland, he was appointed to lead the Canadian delegations to the Geneva and Havana Conferences. An account of the creation of GATT and its operation until 1962 is in his study *Canada's Approach to Trade Negotiations*; see also D. Wilgress, *Memoirs*, for accounts of his participation in GATT during the early years.

15.   In the mid-1960s, J.H. (Jake) Warren of Canada served as Chairman of the GATT Council and also as Chairman of the Contracting Parties. At later dates, Warren was Deputy Minister of Industry, Trade and Commerce in Ottawa, Canada's High Commissioner in London, Canadian Ambassador in Washington, and Canadian Co-ordinator for Trade Negotiations during the Tokyo Round. The former Canadian Ambassador in Geneva, D.S. McPhail, served as Chairman of the GATT Council in 1980–81 and Chairman of the Contracting Parties in 1981–82.

16.   In 1969 Wyndham White was succeeded as Director-General by Olivier Long of Switzerland. In 1980 Long was succeeded by the present Director-General, Arthur Dunkel, also of Switzerland.

17.   Dam, *The GATT*, p. 335.

5

The Havana Charter: What Was Lost

If the Havana Charter and the International Trade Organization (ITO) had come into being in the early post-war years, as planned, the world-trade system would have developed as a more unified process, with a firmer institutional base and with a number of additional rules in trade and trade-related areas.[1]

As we noted in the previous chapter, the central commercial policy rules that were contained in Chapter IV of the draft Charter for the ITO were largely carried over into the General Agreement on Tariffs and Trade; and GATT has remained since 1948 as the main element of the world-trade system. When the Havana Charter and the proposed ITO were abandoned, the provisions of several other sections of the Charter were preserved, in one way or another, elsewhere within the United Nations (UN) system. Several other features of the Charter emerged in modified forms at later dates within the GATT, the Organisation for Economic Co-operation and Development (OECD) and the United Nations Conference on Trade and Development (UNCTAD). Some other elements of the Havana Charter have their parallels in newer initiatives for international co-operation in trade and economic areas; these initiatives are under discussion at the present time. It is therefore of more than historic interest to look at the elements of the Havana Charter that were not carried over into the General Agreement on Tariffs and Trade.

It is likely that from the start, the Havana Charter and the ITO would have attracted a larger membership than the GATT, and thus the trade system would have been spared the recurring pressures over succeeding years for a more comprehensive world-trade organization than GATT provided, despite the progressive growth in GATT membership. If the ITO had existed, it seems unlikely that UNCTAD would have come into being in the mid-1960s. It cannot be assumed, however, that the Soviet Union would have joined ITO, since it absented itself from the Havana Conference, which it denounced as an American effort to achieve dominance over the world economy. China played an active role at the Havana Conference and was also a founding member of GATT; but it seems likely that China would have withdrawn from participation in the ITO, as it did, within several years, from GATT. The ITO, in addition to attracting a larger membership, would have been established more securely as a specialized agency of the United Nations, with a stronger institutional base and probably, also, with far greater resources than GATT enjoyed, especially in its earlier years.

The Havana Charter would also have had important consequences in terms of United States (US) trade policy and domestic trade legislation, consequences that would have been welcomed in Canada. As an international treaty involving the United States (USA) and approved by Congress, the Charter would presumably have required early changes in several US trade practices— its system of countervailing duties, for example—to bring them into conformity with its rules. Unlike the General Agreement, the Charter contained no 'grandfather' clause of the kind in the GATT Protocol of Provisional Application, which enabled GATT members to maintain existing trade practices that, in fact, violated GATT rules. For its part, Canada would presumably have been obliged, without delay, to bring a number of its own trade practices into line with the Charter; it might have been required, for example, to change its anti-dumping system and its system of valuing imports for customs purposes.

The main provisions of the Havana Charter that were left out of the General Agreement included those following.

Economic and Trade-Policy Co-operation

Chapter II of the Havana Charter, entitled "Employment and Economic Activity," contained several provisions designed to encourage co-operation among member countries, in broader areas of economic and trade policy. Members would have committed themselves, among other obligations, to "take action designed to achieve and maintain full and productive employment and large and steadily growing demand." They would also have committed themselves to ensure that domestic "measures to sustain employment, production and demand . . . [would] be consistent with . . . this Charter, and would not create balance-of-payments difficulties for other countries." In the event of "the international spread of a decline in employment, production or demand," the ITO, as an organization, was authorized to initiate international consultations aimed at "appropriate measures" (p. 6).

This Chapter reflected prevailing fears in many countries about a post-war slide into another economic depression such as occurred during the 1930s, and especially a depression in the United States; it also reflected the fact that at the time, many countries, including Canada, were aiming at a full-employment policy. The Chapter did not, however, give the ITO a particularly large role in the co-ordination of economic and trade policies among member countries. This was to be one of the main functions of the UN Economic and Social Council (ECOSOC). In any event, ECOSOC was never able to play this role very effectively.[2] Since the early 1960s, the industrialized countries have used OECD as a framework for continuing consultations in economic areas and, to some extent, in trade areas. Since the mid-1970s, annual meetings at the summit level have provided an additional framework for consultations on broad economic and trade policies among a smaller group of the world's leading economic powers, including Canada.

Co-ordination of trade policies among member countries, as distinct from broader economic policies, would doubtless have been carried further within ITO than it has within GATT, at least until recently. In earlier periods, the relatively lengthy annual sessions of the GATT Contracting Parties were attended by senior officials or trade ministers from capitals, and these sessions provided regular occasions for informal consultations on trade-policy issues beyond those appearing on formal agenda. Such opportunities for discussions and consultations on broader trade-policy issues declined after member countries began to carry out most of their GATT business through diplomatic missions in Geneva, although successive rounds of tariff-and-trade negotiations attracted senior trade officials and ministers from capitals. As we noted in the previous chapter, a deliberate effort has been made since the mid-1970s to strengthen GATT as a mechanism for regular consultations on broader trade-policy issues and developments, within the Consultative Group of Eighteen.

Restrictive Business Practices

The Havana Charter contained elaborate provisions, in a separate Chapter V, covering restrictive business practices that affect international trade. These provisions would have imposed a set of obligations on member countries with respect to their domestic control over such practices. They would also have provided international procedures for dealing with complaints and would have given ITO, as an organization, a positive role in the investigation of restrictive business practices affecting international trade, the settling of disputes, and the development of new international codes and arrangements in this area. Efforts were made in the late 1950s to draw up a code of rules on restrictive business practices within the GATT framework, but these efforts did not succeed because of lack of interest in the leading GATT-member countries. In the 1970s, the spread of multinational corporations gave rise to new international concerns about restrictive business practices and led to the adoption of several non-binding sets of guidelines in the OECD and in the United Nations. (See Chapter 10, below). These guidelines, however, are less binding and less comprehensive than the provisions on restrictive business practices that would have come into force if the Havana Charter had been adopted.

International Commodity Arrangements

Problems of trade in primary products occupied a central place in the negotiations for the Havana Charter. Trade in primary products was an area of special concern for delegations at the Havana Conference from traditional exporters, including Canada, of primary products and of agricultural products. After the Havana Charter and the ITO were abandoned, these issues were pursued in other parts of the UN system, but only in a minor way in GATT. (See Chapter 11, below.) Chapter VI of the Havana Charter would have provided an international framework of rules and procedures for the negotiation and operation of agreements, among exporting and importing countries, to govern trade in particular primary and agricultural products. These rules and procedures would have been aimed at stabilizing the international prices and markets for these products. Chapter VI represented, in effect, a 'code within a code' for primary commodity agreements. It laid out in detail the economic and trade conditions under which such agreements were appropriate; it gave ITO authority to conduct research in this area of trade and to make arrangements for international negotiations; and it established a set of principles and rules to govern the terms of commodity agreements. In addition, the ITO would have been authorized to settle disputes in this area if dispute procedures under particular arrangements did not lead to settlement.

In the absence of the ITO, arrangements were made for the United Nations itself to assist in negotiations for commodity agreements, and special UN committees were established to debate broader issues relating to commodity trade. These UN arrangements, however, were widely regarded as inadequate by both the proponents and the opponents of commodity agreements. Pressures exerted by the developing countries for new institutional arrangements in this area became one of the main forces behind the creation of the UNCTAD system. Since the mid-1960s, UNCTAD has taken over, in general, the functions that would have been assigned to the ITO in this area, although within UNCTAD, problems of commodity trade have tended to be limited to those of special interest to developing countries.

International Investment

Article 12 of the Havana Charter set out a number of general principles and rules relating to international investment. The Article gave encouragement to the international flow of capital as a means of "promoting economic development and reconstruction, and consequent social progress"; but it also spelled out the rights of member countries to control the inflow of foreign capital and to set conditions for foreign investors. One obligation that would have been assumed by member countries was to enter into consultations and negotiations with other members, at their request, in order to conclude, "if mutually acceptable," bilateral or multilateral agreements covering foreign investment.

No international rules in this area have so far been inserted into the GATT system, but in OECD and in the United Nations, several non-binding codes and declarations have been developed that relate to international investment. The United States has recently suggested that rules in this area might be developed within GATT, but it is far from clear whether or in what way such rules could emerge in GATT.

Preferences among Developing Countries

Article 15 of the Havana Charter would have permitted exchanges of tariff preferences among developing countries which are contiguous or in the same geographic area. Other preferential arrangements among developing countries were provided for, but these would have required special approval by the ITO. Under GATT, a somewhat different dispensation was made, but not until 1971. This arrangement was limited to the exchange of tariff preferences among developing countries which adhered to a special Protocol. In 1979, as an outcome of the Tokyo Round, GATT gave its blessing to a broader system of tariff-and-trade preferences among developing countries, on a regional or on a global basis. (See Chapters 9 and 14, below.)

Fair Labour Standards

Under Article 7 of the Havana Charter, member countries would have recognized that "unfair labour conditions, particularly in production for export, create difficulties in international trade." Moreover, they would have accepted a general commitment to take "whatever action may be appropriate and feasible to eliminate such conditions" within their own countries and to co-operate in this regard with the International Labour Office. Trade disputes arising from unfair labour conditions would have been referred to the ITO for settlement.

It is difficult to imagine how these ITO provisions would have worked in practice. 'Low-cost' imports emerged as an important issue in GATT during the 1950s, in connection with Japan's accession to GATT, and the issue led to the special arrangements that have been developed within the GATT framework for trade in 'low-cost' textile products. These arrangements, however, have focused on price problems and not on conditions of labour in exporting countries.

In recent years, several initiatives have been launched, supported generally by organize labour in industrialized countries, and aimed at introducing into the GATT system special rules to deal with trade problems arising from 'unfair labour conditions,' including restraints on trade-union activity. The generally negative response to these proposals indicates that it would be difficult, at this stage, to devise in GATT a broadly acceptable set of rules covering this area.

Institutional Elements

Following the abandonment of the ITO, GATT evolved as a world-trade organization in the narrower area of commercial policy, but on a somewhat fragile basis. An effort was made during the mid-1950s to restructure GATT more firmly as an Organization for Trade Cooperation (OTC), but this attempt did not succeed. Efforts in the mid-1960s, within the United Nations, to create a new and more universal world-trade organization led to the creation of the UNCTAD system, but UNCTAD has not developed into anything resembling the proposed ITO.

It can be argued that the absence of a rigid and formalized institutional structure has been one of the strengths of the GATT system, permitting it to respond more easily and flexibly to the changing conditions of world trade than would have been possible for a larger and more cumbersome, specialized, UN agency. In recent years GATT has, in fact, developed a stronger institutional base, with more adequate personnel and other resources than it possessed in past years. This process has been reinforced by the outcome of the Tokyo Round, which will impose new responsibilities on GATT as an organization. In the future, new possibilities may emerge for a reordering of the organizational structure for trade co-operation, and this may involve a merger of GATT and UNCTAD. There seems, however, to be no immediate prospect of such a development.

Notes

1. The full text of the Havana Charter for an International Trade Organization was published in *Canada Treaty Series, 1948*, No. 32 (Ottawa: King's Printer, 1949). A detailed examination of the Havana Charter and of the negotiations leading to its adoption is in Clair Wilcox, *A Charter for World Trade*. Wilcox led the US delegation at the Havana Conference. A detailed analysis of the Charter and a comparison with the General Agreement on Tariffs and Trade is in W.A. Brown, *The United States and the Restoration of World Trade*.

2. The functions and operations of the UN Economic and Social Council until the late 1960s are examined in W.R. Sharp, *The United Nations Economic and Social Council*.

6

GATT Tariff Negotiations

Most tariff negotiations within the GATT system have taken place during seven successive 'rounds' of negotiations. All or most GATT countries have participated, at least nominally, in these rounds, as have also some countries that are not GATT members. These rounds of GATT tariff negotiations have been 'multilateral' in scope, partly because they involved the participation of many countries, and partly because of the techniques and procedures used in the negotiations. The seven rounds of tariff negotiations were as follows:

- 1947 — Geneva (parallel with the negotiation of the General Agreement)
- 1949 — Annecy, France
- 1950–51 — Torquay, England
- 1955–56 — Geneva
- 1961–62 — The 'Dillon Round' in Geneva
- 1964–67 — The 'Kennedy Round' in Geneva
- 1973–79 — The 'Tokyo Round' of Multilateral Trade Negotiations (MTN) in Geneva.

In terms of the liberalization of world trade, the first 1947 round in Geneva, the Kennedy Round, and the Tokyo Round were by far the most important. Tariff cutting as a result of the other GATT rounds was more limited.

Negotiating Rules and Techniques

The agreements concluded among GATT members to reduce their tariffs are at the heart of the GATT system. Most of these agreements have involved not only the reduction of tariffs, but also the 'binding' of the reduced tariffs against subsequent increase. (Negotiations may also involve binding tariffs that are already low or existing zero rates.) The binding of a tariff under GATT represents a formal commitment not to increase the tariff except in accordance with rather strict rules. Among other benefits, the original negotiating partner, as well as other major suppliers of the product concerned, acquire 'rights' with respect to the bound tariff. These countries are then entitled to be compensated for any increase in the tariff rate, and may demand that the country concerned cut tariffs on other of their exports. If agreement cannot be reached, they are entitled to retaliate, subject to disapproval by the Contracting Parties: they may increase their own tariffs on exports from the offending country or take some other retaliatory measure.[1]

These 'rules of the game,' which are set out in Articles II and XXVIII of the General Agreement, were designed to reinforce the stability of tariffs within the system and to place 'road-blocks' in the way of undoing the tariff liberalization achieved under GATT negotiations, without entirely precluding the possibility of increasing bound rates. The rules thus provide 'open seasons' for the renegotiation of bound rates—a process that normally takes place at three-year intervals—and the Contracting Parties may approve, 'in special circumstances,' the renegotiation of bound rates at other times. Over the years, Canada has renegotiated a number of tariffs that had been bound in earlier negotiations, including many of its tariffs on fruit and vegetables.

In several other exceptional circumstances, a member country may increase a bound tariff if its action is consistent with GATT rules. For example, a country may impose a special duty on imported products from a trading partner in retaliation for a trade measure taken by that partner which impairs its own GATT rights.[2] Moreover, as we noted in the previous chapter, the safeguard rules of Article XIX also permit a member country to raise a bound tariff (or impose some other restrictive import measure) in circumstances where imports are causing or threatening serious injury to domestic producers.

By any standard, the GATT rules and techniques for reducing tariffs on international trade have been highly successful, at least for the tariffs of the industrialized countries in the GATT system, although in some sectors, tariffs remain significant barriers to trade. The GATT Secretariat estimated that prior to the Tokyo Round, over 50,000 tariff items had been reduced and/or bound by GATT-member countries; and it has reported that nearly 27,000 tariffs were cut further by industrialized countries as an outcome of the Tokyo Round. By comparison, only an insignificant number of tariffs have been increased within the GATT system since 1947.

The earlier GATT rounds were conducted on an 'item-by-item' basis. Pairs of participating countries bargained reductions in tariff rates on particular products in their own schedules as 'concessions,' in return for reductions in the rates of other countries on products of export interest; the lower tariff rates thus negotiated were then applied by the countries concerned, on a multilateral basis, to imports of similar products from all other GATT members, under the most-favoured-nation (MFN) rules. Simultaneously, other pairs of countries were bargaining down each other's rates on products of interest to them, and the resulting lower rates were similarly 'multilateralized,' As a result of this system, which was admittedly cumbersome and time-consuming, trade liberalization spread throughout the GATT system, with indirect benefits flowing to all countries as a result of the MFN rule. Very often, pairs of countries would bring into their bilateral negotiations other countries which would stand to gain significant indirect benefits from the results of their bargaining, in an effort to induce these countries to make their own concessions as part of a 'plurilateral' deal.

While this negotiating technique encouraged general trade liberalization, it also had several limitations. GATT members were under no firm obligation to reduce their tariffs, or even to enter into negotiations except with the 'principal suppliers' of an imported product. A smaller supplier, however important its export interest, might not be able to persuade a large importer to enter into negotiations on tariffs that obstructed its exports. Smaller countries generally had less to offer and thus less leverage in bargaining down the tariffs of larger importing countries. The item-by-item technique placed at a special disadvantage smaller countries that are also world exporters of labour-intensive products; and the relative weakness in bargaining strength of those smaller countries explains, in part, the continued high tariffs of the major importing countries, including Canada, on labour-intensive products such as textiles, clothing, footwear and a variety of standard manufactures. The principle of reciprocity underlying item-by-item negotiations thus presented some special obstacles to bargaining between countries of unequal size and by developing countries. It was widely accepted from the start, however, that larger industrialized countries could not expect full reciprocity from developing countries, especially the weaker ones. The inability of developing countries to reciprocate fully in negotiations was recognized more formally in the GATT system as an outcome of the Tokyo Round.[3]

In addition, countries whose tariffs were already at low levels were at a disadvantage in item-by-item bargaining with high-tariff countries. However, the GATT negotiations system incorporated a rule which, to some degree, adjusted the balance for low-tariff countries; it was accepted from the start that a binding against increase of a low duty or of duty-free treatment is, in principle, equal in value to the reduction of a high duty.[4]

Item-by-item negotiations—and, indeed, the GATT system generally—have another feature that has, to a degree, discouraged import liberalization.

Within the GATT, a tariff concession tends to be regarded by the country making it as a 'loss' and a concession by another country as a 'payment' for the loss, even where it may be in the best interest of a country to reduce its own rates. The system does not encourage countries to make unilateral reductions of tariffs, but rather to preserve their bargaining power for future negotiations.

From the beginning, the merits of this item-by-item approach to tariff negotiations were debated within GATT, as were the merits of an alternative 'linear' approach to tariff negotiations. The linear approach involves that all countries simultaneously reach agreement, in advance, on some formula for across-the-board reductions by agreed percentages. Until the mid-1960s, United States (US) trade legislation did not permit that country to negotiate on a linear basis, but such a system was used during the 1950s by members of the European Community (EC) and of the European Free Trade Association (EFTA), to achieve internal free trade within these areas. Following a change in US legislation, this linear approach was employed during the Kennedy Round and the Tokyo Round, but not by all participants and not in all areas of trade.[5]

This linear approach also has its problems. One arises from the 'disparities' of average tariff levels among countries; countries with relatively low tariffs, such as the Nordic countries, have objected that a formula involving the same percentage cut by all countries will not produce a balance of advantage for them. Another problem arises from the desire of most countries to exclude from tariff negotiations certain 'sensitive' areas of domestic production, where reductions in protection would be politically difficult at home. The Kennedy Round and the Tokyo Round involved separate and difficult negotiations on 'exceptions lists' drawn up by individual participants and usually covering textiles, clothing, footwear, certain chemical products, and many agricultural products. Indeed, negotiations in the agricultural sector during both these rounds largely took place on the traditional item-by-item basis. A third problem arises for countries such as Canada, whose exports consist largely of resource-based and agricultural products for which tariffs throughout the world tend to be low, but whose imports cover a wide range of manufactured products on which tariffs are generally high. In the Kennedy Round, but not in the Tokyo Round, it was recognized that these countries had 'special trade structures,' and Canada, Australia, New Zealand and South Africa did not negotiate on a linear basis, but on the traditional item-by-item basis.[6] Canada had a further difficulty with the linear approach, arising from the fact that it led to relatively small cuts in the low or 'nuisance' tariffs that face a number of important Canadian exports in the larger industrialized countries. Even at relatively low levels, these tariffs can give substantial 'effective protection' to processing industries in importing countries. In the Tokyo Round, the United States (USA) had authority to eliminate its tariffs entirely where rates were below 5 per cent. The EC and Japan, however, blocked proposals for any general elimination of low tariffs. Developing countries generally also considered that they were unable to join in linear reductions of tariffs, and to the extent that they participated in tariff negotiations during the Kennedy and Tokyo Rounds, they negotiated their own tariffs on an item-by-item basis.

Neither the item-by-item approach nor the linear approach has been well suited to achieving trade liberalization in certain sectors of trade where groups of countries have special and large interests as exporters or importers, or both, of such goods as non-ferrous metals, forest products, steel, chemicals and certain high-technology products. In these areas there can be a wider interest in achieving completely free trade. During the Kennedy Round, efforts were made to reduce substantially or remove at once all barriers to trade among groups of industrialized countries in selected sectors such as steel and chemicals, but these efforts met with limited success. During the Tokyo Round, Canada took the lead in pressing for a 'sector approach' to negotiations, on a 'vertical' basis, in selected sectors such as non-ferrous metals and forest products. The object was to negotiate at one time the removal not only of tariffs, but also of all other trade barriers in these sectors, and to cover the processed and manufactured forms, as well as the raw materials, within the framework of special agreements. Indeed, as we shall discuss in Chapter 14, below, this sector approach to trade liberalization became a major part of Canada's overall objectives during the Tokyo Round.

Canada's Tariff Structure

Within the multilateral trade framework, most Canadian trade is conducted on the basis of the most-favoured-nation rule, and most of Canada's imports enter under the MFN rates in the Canadian customs tariff schedule. These rates, with some exceptions, have been progressively lowered in successive rounds of GATT negotiations, in exchange for tariff concessions by Canada's trading partners in GATT, and especially by the United States. Most of these reduced MFN rates applied by Canada have been 'bound' against increase under GATT rules.

The customs tariff has traditionally been Canada's main trade-policy instrument, although in recent periods, Canada has also made considerable use of quantitative restrictions and other non-tariff trade-policy measures.[7] Moreover, for most of this century, the customs tariff has been employed largely to give protection against imports, especially for Canada's manufacturing industries and certain agricultural sectors, as distinct from its function of producing revenue for the federal government, which was an important function of the customs tariff before the First World War.[8]

Canada's customs tariff is chiefly governed by two pieces of federal legislation dating back to the mid-19th century:

- The Customs Act, which provides for the general administration of the customs tariff, and covers such matters as the valuation of goods for customs purposes and procedures for the entry of imports into Canada.

- The Customs Tariff (An Act respecting the duty of customs), which sets out in a schedule the rates of duties applicable to various classifications of imported goods, and provides authority for changing these rates. The Customs Tariff also provides for the use of countervailing duties and for the use, in specified circumstances, of tariff 'surtaxes' on imports causing or threatening injury to Canadian producers.

In addition, a separate Anti-dumping Act was adopted in 1968, which governs the use of special dumping duties. Canada's anti-dumping system, which was established early in the twentieth century, was taken out of the Customs Tariff and related provisions of the Customs Act, changed in important ways, and adopted as a separate Anti-dumping Act.[9]

Canadian customs duties are levied on the value of the imported product (on whatever basis Revenue Canada may determine this value under the Customs Act) at the point of direct shipment to Canada. As described in a recent Tariff Board Report, "the value is a f.o.b. value, excluding subsequent freight, brokerage and insurance charges." The Report observes that in contrast to the Canadian system,

> Most countries levy duties on a c.i.f. basis, thus including all charges up to the point of entry. The latter system, by levying duty on freight, compounds the comparative competitive disadvantage which distance tends to impose upon goods originating in far-off areas. This is not so in the case of the Canadian system which, by ignoring the freight element for duty purposes, is neutral in this respect.[10]

Schedule A to the Customs Tariff sets out rates of duty which apply to imported goods; the rates are widely different for particular products and can vary in accordance with the country of export. When the Tokyo Round cuts are fully implemented, the average rate on industrial products will be about 9-10 per cent. The rate structure is complex, but may be summarized for present purposes as follows:

- The highest rates are the 'General' rates, but these are now applied to goods from only a handful of countries that are neither members of GATT nor nations with which Canada has trade agreements; they are Albania, East Germany, North Korea, Lybia, Oman and Saudi Arabia.[11]

- The MFN rates are generally applied to goods from GATT-member countries and countries with which Canada has trade agreements; these rates, as noted above, are applicable to most dutiable imports from Canada.

- British Preferential (BP) rates are lower, but not uniformly lower, than the corresponding MFN rates and are applicable to most, but not all, imports from Commonwealth countries. These BP rates have declined in importance in Canada's tariff system over recent years.[12]

- General Preferential Tariff (GPT) rates have been applied since 1974 to many, but not all, imports from developing countries. These are one-third lower than the corresponding MFN rate, or the equal of the BP rate, whichever is lower.[13] (See Chapter 10, below.)

Many imports enter Canada free of customs duty, and other imports may qualify for drawbacks and remissions of customs duties. At present, about two-thirds of total imports are effectively duty free; this proportion is somewhat higher for Canada than for most other countries. On the other hand, the average rate of Canadian customs duties, where these exist, is somewhat higher than the average rates of many of its trading partners. This is partly because of the high proportion of imported manufactured goods, in relation to total Canadian imports, on which duties have been preserved at generally higher levels than in the United States, the European Community, most other western European countries and Japan. Comparisons of average levels of duties among various countries, however, are difficult to make and can be misleading.

Tariff Reductions Under GATT

In terms of trade liberalization, the most substantial tariff cutting under GATT has taken place in the initial negotiating conference held at Geneva in 1947, the 1964–67 Kennedy Round, and the 1973–79 Tokyo Round. Only meager results were achieved in the four negotiating rounds held between 1948 and 1964. This uneven progress in tariff cutting under GATT is explainable chiefly in terms of the authority to reduce US tariffs, which the US Congress periodically gives to the Administration. It is this authority which, as we noted earlier, has essentially determined both the timing and the scope of successive GATT rounds of negotiations. For the 1947 round, for the Kennedy Round, and for the Tokyo Round, US negotiators had authority to negotiate reductions, with some exceptions, up to 50-60 per cent of existing US rates. Their negotiating authority during the four rounds of negotiations held between 1948 and 1964 was much more limited, and the overall results of these negotiations were correspondingly meager.

While successive rounds of GATT negotiations have greatly reduced tariffs imposed by the main trading countries, it is difficult to measure with any precision the results of these negotiations for the trade system generally or for individual countries. Moreover, comparisons of the incidence of tariff protection can be very misleading over period of time and among countries with different tariff systems and different patterns of trade. Nevertheless, some crude comparisons indicate the extent of tariff reductions within the GATT system. Between 1941 and 1945, US customs collections represented about 32 per cent of the value of dutiable imports; this ratio was reduced to 12-13 per cent in the period between 1950 and 1965; and by 1980, following the cuts of the Kennedy Round and the initial Tokyo Round, the ratio had fallen to 6 per cent.[14] Canadian duties represented about 21 per cent of the value of dutiable imports in 1946; this ratio fell to 17-18 per cent after the first round of GATT negotiations and remained in this range until the late 1960s, when, as a consequence of Kennedy Round tariff cuts, the average was reduced to the 14-15 per cent range.[15] Altogether, before the Tokyo Round, tariffs in the manufactured-goods sector had been reduced as a result of GATT negotiations, by about 60 per cent for Canada, the United States and the European Community, and by about 50 per cent for Japan.[16]

The GATT Director-General has reported that as a result of the Tokyo Round, the level of tariffs of the industrialized countries on industrial products would be further reduced by one-third, measured on the basis of customs collections, and that the total value of trade affected by MFN tariff cuts by all countries amounted to about US $155 billion annually. He also reported that the weighted average of post-Tokyo Round duties in the finished-manufactures sector would be 5.7 per cent for the USA, 8.3 per cent for Canada, 6.0 per cent for Japan, 6.9 per cent for the European Community, and 4.9 per cent for Sweden.[17]

While this record of tariff cutting under GATT is impressive, it is incorrect to conclude, as many have done, that tariffs are no longer important barriers to world trade or to Canada-USA bilateral trade. Since 1948, tariff walls have come down substantially, especially those surrounding the industrialized countries; but within today's generally low-tariff trading world, some pockets of high tariffs remain almost intact, to provide continued protection for sensitive domestic sectors against international competition. For example, US tariffs on many textile, apparel and rubber-footwear products remain over 30 per cent, and Canadian tariffs in these areas remain in the 20-25 per cent range. High US tariffs also stand on many tableware items, in the chemicals sector, and for many medical/optical instruments. Canadian tariffs remain in the 15-20 per cent range for many consumer-type manufactured goods. Further, most industrialized countries maintain systems by which tariffs increase in accordance with the degree of manufacture, and such tariff escalation can result in very high levels of 'effective protection' for their manufacturing industries. Most developing countries maintain high tariffs on their imports for protective reasons, as well as for revenue and balance-of-payments purposes. Thus there is plenty of scope for further progress towards tariff liberalization within the GATT system.

Notes

1. The legal and technical rules with respect to tariff commitments under GATT are fully discussed in John H. Jackson, *World Trade and the Law of GATT*, Chapters 10 and 23, and in K.W. Dam, *The GATT: Law and International Economic Organization*, Chapter 6.

2. See Chapter 4, note 12, above.

3. A somewhat qualified recognition of the inability of developing countries to reciprocate in tariff negotiations during the Tokyo Round was written into the Declaration that launched the Round, and was restated in a Decision adopted by the Contracting Parties following the conclusion of the Tokyo Round. See "Declaration of Ministers" in GATT, *Basic Instruments and Selected Documents* (BISD) *Twentieth Supplement*, pp. 19-22, and "Decision of 28 November 1979; Differential and More Favourable Treatment, Reciprocity and Fuller Participation of Developing Countries" in GATT, BISD *Twenty-sixth Supplement*, pp. 203-205.

4. This rule is expressed in paragraph 2(*a*) of Article XXVIII *bis* of the General Agreement.

5. For an analysis of the provisions of the US Trade Expansion Act of 1963 relating to linear tariff negotiations and the difficulties with this technique during the Kennedy Round, see J.W. Evans, *The Kennedy Round in American Trade Policy: The Twilight of the GATT?*, pp. 151-53 and 184-202; also E. Preeg, *Traders and Diplomats: An Analysis of the Kennedy Round of Negotiations Under the General Agreement on Tariffs and Trade*, pp. 47-49 and 60-70.

6. A report by the Minister of Finance on Canada's participation in the Kennedy Round is contained in *Minutes of Proceedings and Evidence*, House of Commons Standing Committee on Finance, Trade and Economic Affairs, 16 January 1968. Evans, *The Kennedy Round*, pp. 287-89 contains a discussion, from a US perspective, of the contributions to the outcome of the Kennedy Round of Canada and other countries which claimed 'special trade structures' status.

7. G.A. Elliott, *Tariff Procedures and Trade Barriers: A Study of Indirect Protection in Canada and the United States*, and G. Blake, *Customs Administration in Canada* contain useful, if somewhat dated, examinations of Canada's tariff system and its administration.

8. While Canadian tariffs are now generally maintained chiefly for protectionist purposes or as leverage for future bargaining, the revenue from customs duties is not insignificant; it amounted to over an estimated $3 billion in 1980–81, and may increase to over $4 billion in 1983–84. See *Minutes of Proceedings and Evidence*, House of Commons Standing Committee on Finance, Trade and Economic Affairs, 3 February 1981, p. 36A:1.

9. Canada's anti-dumping system is examined in detail, in the context of the 1967 GATT Anti-Dumping Code, in R. de C. Grey, *The Development of the Canadian Anti-Dumping System*.

10. Canada, Tariff Board, *A Report of an Inquiry by the Tariff Board Respecting the GATT Agreement on Customs Valuation*, Part 1: *Proposed Amendments to the Customs Act*, p. 6.

11. In September 1983, Hazen Argue, the Minister responsible for the Canadian Wheat Board, announced that he had signed an agreement with East German authorities, under which Canada would extend MFN tariff rates to imports from East Germany; in exchange, that country would undertake to purchase three million tonnes of grain from Canada over a three-year period.

12. The decline in importance of the BP rates is, in part, because the margins between these rates and the MFN rates have generally been narrowed as an outcome of successive GATT tariff negotiations. Moreover, BP rates that are applicable to imports from developing members of the Commonwealth have, in effect, been subsumed by equivalent rates under Canada's General Preferential Tariff, which was introduced in 1974. Further, since 1 January 1982, Britain and Ireland are no longer entitled to BP tariff treatment, following the entry of these countries into the European Community in 1973; as a consequence of this move, they withdrew tariff preferences for Canadian exports and imposed the Community's common external tariff on imports from Canada. The withdrawal of BP rates on imports from Britain and Ireland was effected by Bill C-50, approved by the House of Commons in April 1981.

13. See Chapter 10, below, for a further discussion of the Generalized System of Preferences. A detailed recent study of Canada's General Preferential Tariff is in G.H. Forrester and M.S. Islam, "The Generalized System of Preferences and the Canadian General Preferential Tariff."

14. US Department of Commerce, Statistical Abstract of the United States, annual issues. See also Evans, *The Kennedy Round*, pp. 12, 283.

15. J.H. Young, *Canadian Commercial Policy*, p. 49; also annual issues of *Canada Year Book*.

16. Canada, Department of Industry, Trade and Commerce, *Canada's Trade Performance 1960–1977*, Volume 1: General Developments, pp. 167–68.

17. GATT Director-General, *The Tokyo Round of Multilateral Trade Negotiations, Supplementary Report*, pp. 30-33.

7

Regional Trade Groups and Preferential Arrangements

ATT provides the only international rules over the formation and operation of regional trade groups and preferential trade arrangements. However, the effectiveness of the GATT rules governing these arrangements has
been questioned. The rules have been abused and stretched by a number of
regional trade groups and preferential arrangements, and as a result, the basic
most-favoured-nation (MFN) principle has been further eroded within the
trade system. Nevertheless, the GATT rules and procedures have provided
models for the formation and operation of regional trade groups, some measure
of control over them, and a basis for outside countries to seek to protect their
trade and economic interests. Since the mid-1950s, a large part of the GATT
agenda has been devoted to efforts to control the growing regionalization of
world trade, and these efforts have also been pursued in successive rounds of
GATT tariff-and-trade negotiations. Canada has played an important role in
these efforts, in line with its major interests in world trade and as a staunch
supporter of the MFN principle in GATT.

The basic GATT rules on MFN and non-discrimination were written into
Article I of the General Agreement and appear also in a number of other
Articles governing particular trade measures. The architects of the General
Agreement, however, inserted several exceptions to these basic rules. One
exception, placed in Article I itself, permitted the continuation of tariff
preferences within the system that had existed in 1939, but prohibited any
enlargement of existing margins of preference or the introduction of new

preferences. Such existing preferences included the system of British tariff preferences exchanged in the pre-war period among Commonwealth countries, including Canada, as well as trade preferences within the French colonial system. Another major exception was provided from the start for countries which form customs unions or free-trade areas; and specific rules and conditions for such arrangements are set out in Article XXIV.

Since the General Agreement was concluded, a number of customs unions and free-trade areas have been established which are in varying degrees compatible with the models established under Article XXIV. The customs-union and free-trade-area models have been developed especially within the process of post-war integration in Western Europe and among certain groups of less-developed countries. Several other preferential trade arrangements which are not designed as customs unions or free-trade areas have also been created among GATT members or between GATT members and outside countries. For some of these, the GATT Contracting Parties have granted special dispensations in the form of 'waivers' under the provisions of Article XXV; these waivers require approval by a two-thirds-majority vote.

Customs Unions and Free-Trade Areas

Article XXIV of the General Agreement provides an exemption from the MFN rules, not only for members of full-fledged customs unions and free-trade areas, but also for countries that conclude 'interim arrangements' designed to lead to the formation of customs unions or free-trade areas. In practice, most regional trade arrangements when presented in GATT, have been in the form of such interim agreements.

Article XXIV defines a 'customs union' as an arrangement whereby member countries not only remove tariffs and other barriers to their internal trade, but also establish a common external tariff that is applicable to imports from outside the area. Within a free-trade area, on the other hand, the member countries retain their individual national tariffs, while removing tariffs and other barriers to internal trade. A customs union thus involves a higher degree of integration of trade and trade-related policies among member countries, which may extend to political and social areas as well, although within a free-trade area, a certain degree of harmonization of trade policies may also be required. Because the parties to a free-trade area usually have different levels of tariffs on imports from outside countries, they adopt 'rules of origin' designed to prevent outside goods from entering a member country with a low tariff, in order to move on into another member country with a higher tariff; these rules of origin can have significant consequences for the trade interests of outside countries.

Other rules in Article XXIV that govern the formation and operation of customs unions and free-trade areas include the following:[1]

- Tariffs and other "restrictive regulations of commerce," with certain specified exceptions, must be removed on "substantially all the trade" within the area.

- After the formation of the customs union or free-trade area, tariffs and other barriers on imports from outside the area must not be higher or more restrictive than before its formation.

- Countries which conclude interim agreements leading to the formation of customs unions or free-trade areas are required to submit their plans and schedules to the GATT Contracting Parties for examination. Among other requirements, interim agreements must be designed to lead to the full-fledged arrangement within a reasonable period of time.

- If the GATT Contracting Parties consider these plans unreasonable, they may make recommendations to the proponents, and the latter may not proceed without modifying their plans acceptably.

As part of GATT efforts to control the operation of regional trade groups, procedures have been adopted for regular reporting by their members, usually every two years. Nominally, at any rate, these procedures offer opportunities for outside countries to exert continuing supervision over them. Further, outside countries retain the ultimate right to retaliate against countries which operate preferential trade policies that are not determined to be customs unions or free-trade areas in accordance with the rules of Article XXIV.

One might ask why the GATT rules were drawn up in terms so firmly opposed to new trade preferences and discrimination, while permitting the formation of customs unions and free-trade areas. In part, the reason was that from the beginning, it was recognized that the post-war trade system would have to accommodate several customs unions already in existence or in the process of being formed, such as the Benelux Union. But a broader economic justification was also advanced as appears from the following passage from a study by the head of the United States (US) delegation at the Havana Conference:

> Preferences have been opposed and customs unions favored, in principle, by the United States. This position may obviously be criticized as lacking in logical consistency. In preferential arrangements, discrimination against the outer world is partial; in customs unions, it is complete. But the distinction is none the less defensible. A customs union creates a wider trading area, removes obstacles to competition, makes possible a more economic allocation of resources, and thus operates to competition, makes possible a more economic allocation of resources, and thus operates to increase production and raise planes of living. A preferential system, on the other hand, retains internal barriers, obstructs economy in production, and restrains the growth of income and demand. . . . A customs union is conducive to the expan-

sion of trade on a basis of multilateralism and non-discrimination; a preferential system is not.[2]

Accordingly, an exemption from the MFN rule for customs unions was written into Article 44 of the draft of the Charter of the International Trade Organization (ITO) as it was prepared in advance of the Havana Conference; and an identical exemption was carried into Article XXIV of the General Agreement, which was brought into force in advance of the proposed ITO Charter. The process by which this exemption was extended to include free-trade areas, as well as customs unions, if of special interest from a Canadian perspective. The change appears to have been proposed during the Havana Conference, primarily to accommodate a possible Canada-United States (USA) free-trade arrangement, or 'partial customs union,' that was then under discussion between Ottawa and Washington. The discussions were broken off after a few months, at the insistence of Prime Minister King; but meanwhile, Article 44 of the Havana Charter had been broadened to accommodate free-trade areas as well as customs unions, and Article XXIV of the General Agreement was correspondingly amended.[3]

Over the post-war period, and especially since the late 1950s, a large number of regional trade arrangements have been brought before GATT as customs unions and free-trade areas within the scope of Article XXIV. With a few exceptions, these regional trade arrangements fall into two main groups:

- The European Economic Community and the network of free-trade arrangements and preferential trade arrangements that now surround the Community

- Regional trade arrangements concluded among groups of less-developed countries.

Almost all of these were brought to GATT as 'interim agreements,' rather than as full-fledged customs unions or free-trade arrangements. Of these, a number subsequently evolved more or less as required by Article-XXIV rules; others are still in the process of evolution, and the future of some of these is uncertain; still others have been abandoned for one reason or another.

The GATT procedures for dealing with these regional arrangements have followed a generally similar pattern. The member countries are obliged to submit details of their arrangements, along with plans and schedules for removing internal trade barriers and, if a customs union is planned, for establishing a common external tariff. Special working parties, on which Canada is invariably represented, are established to review the arrangement in question. The arrangement is scrutinized against the tests of Article XXIV, and outside countries may seek to have it modified where inconsistencies with the rules are found, or where damage to outside trade interests is identified. In some instances, the member countries have adjusted their plans as a result of outside pressure. In practice, only a few customs unions and free-trade areas have been determined to meet fully the tests of Article XXIV: these include the Caribbean Economic Community and the earlier Anglo-Irish Free Trade Area. Some other arrangements have given rise to disagreement about their consistency with Article XXIV, but have nevertheless been put into place and continue to operate without formal GATT approval; these include the European Community (EC) and the European Free-Trade Association (EFTA).

European Integration

The European Economic Community was formed in 1957, by the Treaty of Rome, among France, Germany, Italy, Belgium, the Netherlands and Luxembourg; it has subsequently been enlarged to include Britain, Ireland, Denmark and Greece, and negotiations for the accession of Spain and Portugal are in progress. As negotiations to form the Community were proceeding, discussions took place within the Organization for European Economic Cooperation (OEEC) to link the Community with a wider free-trade arrangement embracing other Western European countries. When this effort failed, the separate European Free Trade Association was formed, in 1959, among Britain, Denmark, Sweden, Norway, Switzerland, Austria and Portugal; EFTA was later extended to include Finland as well.[4]

Canada had special concerns about the formation and operation of the European Community, in view of the importance of its trade with the member countries and the large role these occupy in the world-trade system. In GATT examinations of the EC, as well as in separate negotiations about its trade policies, Canada, in association with other outside countries, strongly pressed its trade interests on the basis of the GATT rules.

One initial Canadian concern about the EC, shared by others, was the levels of its common external tariff. Generally, the amount of this tariff was arrived at by averaging the individual rates applied by the six member countries; the process thus involved general increases in the rates of the traditionally low-tariff members, that is, Germany and the Benelux countries; these two countries represented more important export markets for Canada than did France and Italy, which had relatively high tariffs. Many of the rates to be increased had also been 'bound' by the individual member countries in previous GATT negotiations. Negotiations with respect to the establishment of the EC common external tariff occupied a large part of the Dillon Round in 1961–62.

From the beginning, another serious and continuing concern for Canada and other outside countries arose from the Community's Common Agricultural Policy (CAP), which was generally designed to increase levels of self-sufficiency, within the EC area, of a range of staple products, including wheat and other grains, dairy products, meat, sugar and oil seeds. Under the

CAP, substantial subsidies are provided for Community producers of these products, which often generate surpluses that are then exported to world markets at low and subsidized prices. Imports are held back by a variety of controls, including a system of 'variable levies' designed to protect domestic producers from outside competition. (See Chapter 12, below.)

A third element of the Community, which has been widely regarded as inconsistent with GATT rules and has caused conflict with other GATT members, is the network of free-trade and preferential trade agreements which the Community concluded with Greece, Spain and Portugal, in anticipation of their eventual membership in the Community; with neighbouring members of the European Free Trade Association; with a long list of Mediterranean countries; and with a large number of former colonial territories, first in Africa and later in the Caribbean and the Pacific areas.

During the 1960s, the Community concluded trade agreements with Greece, Spain and Turkey, which anticipated eventual full membership in the Community for these countries. These agreements, however, contained a number of elements that were widely regarded by outside countries as simply preferential in nature and thus inconsistent with the Article XXIV and other GATT rules. Greece eventually joined the Community as a full member in 1981; Turkish membership is not now under discussion; and negotiations for full membership are continued with Spain and with Portugal.

Following the entry of Britain, Ireland and Denmark into the Community in 1973, the Community concluded free-trade agreements with the EFTA countries that had not joined the EC: that is, Norway, Sweden, Finland, Austria, Switzerland and Portugal. These agreements exclude free trade in agricultural products and, largely on these grounds, have been criticized in GATT as falling short of free-trade agreements as defined in Article XXIV. The agreements, however, have greatly enlarged the area of industrial free trade within Western Europe and have given these countries free access to a much enlarged, internal, Western European market.

Since the 1960s, the Community has followed a policy of establishing a network of special trade and economic relationships with virtually all of the 'southern' Mediterranean countries: that is, those countries other than Greece, Spain, Portugal and Turkey that border on the Mediterranean. These relationships clearly constitute preferential trade arrangements, and do not anticipate an evolution of free-trade or customs-union arrangements within the scope of GATT Article XXIV. These agreements have been widely regarded by outside countries as contrary to the GATT rules. The Community has argued, however, that they are justified by the special provisions of Part IV of the General Agreement, since the Mediterranean countries concerned are all in the less-developed group. (See Chapter 10, below, for a discussion of Part IV of GATT.)

From the start, the Treaty of Rome, which established the Community, provided for the 'association' of a group of colonies or former colonies, mainly in Africa, of France, Belgium, the Netherlands and Italy. These countries and territories became entitled to free access to the Community area for most of their exports, and they extended various 'reverse preferences' to their imports from the Community. In the 1960s the arrangements with a group of newly independent 'associated states' in Africa were recast under the first and second Yaoundé Conventions. After Britain's entry into the Community, the Yaoundé Convention was subsumed in the Lomé Convention of 1975, in order to take in a group of British colonies and former colonies, as well as a few additional African countries.

Exports from this larger group of developing countries in Africa, the Caribbean and the Pacific, which are known as the 'ACP' states, plus various French, Dutch and British colonial areas, generally enter the Community market free of customs duties and other restrictions, except for products falling under the Common Agricultural Policy, for which special rules exist. The ACP countries include only a partial list of developing Commonwealth countries and British colonies. Among the exclusions are India, Malaysia, Sri Lanka, Singapore and Hong Kong; Pakistan is also excluded. The ACP countries have no obligation to extend 'reverse preferences' to their imports from the Community, although some such preferences may exist in one form or another. The Lomé Convention involves no special trade arrangement among the ACP countries themselves. These arrangements were extended to 1985 under Lomé II, concluded in 1979.

Like the arrangements that preceded it, the Lomé Convention has been widely criticized as contrary to the rules of GATT; and the excluded developing countries, in particular, have complained about the preferential access to the enlarged Community market which is enjoyed by the group of ACP countries. The Community and the ACP countries have argued that the Lomé arrangements, like those between the Community and the southern Mediterranean countries, are justified under the special rules for developing countries in Part IV of the General Agreement.[5]

The creation of this new, large, European, trading system which is centred on the European Community has had profound effects on the broader world-trade system, involving, among other changes, a realignment of power relationships, which has diminished somewhat the role and influence of Canada within the system. The formation of the Community itself involved costs for non-member countries, including Canada, as imports were diverted from outside sources to tariff-free sources within the Community. The area of tariff preference was greatly extended by the enlargement of the Community in the early 1970s, particularly by the entry of Britain, as well as by the creation of the wider area of tariff-free trade for industrial products, under a network of free-trade and other preferential trading arrangements discussed above. Britain's entry into the Community not only extended the area of discrimination against Canadian exports to include Britain, but also involved the loss of traditional tariff preferences in the British market for a range of Canadian exports. For these products, the levels of British tariff increased from lower preferential rates (which for some products were set at zero) to the higher levels of the Community's common external tariff. Other Commonwealth countries were similarly affected.

More serious, probably, has been the impact of the Common Agricultural Policy, in view of the traditional importance of Western Europe, and especially Britain, as markets for a range of Canadian farm exports. The increased domestic production generated by the CAP not only replaced imports of many products, but also led to increased EC exports of surplus production, at subsidized prices, to third countries. While the Community remains Canada's largest export market for agricultural products, these exports now consist largely of wheat, animal feeds and oil seeds; traditional large markets in Britain and Western Europe for wheat flour, cheese and apples have greatly declined.[6]

The expansion of economic activity and incomes attributable to the process of integration has offset the adverse trade effects arising from the process of economic integration in Western Europe, for Canada and other outside countries. The net effect of European integration on Canadian trade is perhaps impossible to measure, and the costs and benefits are doubtless unevenly distributed across the range of Canadian trade interests.

Regional Trade Groups among Developing Countries

We noted earlier that the formation of regional trade groups in the post-war period has mainly involved, first, the process of economic integration in Western Europe and, secondly, the establishment of a variety of trade and economic arrangements among developing countries. A free-trade area between Australia and New Zealand has also been in the process of formation for a number of years. In addition, Finland and a number of Eastern European countries, including the Soviet Union, have concluded free-trade arrangements, for reasons which appear to be largely political, and which are especially difficult to reconcile with GATT rules because of the state-trading systems of Finland's partners.

Among developing countries, attempts to develop free-trade and customs-union arrangements have had mixed results. Such arrangements have been more common in Latin America and in Africa than among Asian countries.

The Latin-American Free Trade Association (LAFTA), which existed for two decades until it was dissolved in 1980, never succeeded in liberalizing more than a small proportion of intraregional trade, and progress in this direction almost came to a halt during the 1970s. The relatively less-developed members of LAFTA, in particular, complained that they gained unequal benefits from internal liberalization, and in 1969 a group of these countries formed a subregional 'Andean' group which aimed less at trade liberalization than at co-ordinating their industrial development on a regional basis. The original members of the Andean group were Bolivia, Chile, Colombia, Ecuador and Peru. Venezuela joined the group in 1973, and Chile withdrew in 1976. The Andean arrangement has not been submitted to GATT for examination. In 1980, when LAFTA was finally dissolved, a looser arrangement was concluded among Latin America countries, which does not call for internal trade liberalization on an area-wide basis, but permits the establishment of narrower or bilateral trade deals in the area. This new arrangement is called the 'Latin American Integration Association' (LAIA); its future development is unclear.

On the other hand, both the Central American Common Market and the Caribbean Common Market (CARICOM) have emerged from earlier free-trade-area arrangements as full-fledged customs unions. These unions follow the lines of the GATT Article-XXIV model, but have more definite plans for a high degree of internal trade liberalization and unified, common, external tariffs on imports from outside countries. A GATT working party, after an examination of CARICOM, agreed, in 1977, that it "constituted an interim agreement leading to the establishment of a customs union and as such was consistent with the provisions of Article XXIV of the General Agreement."[7]

Only a few of the many regional trade and economic arrangements among African countries have been brought before GATT as arrangements falling under the provisions of Article XXIV. This is partly because many such arrangements have involved only non-members of GATT, and partly because, for the most part, they have been essentially preferential arrangements covering selected areas of regional trade. Among those that have been formed are the Economic Community of West African States (ECOWAS) and the Central African Customs and Economic Union (UDEAC). An Association of South-East Asian Nations (ASEAN) was developed in the mid-1970s among Indonesia, Malaysia, Singapore, the Philippines and Thailand. On the trade side, the Association does not aim at establishing a full free-trade area or customs union, but rather involves exchanges of trade preferences among its members. It was presented in GATT as a preferential trade arrangement, and in 1979 the Contracting Parties adopted a Decision to the effect that these arrangements were consistent with Part IV of the General Agreement.[8]

The further development of regional integration arrangements among developing countries has been given new impetus in recent years by the emergence of concepts of increased 'self-reliance' on the part of developing countries, and the concept of 'de-linking' the South from the North. The recently issued Brandt Report, for example, considers that the growth of integration arrangements among developing countries, on a regional, sub-regional or global basis, would be an important dimension of the New International Economic Order. In 1979 a Ministerial Meeting of the Group of 77 in Arusha, Tanzania, called for the building of new sets of relationships among developing countries. Within the United Nations Conference on Trade and Development (UNCTAD), a special working party has been created to pursue measures for strengthening economic integration among developing countries, not only in trade areas, but in other areas as well.[9]

The GATT rules now provide a great deal of latitude for tariff and trade preferences favouring developing countries, apart from whatever general blessing for such arrangements Part IV of the General Agreement may provide. As we shall discuss in Chapter 10, below, a Decision was adopted by the Contracting Parties, in 1971, to release developed countries from their most-favoured-nation (MFN) obligations under Article I, in order to extend tariff preferences to developing countries under the Generalized System of Preferences (GSP), which had been developed within UNCTAD. Canada and other developed countries implemented GSP schemes during the early 1970s. By another Decision, also adopted in 1971, the Contracting Parties permitted developing countries to extend tariff preferences among themselves, under a special "Protocol on Trade Negotiations among Developing Countries"; any such preferences, however, must be extended to all other developing countries on a global basis. Only a relatively few developing countries have signed the 1971 Protocol, and only a modest amount of trade has been liberalized among developing countries under this arrangement.[10]

One outcome of the Tokyo Round, embodied in a GATT Decision taken in November 1979, was to relax further GATT rules governing trade preferences as these apply to developing countries. The Decision sanctioned new "regional or global" arrangements entered into among developing countries

> ... for the mutual reduction or elimination of tariffs and, in accordance with criteria or conditions which may be prescribed by the Contracting Parties, for the mutual reduction or elimination of non-tariff measures, on products imported from one another.[11]

Any such preferential arrangements must be submitted to GATT for examination; the parties to them are obliged to consult with outside countries which may be affected; and outside countries may enlist the help of the Contracting Parties in order to reach satisfactory solutions to problems arising from particular arrangements.[12] These more relaxed Tokyo Round rules open the way to the possible formation of a new generation of preferential trade arrangements between pairs, or among groups, of developing countries.

GATT Waivers for Regional Trade Arrangements

As we noted earlier, the GATT Contracting Parties have granted several waivers under the provisions of Article XXV of the General Agreement to permit bilateral and regional trade arrangements which are not designed to create free-trade areas or customs unions, and hence would not be covered by

Article XXIV. Among these was a waiver, granted in 1952, to accommodate the formation of the European Coal and Steel Community; this waiver liberalized trade in these products among the six countries that subsequently established the broader European Community. Another such waiver was granted in 1965 to the United States, to permit it to remove tariffs on imports of automotive products from Canada on a preferential basis under the Canada-USA Automotive Agreement. Canada needed no similar waiver, since it offered to extend to other countries the same kind of terms with respect to imports of automotive products as those it extended to the United States.

Approval for waivers covering preferential trade arrangements is by no means automatic in GATT. The consent of two-thirds of the contracting parties is required. It is true that the USA obtained, without great difficulty, a waiver to cover its participation in the Automotive Agreement, but consent to this waiver reflected, in part, a general view that the trade interests of outside countries would not be seriously affected.[13] It could be far more difficult, however, to obtain the approval of a two-thirds majority in GATT for bilateral or regional trade arrangements of a preferential kind that appeared likely to damage important trade interests of third countries or groups of outside countries.

Effectiveness of GATT Controls

The spread of regional trade groups within the GATT system can be exaggerated. Regionalism has emerged in its most highly developed form within Western Europe; it has centred on the European Community and has extended to neighbouring members of the European Free Trade Association, to Mediterranean countries, and to former colonial areas. The GATT rules, however, imperfectly observed, served as a model for this process of European integration. And while they permitted the development of regional trade arrangements in Europe and elsewhere, they have served to provide some measure of international supervision and control over the process. They have also provided a basis for outside countries to try to correct elements that adversely affected their own trade interests, or to seek compensation where corrections could not be agreed upon. Even if outside countries have not strongly exerted their leverage, the existence of the GATT rules may be judged to have exercised a restraining influence on members of regional trade groups.[14]

Even if it were desirable, it is probably impractical, at this stage, to consider any basic changes in GATT rules in order to limit the formation and operation of regional trade arrangements. At the same time, it might be possible and desirable to develop more effective procedures within GATT for the international supervision of such arrangements, as well as some better standards for correcting features of procedures that adversely affect outside countries. It would seem desirable, for example, to adopt within GATT a new and improved set of guidelines for the operation of regional trade arrangements. It might be possible to embody in such guidelines a stronger commitment by participating countries to correct elements that damage outside countries. It might also be possible to adopt some special built-in procedures for the settlement of disputes arising from the operation of regional trade arrangements.

Proposals for Canada-USA Free-Trade Arrangements

Partly as a consequence of the development of regional trade groups in Western Europe and elsewhere, it has become common to point to Canada as almost the only industrialized country that is not now integrated with a market of at least one hundred million people. There has been a great deal of discussion in Canada about the potential benefits to its economy that might flow from Canadian participation in free-trade arrangements, both in terms of improving access to broader markets for efficient Canadian producers, and also in terms of enlarging its economy through the restructuring of Canadian manufacturing industries that would follow the removal of Canada's own barriers to imports. In the mid-1970s, the Economic Council of Canada saw, as the best choices for the country, the elimination of trade barriers by Canada and other nations, either on a broad multilateral basis or else within a large area encompassing the United States, the European Community and Japan. Because neither of these options appeared attainable, the Council favoured a free-trade area with the United States as the most practical course.[15]

The case for Canada's negotiating a free-trade area with the United States has recently been made in forceful terms in a report by the Standing Senate Committee on Foreign Affairs. The Committee recommended that the two countries should submit to GATT, under Article XXIV, a plan and schedule for the formation of a free-trade area covering non-tariff barriers as well as tariffs, with an exception for trade in agricultural products.[16] The recommendations of this Senate Committee have not drawn much support from the Canadian government; and the desirability and practicality of embarking on such negotiations have been questioned on a number of grounds, including doubts about whether the United States would favour such arrangements.[17]

On the basis of the discussion in this chapter of the present study, and without entering into the merits of free-trade between Canada and the USA, it would seem desirable to draw a distinction between, on the one hand, the desirability of removing or reducing barriers to actual and potential bilateral trade and, on the other, the desirability of removing these barriers on a preferential basis or within the framework of a formal free-trade area modelled on GATT Article XXIV rules. This distinction was drawn in a recent study of new arrangements to deal with a number of major Canada-USA trade issues in the 1980s, as follows:

> It is important to understand that whether these bilaterally negotiated arrangements are extended to others on a most-favored-nation basis or on some basis of reciprocity (for example, on a "conditional" most-favored-nation basis) is a question to be decided issue by issue, case by case. To argue that we should be willing to negotiate bilaterally is not to say that we should seek preferential arrangements. This is a separate issue. . . .[18]

In the context of the present study of the world-trade system, it is desirable that further consideration should be given to the consequences for that system as a whole, which could arise from the formation of a bilateral and preferential free-trade area of the classical kind between Canada and the United States. Because both countries, but particularly the United States, play a large role in the world-trade system, the consequences of such an arrangement for third countries could be substantial, and even greater than they would have been at earlier periods. Moreover, the precedents set by the movement towards European economic integration in the 1950s and 1960s, with all the broader political and security elements that surround this process, are not necessarily adaptable to the formation of a bilateral and preferential Canada-USA free-trade arrangement in the 1980s.

Notes

1. For detailed discussions of GATT rules governing customs unions and free-trade areas, see J.H. Jackson, *World Trade and the Law of GATT*, Chapter 24; a list of regional arrangements presented in GATT as of 1969 is on pp. 592-99. See also K.W. Dam, *The GATT: Law and International Economic Organization*, Chapter 16. A more detailed analysis, including an examination of the main regional groups, as of the mid-1960s, is in G. Patterson, *Discrimination in International Trade: The Policy Issues 1945–1965*, Chapter IV.

2. C. Wilcox, *A Charter for World Trade*, pp. 70-71.

3. For a review of the Canada-USA discussions in 1947–48 of a possible free-trade arrangement, see R.D. Cuff and J.L. Granatstein, *American Dollars–Canadian Prosperity: Canadian-American Economic Relations 1945–1950*, Chapter 3. Wilcox, *A Charter*, p. 71, makes a brief reference to the change made to Charter Article 44, without any mention of these Canada-USA discussions. At the conclusion of the Havana Conference, an amendment to Article XXIV of the General Agreement was made by a "Special Protocol"; the text is in *Canada Treaty Series, 1948*, No. 12.

4. For a brief account of the formation of the EC and EFTA and the examination of these arrangements in GATT, see G. Curzon, *Multilateral Commercial Diplomacy*, pp. 273-86.

5. D. Swann, *The Economics of the Common Market*, contains an examination of the structure and operation of the economic elements of the European Community. For a survey of the network of free-trade and preferential-trade agreements linked to the Community, see P. Coffey, *The External Economic Relations of the*

EEC. For details of the Lomé Convention, see "Lomé II Dossier," a reprint from *The Courier* 58 (November 1979). An account of the examination in GATT of the Lomé Convention is in GATT, *Basic Instruments and Selected Documents, Twenty-third Supplement*, pp. 46-55.

6. See Bertrand Nadeau, "L'Entreé de la Grande-Bretagne dans le marché commun et les exportations agricoles du Canada à ce pays." A brief discussion of the implications for Canadian exports of economic integration in Western Europe is in R.J. Wonnacott, *Canada's Trade Options*, pp. 4-9. See also L.A. Fischer, "The Common Agricultural Policy of the EC: Its Impact on Canadian Agriculture," and T. Cohn, "Canada and the European Economic Community's Common Agricultural Policy: The Issue of Trade in Cheese."

7. GATT, *Basic Instruments and Selected Documents, Twenty-fourth Supplement*, pp. 68-72.

8. The Decision of the GATT Contracting Parties with regard to the ASEAN agreement is in GATT, *Basic Instruments and Selected Documents, Twenty-sixth Supplement.*

9. See Independent Commission on International Development Issues (Brandt Commission), *North-South: A Programme for Survival*, pp. 133-35. For recent studies of regional trade and economic arrangements among developing countries, see E. Nicol, L. Echeverria and A. Peccei (ed.), *Regionalism and the New International Economic Order.*

10. The text of this Protocol is in Gatt, *Basic Instruments and Selected Documents, Eighteenth Supplement*. Successive issues in this series contain accounts of exchanges of tariff preferences under the Protocol.

11. GATT, *Basic Instruments and Selected Documents, Twenty-sixth Supplement*, p. 203.

12. A "Decision on Differential and More Favourable Treatment and Reciprocity and Fuller Participation of Developing Countries" was adopted by the GATT Contracting Parties at their Session of 26-29 November 1979, as one of the four so-called 'Framework Decisions' that emerged from the Tokyo Round. This Decision, among other things, provides a new basis for regional and global preferential trade arrangements among developing countries. The text is in GATT, *Basic Instruments and Selected Documents, Twenty-sixth Supplement.*

13. For an account of this waiver, see GATT, *Basic Instruments and Selected Documents, Thirteenth Supplement*, p. 112.

14. The economic integration of Western Europe, of course, has evolved on the basis of broader political and security concepts which have enjoyed wide support within and outside Western Europe, including general support by Canada. The process would doubtless have proceeded whether or not GATT rules on customs unions and free-trade areas had existed to accommodate it. It is significant that neither the United States nor Japan has pursued the Western European example and sought to create (or re-create) new regional trade groups centred around the large domestic markets of each, although the US Administration has recently proposed the establishment of special preferential trade arrangements with countries of the Caribbean basin, and also with a group of central American countries and with

Israel. These arrangements appear to have been proposed largely for political and strategic reasons. If they go forward, they could raise difficult issues in GATT.

15. Economic Council of Canada, *Looking Outward: A New Trade Strategy for Canada*, Chapters 8 and 9. See also Wonnacott, *Canada's Trade Options* and R. Dauphin, *The Impact of Free Trade in Canada*.

16. Canada, Parliament, Senate, Standing Committee on Foreign Affairs, *Canada-United States Relations: Volume III, Canada's Trade Relations with the United States*.

17. See, for example, A.R. Moroz and K.J. Back, "Prospects for a Canada-United States Bilateral Free Trade Agreement: The Other Side of the Fence."

18. R. de C. Grey, *Trade Policy in the 1980s: An Agenda for Canadian-U.S. Relations*, p. 8.

8

The Organisation for Economic Co-operation and Development

The Organisation for Economic Co-operation and Development (OECD) and its predecessor, the Organization for European Economic Cooperation (OEEC), have played a significant role in the world-trade system for over thirty years, although trade issues have occupied only part of a much broader range of activities of both organizations. From 1948 to 1960, the earlier OEEC focused mainly on the reconstruction of the war-damaged economies of its Western European members. Canada and the United States were closely involved as associate members. The successor OECD has had a broader base of membership and a wider range of activities. From its beginning in 1960, Canada and the United States have been full members; Japan, Australia and New Zealand became members in the early 1970s. The twenty-four member countries thus constitute a kind of 'club' of the world's most highly developed and richer countries. OECD represents one of the poles of the North-South alignment that has characterized international approaches to economic, trade and development issues over the past decade. It also represents a pole of the East-West alignment in economic and trade areas.

Unlike GATT, OECD is not based on a set of agreed and binding rules, although it has evolved common approaches to a number of economic and trade-policy issues, mainly in the form of recommendations and voluntary codes or guidelines. In the trade area, as in its numerous other areas of activity, the OECD provides a mechanism for continuing exchanges of information and consultations on issues of common concern, creating opportunities for its members to seek to influence the formulation and implementation of one another's trade policies. In support of these activities, OECD maintains a sizeable Secretariat at its headquarters in Paris, and carries out extensive programs of research, analysis and publications.[1]

Post-war Reconstruction of Europe

Canada was closely involved from the beginning in post-war efforts to recon-struct the war-damaged economies of Britain and other Western European countries which were major traditional markets for a range of Canadian exports. Canada had a large interest in the early restoration of its export markets in Western Europe, so that export earnings in Europe could be used to cover post-war deficits in Canada's trade with the United States (USA). A Canadian government report in 1948 described the disruptive effects of the war in the following terms:

> Canada's historic international trade rested on a triangular pattern with the United Kingdom and the United States. This pattern has to-day almost disappeared. Before the war Canadian exports to the United Kingdom were greater in value than her imports from that country. Canadian imports from the United States were greater in value than her exports to that country. Largely from the earnings of her invest-ments abroad, the United Kingdom was able to achieve a surplus with the United States; and Canada, therefore, was in a position to utilise a portion of this surplus in meeting her indebtedness to the United States. This triangular relationship was seriously weakened by the impact of the First World War and has been almost totally destroyed by World War II. The remnants of the structure are now being maintained by a huge volume of loans, credits and grants from both Canada and the United States to the United Kingdom and to other Western European economies.[2]

The Canadian and United States (US) assistance programs for Western Europe, and their close association with OEEC, were thus regarded as means of hastening the restoration of a multilateral pattern of trade and the convert-ibility of European currencies. These were major Canadian objectives in the post-war period.

Canadian assistance to Western Europe's recovery was generous. As the war came to an end, Canada made gifts of large quantities of food, medical supplies and other necessities to liberated countries of Western Europe under military relief programs and through United Nations (UN) programs directed by the United Nations Relief and Rehabilitation Administration (UNRRA). After 1944 Canada also extended loans amounting to about six hundred million dollars, on concessional terms, under the newly adopted Export Credits

Insurance Act, to France, Belgium, Netherlands, Norway and some other war-damaged countries.

In the spring of 1946, the United States made to Britain a loan amounting to $3750 million, on concessional terms. The loan agreement embodied, as well, a renewed commitment by Britain to support the kind of multilateral and non-discriminatory, post-war, world-trade system that was the object of the US policy that was to be established under the proposed Havana Charter and the International Trade Organization (ITO). The US loan agreement also obligated Britain to make sterling convertible by March 1947, a condition that proved quite unrealistic.

About the same time, Canada also extended a loan to Britain amounting to $1250 million. This amount was substantially larger, in relation to Canada's economic strength, than the US loan. The terms of the Canadian loan were parallel to those of the US loan agreement, but no date was proposed for sterling convertibility.

Loans and other assistance on this scale imposed severe strains on Canada's balance of payments. Exports financed by these means did not earn cash that could be converted to pay for imports from the United States. Canada quickly developed a serious dollar problem of its own. Between May 1946 and November 1947, Canada's reserves of gold and US dollars fell from almost $1.7 billion to $500 million. As a consequence, the government imposed severe foreign-exchange controls and import restrictions in November 1947. Ironically, these restrictions were imposed on the very day Prime Minister King, in glowing terms, announced on the radio from London the successful conclusion of the GATT negotiations in Geneva.[3] These controls and restrictions were relaxed relatively quickly, however, following an upturn in Canadian exports to the United States during 1948–49, and an increase in dollar earnings by Canada from exports to Western Europe, financed, in part, under the Marshall Plan. Under its Marshall Plan program, the United States provided almost thirteen billion dollars' worth of grant aid to Western European countries between 1948 and 1952, in support of reconstruction efforts. A significant part of this aid was made available so that Western European countries could pay in US dollars for imports from Canada and other 'offshore' sources.

Establishment of OEEC

One of the conditions attached to US aid under the Marshall Plan was that the European recipients would co-ordinate their individual post-war reconstruction programs. For this purpose the countries concerned established a permanent organization in Paris, in the form of the Organization for European Economic Cooperation. Canada and the United States became associate members, and Canada was closely associated with most of its activities.

The OEEC was also given a broad mandate to support the growth of industrial and agricultural production in Europe, to study possibilities for the development of customs unions and free-trade areas in Europe, and to encourage the expansion of intra-European trade. The OEEC approach in the trade area was quite different from the GATT system. That system involved binding commitments by governments to adhere to a set of agreed rules, and negotiations aimed at trade liberalization through tariff cutting. OEEC functioned through a process of continuous consultation among member countries on trade and other areas of common interest. Over a period, this process of consultation was refined and extended to broader economic policies; it led to the member countries adopting, not always unanimously, recommendations, codes and guidelines aimed at influencing the formulation and operation of the policies of the member countries.

Thus a Code of Liberalization of Trade was developed in 1950, applicable to the European members, but not to Canada and the United States. Under the Code, the member countries undertook to dismantle, in stages, the widespread quantitative restrictions that impeded intra-European trade. The Code did not apply to tariffs, and it left substantial disparities in levels of tariffs imposed by member countries on imports from one another. The obligations under the Code were not legally binding, and were unevenly observed among OEEC-member countries. Nevertheless, over the decade of the 1950s, trade among the OEEC members in most industrialized products, although not in agricultural products, was largely freed from quantitative restrictions. This trade liberalization was not extended to outside countries, including Canada, or was extended to them at a slower pace; thus there occurred a growth of discrimination against imports from outside the OEEC area, a development which caused increasing concern to Canada. The OEEC trade code was reinforced by other codes calling for the liberalization of invisible transactions and flows of capital within the OEEC area; and the progressive relaxation of controls on intra-European payments was supported by the creation of a European Payments Union (EPU), to which the United States contributed $350 million. By the end of the 1950s, the economic recovery of Europe had proceeded to a point where the OEEC countries made their currencies partly convertible into currencies of other countries, and in 1961 most of them restored full convertibility.

Canada was somewhat less willing than the United States to allow its broad support for Western European recovery to override its objections to discrimination against Canadian exports. Through the 1950s, in OEEC, GATT and the International Monetary Fund (IMF), as well as through other channels, Canadian protests grew louder as the OEEC-member countries progressively dismantled quantitative restrictions against one another's exports without giving equal treatment to Canada. The campaign against trade discrimination by Western European countries progressively shifted from OEEC into GATT, where a special Balance-of-Payments Committee was established in 1955, and where discrimination by OEEC-member countries in the use of quantitative restrictions could be challenged on the basis of the stricter rules of the General Agreement.

Canadian concern about discriminatory European import restrictions were increased in the later 1950s by the evolution of plans for new customs-unions and free-trade-area arrangements within Europe. There were particularly serious misgivings in Canada about the prospect of British participation in these European groupings, since Britain was Canada's major market in Europe and many important Canadian exports enjoyed long-standing tariff preferences in that country. During the late 1950s and early 1960s, the Diefenbaker government took a particularly strong position against losing preferential access for Canadian exports to Britain and, more generally, against new or continued Western European arrangements that discriminated against Canadian exports.[4]

OEEC Becomes OECD

By the end of the 1950s, European reconstruction had been largely accomplished. Industrial and agricultural production was running far above pre-war levels; exports had revived; dollars were flowing into the area in large amounts; Western European currencies had been made externally convertible; and internal trade had been largely freed from quantitative restrictions. Among Western European countries, new forms of regional integration had been created with the establishment of the European Community (EC) and of the European Free Trade Association (EFTA). The resurgence of Europe's economic strength had significantly changed earlier post-war relationships with Canada and the United States, bringing a new emphasis on interdependence and partnership. And the task of assisting the developing countries was emerging as a major challenge for North American and Western European countries.

In these changed circumstances, the future role of the OEEC became increasingly uncertain; it was discussed at a series of intergovernmental meetings during 1960, in most of which Canada participated. The outcome was a decision to maintain the organization, but under new arrangements embodied in a Convention signed in Paris in December 1960. There the OEEC members created its successor, the Organisation for Economic Co-operation and Development, with Canada and the United States as full members.

The new organization retained functions in the trade area, but these were more limited. Under pressure from Canada and the United States, the Code of Liberalization of Trade was abandoned. It had served its function in reducing intra-European barriers to trade, but its maintenance might have encouraged new forms of trade discrimination by the new-born, European, regional trade groups. It was thus agreed that the new OECD should function in the trade area, as in other areas, through the process of consultation that had been worked out and refined in OEEC, and not under any special trade code.

OECD activities in trade areas have represented only one part of a complex of related activities covering general economic policy, monetary problems, investment flows, agricultural problems, economic development and aid, science, technology, education and other matters. The most important area of OECD work is probably in the co-ordination of general economic policy within the Committee on Economic Policy: this is an area where international co-operation has never developed very successfully within the United Nations framework. Other OECD activities overlap the work of more specialized international bodies within and outside the United Nations family of organizations, including GATT and the United Nations Conference on Trade and Development (UNCTAD). But OECD provides a unique framework where the links between these related policy issues can be analysed and addressed by the leading industrialized countries.

The object of co-operation within OECD is, for the most part, not to achieve common policies among its members. It is, rather, to harmonize national policies; to encourage parallel action in areas of common interest; and through a process of persuasion, to seek changes in national policies that may injure the interests of other members. The OECD process, however, has also served to diffuse confrontations and reduce the threat of retaliation on several specific trade issues. In several areas, such as governments' use of financial incentives to encourage exports, member countries have been able to agree on guidelines and other 'rules of the game' to be followed in the operation of their national policies. The forms of co-operation that have evolved within OECD, as well as the work done in OECD in central economic and trade areas, have provided one of the main foundations for the series of annual summit meetings, which have been held since the mid-1970s, among a smaller group of leading OECD members, including Canada.[5]

Activities in Trade Areas

Among the numerous other committees and sub-groups in OECD, a Trade Committee was established, which has been used by member countries as a forum for consultations on issues of common interest and for the development of common approaches in various trade areas. To a large extent, the Trade Committee has functioned as a forum for continuing exchanges of information and consultations on trade-policy issues of special interest, while member countries tended to use GATT, rather than OECD, to deal with larger issues and disputes. However, within the Trade Committee and in other OECD bodies, member countries have sought to concert their approaches to a number of specific issues that were subsequently carried over into GATT for further negotiations on a broader multilateral basis; they have also, many times, used

OECD as a forum for dealing with trade issues that fall outside the ambit of GATT; and they have used the OECD as a framework for reinforcing parallel initiatives in trade areas under consideration in Geneva. OECD activities of special interest in trade areas include the following:

Restrictive Business Practices

In 1961 the OECD established a committee of experts on restrictive business practices. At successive meetings, this committee examined national legislation in this area and identified practices that could have adverse effects on international trade. Interest in this area progressively increased as European countries and the European Community developed stronger combines and anti-trust legislation, and as concerns emerged over practices of multinational corporations. In 1967, 1973 and 1979, successive OECD recommendations were adopted, establishing guidelines and procedures for consultations among OECD governments with respect to restrictive business practices with effects beyond national borders, and to legal actions in one country that involved the interests of other members.[6] As we shall note below, in Chapter 9, OECD activities in this area have been overtaken by a more elaborate United Nations "Set of Multilaterally Agreed Equitable Principles and Rules" governing restrictive business practices, which was adopted by a UN Conference in April 1980. It might be noted that between Canada and the United States, bilateral arrangements have existed since 1959, which provide for co-operation in the area of anti-trust and competition policy.[7]

UNCTAD Issues and the Generalized System of Preferences

OECD is used regularly by its members for advance consultations on trade and other issues arising in UNCTAD. Following debates at the UNCTAD Conferences in 1964 and 1968, the industrialized countries used the OECD, during the early 1970s, to work out a common approach for the application of tariff preferences for developing countries. Meetings of OECD members are held regularly to exchange information on the operation of their preferential schemes.

The "Rey Report"

In the early 1970s, a twelve-member group of eminent economists was appointed to examine current international economic, monetary and trade issues, in the wake of the monetary and trade measures taken by the United States in August 1971. The report of this group, named after its chairman, gave strong support to a further strengthening of the multilateral trade system based on GATT, and to further efforts at trade liberalization; the report generally reinforced advance planning for the subsequent Tokyo Round of multilateral trade negotiations.[8]

Trade Pledge

In the aftermath of the 1973 oil crisis and the consequential payments problems for many OECD countries, a Ministerial-level meeting in 1974 adopted a 'Declaration' committing member countries, in dealing with their problems, to avoid the use of import restrictions, measures to subsidize exports, destructive competition in export credits, and export controls. This trade pledge was renewed annually until 1980, when it was replaced by a broader 'Declaration on Trade Policy' at a meeting of Ministers from OECD-member countries. The new Declaration has no terminal date; among other statements, it reaffirms the undertakings of OECD countries to maintain and improve an open and multilateral trade system, to strengthen GATT, to implement fully their commitments made in the Tokyo Round, and to move ahead with further improvements to the GATT system. It also embodies commitments to avoid restrictive trade measures, policies that distort export competition, and internal measures that have protectionist effects. In the context of the 1980 Declaration, OECD countries carry out 'periodic reviews' within the Trade Committee, aimed at examining one another's trade-policy measures with the object of trying to ensure that the Declaration is followed.[9]

Export Credits

The subsidization of exports by means of long-term credits supplied by governments at relatively low interest rates and on other favourable terms has become a major issue among OECD countries in recent years. In 1972 member countries undertook to notify one another in advance about the terms of credits extended for more than five years. In 1976 a 'Gentlemen's Agreement' on the subject was adopted, which was succeeded in 1978 by an 'Arrangement on Guidelines for Officially Supported Export Credits,' commonly called 'The Consensus.' This Consensus set out limits on terms to be offered for long-term credits, including the minimum interest rate that can be offered, with the object of putting all participants on a more or less equal footing. These interest rates, however, have been low in comparison with rates recently prevailing, especially in North America. Since the 1978 Consensus was adopted, the use of export credits as incentives for exports has grown, and wider divergences have emerged among interest rates prevailing in OECD-member countries. Moreover, at earlier periods, export credits on subsidized terms were used mainly to assist sales of capital goods to developing countries and state-trading countries; more recently, such export incentives have also been used to assist exports within the OECD area. In 1980 minimum interest rates under the Consensus were raised slightly, and because of pressure from the United States, negotiations continued on proposals for more substantial increases. In October 1981 agreement was nearly complete on a broader proposal involving increases in minimum interest rates; the differentiation of interest rates on sales to poor countries, to intermediate, and to richer countries; and a change in rules for the prior notification of mixed credits: that is, those that combine export credits and development aid. In July 1982 the rates were further revised upward, and the classification of borrowing countries was revised. One effect was to increase rates for loans to Eastern European countries and newly industrialized countries.[10]

As a country with relatively limited resources to subsidize export transactions, Canada has generally favoured rather strict rules and conditions governing the subsidization of exports. Nevertheless, in 1982, the terms offered by Canada's Export Development Corporation to assist a large sale of subway cars to New York City drew protests from the United States. Canada makes available long-term credits to assist export transactions under the Export Development Act, which was adopted in 1969 to replace the earlier Export Credits Insurance Act, and which is administered by the Export Development Corporation.

Government Procurement Practices

During the 1960s, the OECD Trade Committee examined government procurement policies of member countries and prepared a draft set of guidelines to govern the practices of member governments in this area; these guidelines were aimed at reducing discrimination against non-national suppliers. This draft code was transferred, in the early 1970s, to the Tokyo Round of multilateral trade negotiations, where it became the basis for the Agreement on Government Procurement that was adopted at the conclusion of the Tokyo Round. It has been observed that in the OECD discussions,

> . . . virtually all of the problems that would have to be faced if an international procurement code was to be adopted, surfaced. The OECD discussions resolved many of those problems and framed the remaining issues for resolution in the final year of the negotiations in the MTN.[11]

Agreements on Shipbuilding and Steel

In 1972 a 'General Arrangement' on shipbuilding was adopted among a group of OECD countries concerned. This Arrangement, aimed at reducing government subsidies that detracted from international competition, was succeeded in 1976 by a more elaborate set of 'General Guidelines for Government Policy in the Shipbuilding Industry,' which involved undertakings with respect to export pricing of certain types of ships. The object of these arrangements, which mainly involve European countries and Japan, was primarily to reduce competition for European industries from rapidly expanding Japanese ship-yards. In more recent years, however, new competition in the world market for ships has emerged from the growth of shipbuilding production outside the OECD area, in countries such as South Korea, Brazil and Taiwan.

Somewhat similar arrangements were developed within OECD in the late 1970s, to deal with even more difficult trade issues in the steel sector. These issues arose from falling demand and prices, excess production capacity in many countries, and increased government intervention to support domestic industries and exports, especially in the European Community. In 1978 an OECD Steel Committee was established, and a set of guidelines was adopted, aimed among other purposes, at avoiding trade measures in this area that are inconsistent with GATT rules.[12]

Adjustment Policies

In the OECD Trade Committee and in other OECD committees, exchanges of views regularly take place with respect to 'adjustment policies' followed by member countries. These policies are aimed, in large part, at reducing levels of trade protection for declining or weak industries and accommodating increased levels of imports of manufactured products from developing countries. The object is to formulate a common approach to these problems among the more highly industrialized OECD-member countries; and in 1978 the OECD Council of Ministers approved a set of 'orientations' or criteria on which their adjustment policies should be based. They agreed generally that assistance to ailing firms should be temporary and aimed at the restructuring and rehabilitation of firms, rather than take the form of continuing subsidies to maintain employment and production in obsolete firms and industries, and thus delay the process of adjustment. In 1980 a Special Group on Positive Adjustment Policies was created to analyse and exchange views on adjustment problems in member countries, and to keep under review the adjustment policies and programs of OECD members.[13]

Export Controls

In 1973–74 the upward movement of world prices and temporary shortages of certain raw materials and primary agricultural products stimulated interest among the larger OECD importing countries in strengthening trade rules governing the use of export restrictions and export taxes. The Trade Committee prepared an inventory of export restrictions imposed over recent years and an analysis of the problems involved. Canada and Australia, as major exporters of primary commodities and agricultural products, successfully blocked initiatives for establishing OECD rules and guidelines relating to the use of export controls. During the Tokyo Round, Canada also joined in opposing an extension of existing GATT rules in this area, unless this extension was linked with a reduction of tariff and other barriers that stood in the way of exports by producing countries of more highly processed forms of raw materials and other primary products. It was agreed, however, that the subject would be further considered in GATT.[14]

Trade in Services

As we have noted elsewhere, the GATT rules apply almost entirely to trade in goods, and there are no similar international rules dealing with trade in services, although services represent a large and fast-expanding area of world trade. The United States has advanced proposals aimed at reaching agreement, within the GATT framework, on rules covering barriers to trade in services. In OECD work has been under way over the past year or so, involving the identification and analysis of existing barriers to trade in services. This work in OECD could serve as a basis for any future negotiations in GATT in this area.[15]

Canadian Interests

It is difficult to measure the effects of OECD activities on the broader world-trade system or on Canadian trade interests. Canada initially had serious misgivings about giving OECD any large role in trade areas. As it turned out, OECD has played, until the present time, a relatively muted part in this area but, as indicated above, its activities, on balance, have served to strengthen the broader trade system, rather than to weaken it. OECD has provided a framework for continuing consultations among industrialized countries on trade-policy developments of common concern; and in this process, Canada has been able to use the OECD as an additional means of influencing the development of trade policy in the United States, the EC, Japan, and other OECD-member countries. This same process, of course, has provided an additional means for these countries to influence and to restrain the development of Canada's trade policies. In certain areas, indeed, Canadian trade interests have conflicted with those of OECD members that are importers of resource products and basic foodstuffs. Moreover, as we noted above, Canada and the other resource-exporting members, such as Australia and New Zealand, have opposed efforts to formulate a common OECD approach to commodity-trade issues and to the issue of export controls.

An important function of OECD in trade areas has been to provide, with the aid of its Secretariat, facilities for research and analysis of special trade-policy problems, and for the development of common approaches to these problems, and in the form of agreed and voluntary guidelines or codes. In some cases, these agreed approaches among OECD members have provided models for adoption on a global basis in GATT or in the United Nations. The OECD work on restrictive business practices and on government procurement policies are examples, as are the successive 'trade pledges' against the use of protectionist trade measures. Provided that these OECD efforts reflect broader global trade interests, they can make a constructive contribution to the evolution of the broader trade system; and the OECD process allows Canada a full opportunity to press for early recognition of its own trade interests.

Participation in OECD activities, in trade areas as in other areas, has also provided a general basis for the participation of Canada in the summit meetings which have been held annually since the mid-1970s, in efforts to co-ordinate more closely the economic and trade policies of the leading industrialized countries. It is noteworthy that at these meetings, the heads of government of the participants—the United States, Canada, Japan, France, Germany, Italy and the United Kingdom—have emphasized their commitment to the maintenance of an open trading system as embodied in GATT, and have committed themselves to resist the adoption of protectionist trade measures as a means of dealing with their economic problems.

Canadian interests might be served if some of the OECD functions in trade areas could now be transferred into the global trade system represented by GATT. The GATT Consultative Group of 18 is now well established and could be used with greater effectiveness in the future as a forum for continuing consultations, on a global basis, among the key trading countries. Moreover, a further strengthening of the GATT Secretariat would enable it to take from the OECD some of its programs for research and analysis in trade areas, and this move might encourage the evolution, on a broader multilateral basis, of new approaches to trade policy and the strengthening of world-trade rules that would correspond to Canadian interests in global trade issues.

Notes

1. For an account of earlier OEEC functions and activities, see OEEC, *A Decade of Co-operation: Achievements and Prospects*. The activities of OECD are reviewed in Annual Reports by the Secretary-General, "Activities of OECD"; bimonthly reports on OECD activities are contained in the OECD *Observer*; an early analysis and assessment of OECD is contained in H.G. Aubrey, *Atlantic Economic Cooperation: The Case of the OECD*. An examination of the structure and main

functions of OECD is in M.A. van Meerhaeghe, *A Handbook of International Economic Institutions*, Chapter 6.

2. Canada, Department of External Affairs, *External Affairs* 1 (November 1948), pp. 9-10.

3. These import controls and other measures were announced by the Minister of Finance on 17 November 1947; the text is in Department of External Affairs, *Statements and Speeches*, No. 47/21. See A.F.W. Plumptre, *Three Decades of Decision: Canada and the World Monetary System, 1944–75*, Chapter 4.

4. See Plumptre, *Three Decades of Decision*, pp. 122-27.

5. Aubrey, *Atlantic Economic Cooperation*, pp. 103-105, presents an analysis, made in the mid-1960s, of the process of co-operation within OECD; a somewhat critical recent analysis is in M. Henderson, "The OECD as an Instrument of National Policy."

6. See OECD, "OECD Council Recommendation on Co-operation between Member Countries on Restrictive Business Practices Affecting International Trade," *Observer*, No. 101 (November 1979).

7. These Canada-USA arrangements are set out in the "Fulton-Rogers Understanding" of 1959 and the "Basford-Mitchell Understanding" of 1969. For a discussion of some of the problems in Canada-USA relationships in the anti-trust area, see J.S. Stanford, "The Application of the Sherman Act to Conduct Outside the United States: A View from Abroad."

8. OECD, Secretary-General, *Policy Perspectives for International Trade and Economic Relations*. A senior officer of the Canadian Department of Finance, A.F.W. Plumptre, was a member of the group.

9. The text of the 1974 "Declaration Adopted by the Governments of the OECD Member Countries" is in OECD *Observer* (June 1974). The text of the 1980 "Declaration on Trade Policy" is in OECD *Observer* (June 1980, Special Supplement). For an account of the first 'periodic review' under the 1980 Declaration, see *Activities of OECD in 1980*, pp. 21-22.

10. The 1978 Arrangement on Guidelines for Officially Supported Export Credits is reviewed in the OECD *Observer* (March 1978). The outline for changes on which agreement was nearly reached in October 1981 are in the OECD *Observer* (November 1981). For the Canadian government's approach to the arrangement, see Canada, Department of External Affairs, *A Review of Canadian Trade Policy*, pp. 165-67.

11. M. Pomeranz, "Toward a New International Order in Government Procurement," *Law and Policy in International Business*, 11 (1979), p. 1276.

12. The OECD guidelines relating to production and trade in steel are described in the OECD *Observer* 95 (November 1978).

13. Annex II to the Communiqué issued by the OECD Council of Ministers at the conclusion of its June 1978 meeting contains the text of "Policies for Adjustment: Some General Orientations"; see *Activities of OECD in 1978*, pp. 104-107. For accounts of the Special Group on Positive Adjustment Policies, see *Activities of OECD in 1979*, p. 21, and *Activities of OECD in 1980*, p. 18.

14. GATT, Director-General, *The Tokyo Round of Multilateral Trade Negotiations*, p. 108, and GATT, Director-General, *Supplementary Report*, p. 49.

15. An account of OECD work relating to trade in services is in the OECD *Observer* (July 1981).

9

Low-Cost Imports, Market Disruption, and Restrictions on Textiles and Clothing

For over twenty years, the basic GATT principles of trade liberalization and non-discrimination have been set aside for an important sector of world trade, embracing exports of textiles and clothing by so-called 'low-cost' producing countries. The industries involved are characteristically among the first established in newly industrialized developing countries, to take advantage of relatively low wage rates combined with standard and easily transferable technology, and they are often geared to produce mainly for export markets. These very industries, however, have also been long established in many developed countries where there are large employers of labour—commonly low-skilled labour—often in areas where there are few other means of gainful employment. In many industrialized countries, including Canada, these industries have traditionally been given hefty tariff protection against import competition. Over recent decades, however, the producers of textiles and clothing, along with labour unions in these sectors, have pressed for additional and new forms of protection against 'market disruption' caused by import competition from low-cost sources. In response, governments of most industrialized countries have given these producers special measures of protection against low-cost imports, beyond that offered by normal customs tariffs; these measures have been applied both within and outside the GATT rules. Since the mid-1970s, these restrictions on low-cost imports have increased in many industrialized countries, in circumstances of slow economic growth and high unemployment.

In the textiles and clothing area, a series of special international arrangements has been concluded within the GATT framework, at the insistence of industrialized importing countries. These arrangements allow long-lasting quantitative controls to be imposed, on a discriminatory basis, against low-cost suppliers, without the risk of their retaliation. Since 1973 these arrangements, which have been embodied in the Multifibre Arrangement (MFA), have become progressively more restrictive. The MFA amounts to a negotiated derogation from the normal GATT Article-XIX 'safeguard' rules, which allow the use of special measures to limit "injurious" imports, but only on a non-discriminatory basis, against imports of the product concerned from all sources, for short periods, and subject to the payment of compensation. It is argued that these regular GATT safeguard rules are ineffective in dealing with the special problems caused by the growing volume of exports of textiles and clothing from the developing countries and the state-trading countries of Eastern Europe.[1]

In importing countries, continuing special measures of protection for textile and clothing industries are being challenged increasingly by consumer groups. Within the trade system, controls on trade under the MFA arrangements have become an important part of broader North-South confrontations over the operation of the world economic and trade order. At this point there is some uncertainty about the further extension of the MFA when it expires in 1986.

The issues surrounding 'low-cost' imports and 'market disruption' are not new. They emerged in GATT during the 1950s, at the time of Japan's re-entry into the world-trade system and its demand to be accepted as a full member of GATT.

Japanese Accession to GATT

Japan's exports expanded rapidly during the 1950s, following the post-war reconstruction of its industrial base, with substantial assistance by the United States (USA). These exports were concentrated in a narrow range of standard-technology, labour-intensive, manufactured goods, such as textiles and clothing, footwear, tableware, plywood and, later, optical goods and certain electronic products. These were exported at relatively low prices, reflecting a relatively low-wage structure, an abundant supply of skilled workers, and other features of Japanese industrial and trade policy at the time. The low-wage factor in Japanese export pricing was the main basis for widespread opposition in developed countries in Europe, North America and elsewhere, to the acceptance of Japanese goods on equal terms with those of other countries. Moreover, misgivings about the aggressive marketing of Japanese exports, as well as anti-Japanese sentiment in countries of south-east Asia and elsewhere, stood in the way of the acceptance of Japan as an equal trade partner.

In Britain, many Western European countries, Australia and some other countries, quantitative import restrictions continued to be maintained or intensified against Japan at a time when these restrictions were being progressively dismantled among the OECD members and among sterling-area countries. This discrimination against Japan resulted in a concentration of its exports in other less restricted markets, including Canada. In the 1950s the USA developed a system of bilateral agreements with Japan incorporating 'voluntary export restraints' on a number of products; these restraints were administered by the Japanese government or by industry in Japan. Canada followed suit, and persuaded the Japanese to accept restraint arrangements for a few products, including stainless steel flatware and certain textile and clothing products.

Japan itself maintained a high restrictive import regime, especially for manufactured goods and for food products that competed with Japanese producers. This regime was defended initially on balance-of-payments grounds, but it also gave protection to Japanese producers. These restrictive Japanese import policies were used by other countries to defend their own restrictions against Japan and to hinder Japan's accession to GATT. The Japanese market was open, however, for raw materials and for some basic agricultural products, and it became increasingly important to Canadian exporters of resource products.[2]

By the late 1950s, voluntary export restraints administered by Japan under bilateral agreements had become widespread. These restraints involved undertakings by Japan to place quantitative limits on exports of specified products, or to observe minimum prices, or otherwise to regulate exports of the products concerned. The importing country undertook to refrain, under normal circumstances, from imposing additional restrictions on the same or other Japanese exports and, in some cases, to extend most-favoured-nation (MFN) treatment and other GATT rules to their trade with Japan. These arrangements, however, were usually difficult to negotiate; they involved annual confrontations and continuing friction in bilateral relations. Restraint undertakings were often evaded by transhipments through third countries and in other ways; and Japan complained that its exports were being replaced by exports from other Asian sources. Moreover, in comparison with larger countries with greater bargaining strength, notably the USA, countries such as Canada were at a disadvantage in negotiating bilateral restraint agreements with Japan. Further, it was generally appreciated that these bilateral restraint arrangements, concluded outside the context of the multilateral trade rules, seriously undermined the principles on which the post-war trade system had been built. A 'rightful' place for Japan in the international trading world became a basic objective of US policy and was in line with the broad policies of a number of other countries, including Canada, with important political and trade interests in the Pacific area.

All these conflicting issues with respect to post-war relationships with Japan came together in connection with Japanese efforts, during the 1950s, to accede to GATT as a full member. Japan made an overture to join GATT in 1951, following the signature of a peace treaty with many former war-time enemies. Its application was blocked until 1955, despite strong support from the USA, Canada, Germany and a few other countries. The opposition included most West European countries, led by Britain, as well as a number of developing countries; and it was based fundamentally on protectionist import policies and the desire to continue to apply discriminatory quantitative restrictions against Japanese exports, which GATT rules would have precluded. Proposals were made by opponents of Japan's membership for introducing into GATT rules new provisions for applying safeguard restrictions, on a discriminatory basis, against low-cost Japanese goods, but such proposals were unacceptable, not only to Japan, but to many other countries, including Canada.

In 1954 arrangements were made to open for signature a Declaration under which the signatory countries undertook to base their commercial relations with Japan on the General Agreement, pending formal accession. This Declaration was signed by many GATT members, including Canada. The next year, tariff negotiations were held with Japan in connection with its accession request. When these negotiations had been concluded, Japan formally became a GATT member in 1955. However, the opponents to Japan's membership, including Britain, many West European countries, and a number of developing countries still refused to commit themselves to extend GATT rights to Japan; and for varying periods of years, these countries invoked a little-used provision of the GATT (Article XXXV), which allows an existing GATT member to withhold application of the Agreement from a new member.

Over succeeding years, Japan made strenuous efforts to persuade these countries to apply the General Agreement to their Japanese trade. These efforts were well and consistently supported by Canada and other countries that already applied the General Agreement to Japan, in part because restrictions in other countries caused Japanese exports to concentrate on their more open markets. The situation was generally regarded as highly unsatisfactory and gave rise to continuing friction in GATT. The solutions reached during the 1950s and 1960s involved wider international acceptance of Japan as a full GATT member but, in return, involved a new series of bilateral agreements by some countries, requiring Japan's acceptance of continuing 'voluntary restraints' on its exports, or its acquiescence in continued restrictions by the countries concerned on certain of its exports. Japan was thus obliged to accept continuing discrimination against its exports, although on a progressively reduced scale. These precedents established in connection with Japanese exports provided a basis for parallel restrictive controls on imports from the emerging textile and clothing industries in developing countries and in Eastern European countries.

The Concept of Market Disruption

By the late 1950s, a number of industrialized countries, including Canada, had concluded bilateral arrangements involving export restraints on various products with several Asian exporters, such as Hong Kong, India and South Korea, countries that had emerged as competitive suppliers of textile products, footwear and other light manufactured goods. In GATT, the United States, in 1959, formally placed the issue of 'market disruption' from 'low-cost imports' on the GATT agenda. A report was prepared on measures that GATT members had taken to deal with disruptive imports, and a great variety of restrictions and other measures were found to exist, concentrated on trade in cotton textiles. The Contracting Parties then endorsed an historic definition of 'market disruption,' which had been drafted by the Executive Secretary, Wyndham White. This definition was to the effect that situations of market disruption generally contain the following elements in combination:

- There is a sharp and substantial increase or potential increase of imports of particular products from particular sources.

- These products are offered at prices which are substantially below those prevailing for similar goods of comparable quality in the market of the importing country.

- There is serious damage to domestic producers or threat thereof.

- The price differentials referred to in the second point listed above do not arise from government intervention in the fixing of formulations of prices or from dumping practices.

The GATT Contracting parties then adopted a decision that gave international recognition to this concept of market disruption, as well as to the concept that problems involving market disruption required trade-policy measures beyond those sanctioned by existing GATT rules.[3] A special GATT working party was appointed to find solutions "consistent with the basic aims of the General Agreement." The solution that emerged took the form of new arrangements negotiated within GATT, covering trade in cotton products. The new arrangement legitimized, under specified conditions and circumstances, the conclusion of bilateral restraint agreements between importing and exporting countries, designed to avoid 'market disruption' from imports of low-priced cotton products.

GATT Arrangements for Trade in Textile Products

The initiative for those new and special rules within the GATT framework was launched by the United States, partly to head off opposition by the powerful US textiles industry to new trade legislation being prepared by the incoming

Kennedy Administration as a basis for a new round of GATT tariff negotiations. Another US objective was to induce other major importing countries, notably the European Community (EC), to relax their longstanding restrictions on imports of cotton textiles from the developing countries and Japan. Yet another was to provide a sounder legal basis, under US law and internationally, for the growing number of bilateral restraint agreements, covering cotton products, which the United States was concluding with low-cost suppliers. Accordingly, in 1961, the United States proposed the adoption within GATT of "arrangements for the orderly development of the trade in such products, ... while at the same time avoiding disruptive conditions in import markets."[4] Canada and other importing countries gave general support to the US initiative. The low-cost exporting countries accepted the arrangements with reluctance, but in hopes that the modifications would give them better access to European markets, and because they feared that without new arrangements, the importing countries, and especially the United States, would unilaterally impose new and even more severe restrictions on their exports.

The new international arrangements governing trade in low-priced cotton textiles were adopted in 1961, for a one-year period, in the form of a Short-term Arrangement Regarding Trade in Cotton Textiles. This Arrangement was renegotiated the following year in the form of a more elaborate five-year Long-term Agreement (LTA), which was later extended until 1973. In that year the LTA was replaced by the existing Multifibre Arrangement, which extended the product coverage of the earlier Arrangement to cover synthetic and woollen products, in addition to cotton products.[5] The initiative to convert the LTA into a broader arrangement covering man-made and woollen products again came from the United States which, under pressure from its textile industry, had put in place, during 1971–72, a number of bilateral, 'multifibre,' restraint agreements with Japan and some other exporting countries in Asia. During the 1960s, technological advances had led to the increased use of synthetics to replace or to be blended with natural fibres and fabrics, and the technology involved was fairly easily transferred to developing countries. New industries incorporating advanced technology, and often financed by multinational corporations, progressively were established in Hong Kong, Korea, Taiwan, India and other developing low-wage countries in Asia and elsewhere. Their exports came to occupy a growing share of the markets of the United States and other developed countries, and in these countries domestic industries pressed for increased restrictions covering woollens and synthetics, in addition to cotton products.

The Multifibre Arrangement (MFA)

The 1973 MFA thus greatly enlarged the coverage of the special arrangements within GATT to control trade in low-priced textiles and clothing products.

Extensions of the MFA that were negotiated in 1978 and in 1981 have permitted controls under these arrangements to be applied more severely. The basic purposes of these arrangements, however, have remained constant. These are:

- To establish rules and conditions under which controls may be applied to exports of textiles and clothing from particular low-cost suppliers. These rules and conditions are normally to be applied under bilateral agreements concluded between importing and exporting countries.

- To establish rules which provide some degree of 'orderly' growth of exports falling under these controls, especially exports by smaller developing countries and new entrants into world textile and clothing markets.

- To bring these controls under international scrutiny, within GATT.

The MFA, like its predecessor, is not part of the General Agreement, although it operates within the framework of GATT. Not all GATT members have signed it, and its signatories include several non-GATT countries; Mexico, for example, is a member. On grounds of equity, the MFA requires that importing countries also control imports from non-signatory low-cost suppliers; thus Canada and other importing countries have concluded MFA-type restraint agreements with China and with Taiwan. The suppliers whose exports are controlled under the MFA have all been developing countries and East European countries, but the MFA can also be applied against an industrialized country.

The basic rules governing restraints under the MFA, as concluded in 1973, may be summarized as follows:

- Signatories must notify GATT of all import controls or export restraints on textiles and clothing products, and must bring such measures into conformity with MFA rules.

- All existing restrictions, and any new restrictions, must either be dismantled or justified in terms of 'market disruption' in the importing country concerned. 'Market disruption' is defined in terms of unusually low prices, an increased flow of imports, and serious injury or the threat thereof to a domestic industry.

- Levels of quotas for particular products or groups of products must not involve reductions below levels of quantities of existing imports from the exporting country concerned.

- Quotas must normally be increased annually by at least 6 per cent, but lower growth rates are permitted in exceptional circumstances.

- Restraint arrangements must permit 'swing' among categories of products, so that a part of unused entitlements in one category can be shifted into another; they must also permit some shifting of unused quotas from one year into another.

- Restraints should be avoided on exports of small suppliers and new entrants; and more favourable treatment should be given to these countries and to cotton-producing developing countries, in terms of quota levels, growth rates and flexibility, in the event that restraints are applied against them.

- All measures imposed under the Arrangements are to be scrutinized and kept under review by a Textiles Surveillance Body, whose functions are noted below, for the purpose of determining their conformity with MFA rules.

Under the MFA, permitted bilateral restraint agreements may take either of two forms. Article 3, covering one or only a few products causing market disruption, is designed to accommodate bilateral agreements for short-term periods. However, in situations where agreement with the exporting country cannot be reached, the importing country may unilaterally impose a restriction. Article 4 is designed to accommodate longer-term bilateral agreements covering a broader range of products, and most controls under the MFA are of this kind.

As we noted above, the MFA established a permanent Textiles Surveillance Body (TSB) within GATT, to scrutinize and pass judgement on bilateral restraint agreements concluded under its provisions; to supervise generally the operation of the MFA; and to help settle disputes arising from the operation of the Arrangement. This body consists of an independent chairman and eight members named by the governments of roughly an equal number of exporting and importing countries. In practice, the United States, the European Community and Japan are permanently represented on the TSB, while the other seats rotate among groups of countries with particular sets of interests. The member from Canada alternates with a member named by a group of Nordic countries.[6]

The MFA, from the start, was well suited to accommodate the growing network of comprehensive restraint agreements which the United States concluded, under Article 4, with a long list of developing-country exporters. With its large internal market and a relatively low level of imports, the United States has been able to offer quota arrangements with appealing provisions for growth and with assurances of freedom from additional restrictions over medium-term periods. Progressively, almost all US imports from low-cost sources have been brought within these Article 4 agreements. The European Community and smaller importers, including Canada, have encountered greater difficulty in negotiating restraint agreements with exporting countries under MFA rules. Starting with relatively larger levels of imports from low-cost sources, the European Community, in particular, has resisted granting annual increases in quota levels, and otherwise bringing its restrictive system for textiles from low-cost sources into conformity with MFA rules.

As we noted above, the MFA was extended from the beginning of 1978 for a further four years by a Protocol which weakened the protection offered under the MFA to exporting countries. The Protocol permitted "jointly agreed departures" from basic MFA rules governing base-year quota levels, annual growth of quotas, and flexibility in the administration of quotas.[7] This weakening of the rules, which the European Community insisted on, provided a basis for the subsequent negotiation of a number of restraint arrangements by the Community as well as by other importing countries, including Canada, that were less liberal than the basic rules of the Agreement would require.

A further extension of the MFA was negotiated in late 1981, in circumstances of continued decline of demand and production, and of increased unemployment levels in most importing countries. The European Community in particular, but Canada and other importers as well, pressed for an MFA III that would provide a basis for concluding even more restrictive bilateral restraint arrangements, especially with the larger exporting countries which hold substantial and, in some cases, unused quota entitlements for textiles and clothing. The Protocol extending MFA III that was finally adopted essentially preserves the sanction embodied in MFA II for the conclusion of bilateral restraint arrangements that involve 'reasonable departures' from basic MFA rules governing base-quota levels, annual quota increases, and flexibility in quota administration, especially under arrangements with the larger suppliers. In addition, a number of the largest exporting countries indicated their 'willingness' to negotiate future arrangements that would deal with problems arising from their large quota entitlements. At the same time, MFA III incorporates undertakings by importing countries to give more favourable access to their markets to small suppliers and new entrants and, when restraint agreements are concluded with these countries, to provide more favourable terms for such elements as quota levels and annual growth rates.[8]

The establishment of special rules governing exports of textiles and clothing products reflected a widely accepted view that this sector of trade presents a set of intractable trade issues that the normal GATT rules are unable to deal with; and that in the absence of the MFA, even more severe discriminatory restrictions would be imposed unilaterally by the largest importers. Whatever the merits of views of this kind, it is clear that the whole concept of the MFA has been highly damaging to the liberal trade system, especially as the MFA has operated in practice. Trade restrictions within its framework have tended to increase, rather than diminish, and they have provided a basis for demands from other sectors for special measures of import protection. The trade restrictions under the MFA represent a major strain in overall North-South relationships, as well as strains in a whole network of bilateral relationships within the trade system. Moreover, the MFA has led to the emergence of a cartel-like system of production and trade in textiles and clothing, dominated by the seven largest importers and exporters: the United States, the European Community, Japan, Korea, Hong Kong, China and Taiwan. The negative effects of the system have been disproportionate for smaller importers and exporters. In the circumstances, the future of the MFA is increasingly uncertain.

Canadian Textile-Import Policy

Despite high tariffs on textiles and clothing products, imports into Canada from low-cost sources grew rapidly during the 1960s, and came to occupy a larger share of the domestic market. In response to industry pressures for greater protection from imports, the government negotiated agreements with a number of low-cost exporting countries. These agreements, some of which came under the Cotton Textile Arrangement, and some of which were outside it, covered a range of natural and also man-made textile products. The number of countries with which such agreements were concluded increased from six in 1966 to twenty in 1971.[9] In 1970 the government announced a new Canadian Textile Policy, which combined assurances to the producers that it would continue to give special protection against low-cost imports, with special financial assistance to the industry. The Policy was intended to create conditions "in which the Canadian textile and clothing industries continue to move progressively toward viable lines of production on an increasingly competitive basis internationally."[10]

The Canadian textile policy was translated in 1971 into the Textile and Clothing Board Act which, among other arrangements, established the Textile and Clothing Board (TCB) as a quasi-independent body to examine requests for imposing restrictions on imports of textile and clothing products. The TCB may recommend restrictive measures when it determines that imports are entering Canada "at such prices, in such quantities and under such conditions as to cause or threaten serious and immediate injury" to Canadian producers. Its recommendations, however, do not have to be accepted by the government and, on occasion, have not been followed.

The 1971 Act, moreover, pursuant to recommendations of the TCB, amended the Export and Import Permits Act so as to provide new authority for the government to impose import restrictions on textile products likely to cause or threaten serious damage to Canadian producers. In 1971, acting on a recommendation of the TCB, the government used its new authority to place a global import quota on lower-priced shirts. This global import quota chiefly affected imports from Japan and developing-country suppliers. It was presented as a safeguard measure taken under the traditional rules of GATT Article XIX, and was not imposed within the framework of the Cotton Textile Arrangement.

Canada and the MFA

From 1973 until 1976, Canada operated its import-restraint system for textiles in relative conformity with MFA rules, while continuing to impose a global quota on lower-priced shirts under the GATT Article XIX safeguard rules. Canadian restraints under the MFA took the form of Article 3 agreements with Japan, Hong Kong, South Korea and some other exporters, covering varying numbers of specified textiles products, almost all involving quotas administered by the exporting countries. The number of separate agreements was progressively reduced from a high of twenty in 1971 to eleven in 1975; the number of products subject to control was reduced from nineteen in 1972 to fifteen in 1975.[11]

Canada's policy of adhering to the MFA rules and of following a relatively liberal import policy for textiles was dramatically changed in 1976, when the government imposed global quantitative restrictions, under the Export and Import Permits Act, on practically all imports of clothing, and set quota levels below the levels of existing imports, with no provisions for annual growth. This measure followed the Textile and Clothing Board's presentation of an 'interim report' to the Minister of Industry, Trade and Commerce. In its report, the TCB recommended the immediate imposition of import restrictions, on a global basis, covering almost the whole range of clothing items, with a roll-back in quantities to 1975 levels.[12] Canada notified GATT that these new measures were being imposed, not under the MFA, but under the GATT Article XIX safeguard provisions. In accordance with Article XIX rules, the restrictions were applied to all sources of imports on a non-discriminatory basis.

This comprehensive restriction imposed by Canada on clothing imports aroused strong international criticism, not only from exporters of low-priced clothing, but also from the United States, whose exports of clothing to Canada were restricted under the global quotas. Many countries contended that the Canadian measures violated the letter and spirit of the MFA. Canada's position was that GATT members of the MFA had also preserved their rights to use safeguard measures under the General Agreement; and that the global import quotas were temporary and of an emergency nature, and were fully consistent with GATT Article XIX. However, Canada subsequently agreed to compensate the United States for damage to its exports of clothing as a result of the global quotas.

Beginning in 1979, Canada replaced its global import-quota system for clothing with bilateral restraint agreements under the MFA. These arrangements, covering a comprehensive range of clothing, were concluded first with the largest exporting countries; later, agreements covering a varying range of products were concluded with a number of smaller low-cost suppliers. In overall terms, the new bilateral agreements were nearly as restrictive as the previous global quota, at least for imports from the largest low-cost sources.

During 1979–80 the Textile and Clothing Board carried out a further inquiry covering both textile and clothing products; among its recommendations was one that controls on imports from low-cost sources should be continued on a comprehensive basis for a further decade.[13] In June 1981 the government announced a policy on import controls that was somewhat less restrictive than that recommended by the TCB; it also reallocated funds amounting to more than $250 million for a new adjustment program, to be managed by a Canadian Industrial Renewal Board, for Canada's textile and clothing industries.[14] The government announced in February 1982 that it had concluded or was proceeding with negotiations with seventeen countries for the continuation of bilateral restraint arrangements for five-year periods; it also made public the results of ten of the agreements that it had concluded.[15] In overall terms, these arrangements involve controls on about 90 per cent of Canadian imports of clothing, and on almost 10 per cent of total imports of textiles. The bilateral agreements with the largest low-cost exporting countries, such as South Korea and Hong Kong, cover a comprehensive list of apparel. For the next five years, they will hold quotas for many products as or near existing levels, rather than provide 6 per cent growth, as required under the original MFA rules. The restraint agreements with smaller suppliers cover fewer products, and for the most part will permit import growth of 6 per cent annually, although many of the quota levels are relatively small in absolute quantities. In other respects, as well, the treatment accorded to the smaller suppliers appears somewhat more generous than that accorded to the larger suppliers.

The government's controls on imports of textile and clothing products have not gone unchallenged in Canada. Some of the opposition has arisen from the obvious conflict between Canada's import policies in these sectors, as well as in the footwear sector, and the government's repeated declarations of its sympathy and support for the efforts of Third World countries to accelerate their economic development.[16] Others have protested the high costs to Canadian consumers—who are the real losers—and to the economy generally, resulting from restrictive import quotas, in addition to high tariffs, on textiles and clothing.[17] Moreover, the maintenance of these restrictive import controls causes continuing friction in Canada's bilateral trade and in other relationships with friendly countries which provide growing markets for Canadian exports. Severe as they are, Canada's restrictions on imports under the MFA may be less comprehensive than those imposed by many other industrialized countries, including the United States and the European Community. As long as these large importers continue to maintain highly restrictive trade arrangements with the larger exporters, it is inevitable that strong pressures for similar import controls will be exerted on the anadian government by domestic firms and labour groups.

Notes

1. For general discussions of the issues in GATT surrounding low-cost imports, market disruption, and restrictions on trade in textiles and clothing, see G. Patterson, *Discrimination in International Trade: The Policy Issues 1945–1965*, Chapter VI. See also K.W. Dam, *The GATT: Law and International Economic Organization*, Chapter 17.

2. Japan's restrictive import policies, designed to give special protection to a number of domestic agricultural and manufacturing sectors, combined with other obstacles to the marketing of exports in Japan, continue to weaken the force of Japanese protests about barriers to its exports in other markets.

3. The Decision by the Contracting Parties involving recognition and definition of the special problem of market disruption (19 November 1960) is in GATT, *Basic Instruments and Selected Documents, Ninth Supplement*, pp. 26-28. Point (iv) of the Definition was included in order to distinguish market disruption arising from low-cost exports from disruption arising from dumped or subsidized exports, for which the General Agreement provides other remedies, and from disruption arising from exports by state-controlled economies.

4. Patterson, *Discrimination*, p. 309. See pp. 307-10 for background on the US initiatives of the early 1960s that led to the Arrangements for cotton textiles under GATT; see also GATT, *The Activities of GATT 1961/1962*, p. 29.

5. The Short Term Arrangement Regarding International Trade in Cotton Products was put into place by a Decision of the GATT Contracting Parties on 21 July 1961; the text is in GATT *Basic Instruments and Selected Documents, Tenth Supplement*, pp. 18-22. The Long Term Arrangement Regarding Trade in Cotton Textiles was concluded on 9 February 1962, and entered into force on 1 October 1962; the text is in GATT, *Basic Instruments and Selected Documents, Eleventh Supplement*, pp. 25-41. The Arrangement Regarding International Trade in Textiles (the 'Multifibre Arrangement' or 'MFA') was negotiated during the autumn of 1973 and entered into force on 1 January 1974; the text is in GATT, *Basic Instruments and Selected Documents, Twenty-first Supplement*, pp. 3-18.

6. For a critical assessment of the effectiveness of the Textiles Surveillance Body in supervising the operation of the Multifibre Arrangement, see G.H. Perlow, "The Multilateral Supervision of International Trade: Has the Textiles Experiment Worked?".

7. The Protocol extending the MFA that was negotiated at the end of 1977 came into effect on 1 January 1978; the text is in GATT, *Basic Instruments and Selected Documents, Twenty-fourth Supplement*, pp. 5-8.

8. The Protocol that was negotiated at the end of 1981 extends the MFA for four years and seven months after 1 January 1982. The text is in GATT, *Basic Instruments and Selected Documents, Twenty-eight Supplement*.

9. K. Stegemann, *Canadian Non-Tariff Barriers to Trade*, pp. 10-13.

10. Statement by the Minister of Industry, Trade and Commerce to the House of Commons, 14 May 1970, p. 6953. A detailed discussion of the Canadian Textile Policy during the first half of the 1970s is in C. Pestieau, *The Canadian Textile Policy: A Sectoral Trade Adjustment Strategy?*

11. Pestieau, *Canadian Textile Policy*, p. 35.

12. The full report is in Canada, Textile and Clothing Board, *Clothing Inquiry: A Report to the Minister of Industry, Trade and Commerce*; this report also contains the Board's interim report and recommendations that had been presented the previous autumn.

13. Canada, Textile and Clothing Board, *Textile and Clothing Inquiry: Report to the Minister of Industry, Trade and Commerce*, Vol. 1 and Vol. 2.

14. Government of Canada, News Release: "Government Policy for the Textile and Clothing Sectors," Ottawa and Montreal, 19 June 1981.

15. Canada, Department of External Affairs, *Summary of Canada's Bilateral Restraint Arrangements—Textiles and Clothing*. This document also contains the full text of the Multifibre Arrangement, the Protocol extending the MFA after 1 January 1982, and the text of the Export and Import Permits Act, together with the Import Control List as of 11 February 1982 and notices dated 11 February 1982, regarding a number of General Import Permits.

16. For a critical study of Canada's trade barriers against imports from developing countries, see M.A. Biggs, *The Challenge: Adjust or Protect?*

17. See, for example, G.T. Jenkins, *Costs and Consequences of the New Protectionism: The Case of the Canadian Clothing Industry*. In this study of the costs of quotas and high tariffs on clothing imports, Jenkins found that quotas and tariffs resulted in losses to Canadian consumers, amounting to almost $470 million annually (1979); of these losses, the cost of the quotas alone amounted to about $200 million annually.

10

Developing Countries in GATT and UNCTAD

Within the GATT system, it was agreed almost from the start that all countries should have equal status, nominally at least, irrespective of their size, economic power, importance in world trade, or stage of economic development. At the Havana Conference in 1947–48 there was a lively debate over whether the proposed International Trade Organization (ITO) should have a system of weighted voting, like the International Monetary Fund (IMF) and the International Bank for Reconstruction and Development (World Bank). In the end it was agreed that the ITO and GATT should adopt the one country / one vote system. At the same time, it was generally recognized that less-developed countries should have certain exemptions from the GATT rules and disciplines, and that they would be unable to make a full contribution to trade liberalization. Over time, the distinction between the less-developed countries and the industrialized countries in the GATT system was elaborated and formalized in a number of ways. The process was further reinforced by the creation, in the mid-1960s, of a new and powerful element in the trade system outside GATT, in the form of the United Nations Conference on Trade and Development (UNCTAD), which was designed essentially to help less-developed countries gain a larger and fairer share of the benefits of international trade

For over fifteen years, UNCTAD has generated a greater awareness of the special trade and economic problems of developing countries, and has stimulated international efforts to deal with a range of issues of primary concern to

107

developing countries through co-operative action. The goals of UNCTAD are very different from those of the GATT. The broad objectives of GATT are the liberalization of world trade, non-discrimination in world trade, and the construction of a common body of trade law that is binding on all member countries. By contrast, UNCTAD aims to restructure the trade system so as to increase the benefits of international trade for less-developed countries and thus contribute to an acceleration of their overall development. The operations of GATT and UNCTAD are not necessarily incompatible, but a number of conflicts have arisen between the two bodies largely because of their quite different objectives.[1]

The creation of UNCTAD followed the emergence, in the late 1950s and early 1960s, of many newly independent countries from former colonial status and the increased voicing of complaints by the less-developed countries that the existing world organizations in trade and economic areas, and GATT in particular, were unresponsive to their special interests. A further explanation for the creation of a second organization within the trade system was given by a former Secretary General of UNCTAD, after that organization had existed for several years:

> Is UNCTAD really needed? This question has been overtaken by events. UNCTAD exists: but probably it would not have been established if the international trade organization which was provided for in the charter adopted by the United Nations Conference of Trade and Employment held in Havana in 1948, had materialized.[2]

Developing Countries in the Geneva and Havana Negotiations

At the Geneva and Havana Conferences in 1947–48, the less-developed countries played a prominent role and generally joined together in support of common interests.[3] The group included countries, in Latin America and elsewhere, which had been independent before the war, and a few newly independent countries such as India, Pakistan and Indonesia. On certain issues Australia joined this group. These countries pressed for a number of special exemptions from the regular trade rules, but their efforts were only partly successful. The principal provisions of the General Agreement, which deal with the trade problems of developing countries, were written into Article XVIII, which was extensively revised in 1955; the revisions, however, involved no great changes of substance. In essence, the Article reflects earlier theories of import substitution as an approach to economic development, and thus it provides more freedom to less-developed countries than to industrialized countries to maintain restrictive import regimes by the use of quantitative restrictions and other measures for the purpose of encouraging the establishment of new industries. There is nothing in Article XVIII that deals with the export problems of less-developed countries.

Thus Article XVIII permits a less-developed country greater freedom to raise tariffs which it has reduced or bound under GATT. This provision has had little practical application, however, since most developing countries have reduced or bound few of their tariffs in GATT negotiations; and many developing countries have continued to maintain very high customs duties on imports, for protective, as well as for other, reasons. Another dispensation provided by Article XVIII permits a developing country to impose quantitative restrictions on imports for balance-of-payments reasons, under rules that are somewhat more relaxed than the regular rules of Article XII. A third concession made in Article XVIII:13 to developing countries permits the use of quantitative restrictions "to promote the establishment of particular industries." Restrictions imposed for this purpose, however, were made subject to an elaborate process of consultation, negotiation and approval by the GATT Contracting Parties. In practice, little use was ever made of this exception. Developing countries have been able to maintain quantitative restrictions and other controls on imports on the basis of more easily used rules in Article XVIII, which permit the use of quantitative restrictions for balance-of-payments reasons.

A major objective of the group of developing countries at the Geneva and Havana conferences, which was generally supported by Canada, was to facilitate the conclusion and operation of international commodity agreements aimed at stabilizing prices and other conditions of trade for primary commodities. As discussed in Chapter 11, below, a whole chapter of the Havana Charter was devoted to the principles and mechanisms to govern such agreements, but these provisions were not carried into the GATT Articles, an omission which, from the perspective of the developing countries, considerably weakened GATT as an instrument for trade co-operation. When the Havana Charter was abandoned, arrangements for conducting negotiations for commodity agreements were established within the United Nations and later transferred to UNCTAD.

From the perspective of less-developed countries, the omission from the General Agreement of the Havana Charter of the chapter dealing with restrictive business practices also weakened the GATT. International rules were regarded as needed to reinforce those countries' own efforts to control cartel-like arrangements among large international enterprises based in industrialized countries. Subsequent efforts to reintroduce rules in this area into the GATT were unsuccessful. At a later date, a body of rules in this area was developed within the UNCTAD framework, and other guidelines were also developed within the Organisation for Economic Co-operation and Development (OECD).

At the Havana Conference, the developing countries obtained an exception from the most-favoured-nation (MFN) rule and from the no-new-preference rule, to permit the establishment of new preferential tariff arrangements among adjacent or neighbouring countries in the group. Such an exception was included in the Charter, but was omitted from the General Agreement, although both texts included exceptions for full-fledged customs unions and free-trade areas. As we discussed in Chapter 6, above, the GATT rules governing preferences have subsequently been greatly relaxed for less-developed countries.

As we also noted in Chapter 6, the developing countries have always been at a disadvantage in tariff bargaining under the GATT rules and procedures. One difficulty has arisen from the concept of reciprocity, by which tariff reductions made by one country are expected to be matched by reductions made by another. Although the principle of reciprocity was not always strictly applied to less-developed countries, these countries have often been unable to offer sufficient concessions to bring down tariffs on their exports that are imposed by larger, more powerful, trading countries. The 'principal supplier' rule has also created difficulties. Importing countries are under an obligation to negotiate with the main supplier of a particular product, but not necessarily with others. Developing countries often have difficulty finding products for which they are individually a principal supplier. At later dates, the GATT negotiating rules with respect to reciprocity and principal suppliers were formally modified to take account of the problems of developing countries.

Despite these problems, developing countries have gained substantial advantages from the GATT. Under the MFN rule, their exports have obtained the benefits of all of the tariff cuts resulting from the negotiations among other countries. The GATT rules have provided substantial protection against arbitrary trade measures by larger more powerful countries. At the same time, GATT has not, in practice, imposed particularly onerous disciplines over the trade policies and practices of less-developed countries. Indeed, it is a widely held view that these disciplines have been excessively light.

The inadequacies of GATT from the perspective of developing countries may partly explain the slow growth of membership among those countries during the 1950s; by 1957 almost all industrialized countries had joined GATT, but membership of developing countries had grown only from ten to thirteen. Partly to attract greater interest from less-developed countries and countries which were emerging from colonial status in greater numbers, a special program was launched in GATT, which focused largely on barriers to exports of the less-developed countries that were maintained by the industrialized countries.

Barriers to Exports of Less-Developed Countries

In 1957 a panel of eminent international economists was appointed by the GATT Contracting Parties to examine current trade problems. Their report,

Trends in International Trade, otherwise known as the 'Haberler Report,' after its chairman, focused in large measure on the export problems of less-developed countries, and laid much responsibility for these problems upon the import policies of developed countries.[4] The GATT Contracting Parties thereupon established a special Committee III which, over the next few years, examined in detail trade barriers maintained by developed countries against lists of exports of special interest to less-developed countries, individually and as a group. Committee III brought to light many high tariffs on manufactured goods, such as textiles, clothing, footwear and light manufactures, for which developing countries were seeking export markets; escalating tariff structures which gave high levels of effective protection against the processed forms of raw materials; some very high internal taxes on coffee, tea and cocoa in Western Europe; and many quantitative restrictions, again mainly in Western Europe, on a wide range of manufactured products. In many cases these quantitative restrictions were illegal under GATT rules and involved discrimination against developing-country suppliers. Moreover, the preferences extended by the European Community (EC) to its associated African countries were strongly protested in Committee III by other developing countries that were excluded from these arrangements. In general, Western European countries were the main targets of complaints in Committee III, although Canada and the United States (USA) were criticized for maintaining some high tariffs, especially on textile products and other light manufactured goods.

Because of dissatisfaction with the results achieved in Committee III, a group of developing countries in GATT drew up a special Programme of Action in the early 1960s, which was submitted to a Ministerial-level meeting of GATT in 1963. This Programme represented an ambitious strategy for trade liberalization. It called for, among other changes, the following trade-policy measures by developed countries:

- A standstill on all new tariff and non-tariff measures imposed on exports from developing countries

- Elimination within one year, or within four years at the latest, of all quantitative restrictions that were illegal under GATT rules

- Duty-free entry for tropical products within two years

- Elimination of all tariffs on primary products (date unstated)

- Adoption of a schedule for the reduction or elimination of tariffs on semi-processed and processed products, including a reduction of at least 50 per cent over three years

- Elimination within four years of internal taxes on products wholly or mainly produced in developing countries

- Annual reports on the implementation of the above measures.[5]

At the 1963 Ministerial meeting, this list of requests by the less-developed countries got a mixed reception from the industrialized members of GATT. Ministers from the European Community found many of the requests unacceptable, partly because they tended to weaken the preferential relationships that had been created with the associated African countries. Ministers from the United States and other developed countries accepted the Programme in part or expressed particular reservations. Canada's position was relatively positive. (Many of the proposed measures, indeed, would have benefited Canada's own trade interests if they had been adopted by its main trading partners.) The Minister of Trade and Commerce indicated that Canada would welcome a standstill on tariffs and other trade barriers affecting the exports of less-developed countries; he said that Canada maintained no quantitative restrictions, and supported the elimination of such restrictions by countries that used them. Canada, he assured the meeting, would work, in company with other major importers, for tariff-free treatment of a number of specified tropical products, although its position was reserved with respect to vegetable oils and oil seeds. He stated that Canada had no internal taxes that discriminated against products of special interest to developing countries. He claimed that GATT efforts to eliminate tariffs on primary products were regarded as "particularly important," and that Canada would join with other industrialized countries in efforts "to include, as far as possible, in forthcoming negotiations the proposal to eliminate tariff barriers on exports of semi-processed products" from developing countries. The Minister added that Canada was concerned about the establishment of new preferential arrangements (that is, by the European Community) and expressed the view that to undermine the GATT principle of non-discrimination was unlikely to benefit weaker countries.[6]

In practical terms, the GATT Programme of Action never got off the ground. The industrialized countries were turning their attention to broader tariff and trade negotiations under the Kennedy Round, which was to begin very shortly. The less-developed countries, for their part, were in the process of shifting their attention to alternative plans for advancing their interests at the first United Nations Conference on Trade and Development, which was scheduled to be held in 1964. The momentum in GATT was lost, and has not yet been regained, for a comprehensive strategy aimed at reducing barriers to the exports of the developing countries. Instead, within GATT, efforts were diverted during the mid-1960s to seeking legal and institutional changes to the General Agreement, which would focus on the special trade interests of the developing countries.

Part IV of the General Agreement

The impetus to add to the General Agreement a separate section dealing with the special trade interests of developing countries was, in part, a response to apprehension that the forthcoming UNCTAD Conference might lead to the creation of a new, permanent, world-trade organization that would compete with GATT, at least in areas of special concern to developing countries. The outcome of this concern was the addition to the General Agreement of three new Articles as a separate Part IV entitled "Trade and Development." While the exercise has been widely criticized as failing to bring any substantive gains for the less-developed members of GATT, the Part IV Articles have assumed a considerable symbolic importance, and they have provided a new and firmer footing on which the less-developed countries have based new claims for special and more favourable treatment within the GATT system.

The first of the new Articles, Article XXXVI, contains a series of objectives and principles which add little to those already set out in the General Agreement. Included for the first time, however, was a formal affirmation that "the developed countries do not expect reciprocity for commitments made by them in trade negotiations to reduce or remove tariffs and other barriers to trade of the less-developed contracting parties" (Article XXXVI:8). This principle was restated later, in the 1973 Tokyo Declaration that launched the Tokyo Round and in decisions taken by the Contracting Parties at the conclusion of that Round. However justified in terms of equity, the adoption of this principle does not appear to have been successful in encouraging more active participation of developing countries in tariff negotiations, either in the 1965–67 Kennedy Round or in the 1974–79 Tokyo Round.

The second new Article sets out a number of general undertakings, by industrialized countries in GATT, with respect to trade measures that affect developing countries. These undertakings, however, are expressed in highly qualified terms and with numerous reservations: they are applicable only "to the fullest extent possible—that is, except when compelling reasons, which may include legal reasons, make it impossible. . . ." At best, the Article represents statements of intention, rather than commitments of the usual GATT kind. It is silent on the matter of any preferences for the exports of less-developed countries. Nor does it provide any legal basis for exempting developing countries from trade-policy measures imposed by industrialized countries, such as balance-of-payments restrictions or special import surcharges, safeguard measures imposed under GATT rules, or restrictions on agricultural imports.

The third new Article consists essentially of an endorsement, again, stated in well-qualified terms, of a series of existing or proposed programs of special interest to developing countries, a number of which operate outside the ambit of GATT itself. This Article introduced a somewhat more explicit basis for GATT to concern itself with international commodity agreements, but gave GATT little in the way of a new mandate in this area. In any event, UNCTAD, rather than GATT, has assumed the main role for developing and organizing negotiations for commodity arrangements, although several agreements of a

limited kind, on certain dairy products and beef, have been developed within
GATT, along with certain elements of the International Wheat Agreement.
This Article also established the terms of reference for a new, permanent,
GATT Committee on Trade and Development. This Committee's function has
been to monitor the operation of the new Part IV Articles, and to scrutinize
generally trade measures taken by industrialized countries that affect exports
of less-developed countries.

The Creation of UNCTAD

As we noted above, during the late 1950s, less-developed countries became
increasingly critical of the established bodies within the United Nations (UN)
framework that were dealing with trade and development problems. This
occurred at a time when these countries were coming to form a majority in the
UN General Assembly, as a result of the emergence from colonial status of
many new independent countries. GATT was particularly criticized as being
concerned largely with trade among industrialized countries and ignoring the
trade problems of less-developed countries. The IMF and the World Bank were
held to be dominated by the larger industrialized countries. The UN Economic
and Social Council was criticized, not only for ineffectiveness as a forum for
serious discussion of world-trade and economic problems, but also because its
membership did not reflect the new majority position of the Third World
within the United Nations. The Secretariat in New York, as well, was viewed
as being unrepresentative of the less-developed world, especially on the
economic side.

In the early 1960s, these complaints by developing countries led to
proposals in the General Assembly for a special United Nations Conference
on Trade and Development to focus on issues of special interest to those
countries. This Conference was held in Geneva in 1964. A primary objective
of the developing countries became to create a new permanent institution for
world trade and development within the United Nations system, where their
combined strength was greater than in GATT, IMF or the World Bank, and
where a new body of analysis could be developed upon which developing
countries could pursue their trade and development interests more successfully.

The outcome of the first UNCTAD Conference was greatly influenced by
proposals presented by Raul Prebisch, the Executive Secretary of the UN
Economic Commission for Latin America, in a report titled "Towards a New
Trade Policy for Development." The Conference agreed on arrangements
which included the following elements: UN Conferences on Trade and Development would be held every three years; UNCTAD would establish permanent
institutional arrangements which would absorb existing UN bodies dealing
with international commodity-trade agreements; a new and large secretariat
for UNCTAD would be established in Geneva, away from the influence of

New York headquarters; and a Trade and Development Board with fifty-four members would be established to meet between Conferences and would appoint subsidiary committees to deal with manufactures, shipping, and other issues.[7]

The UNCTAD Secretariat in Geneva grew rapidly in size. It has tended to become an open advocate of the trade and development interests of the Third World, providing a new body for research and analysis of trade and development issues of special interest to these countries, as well as a base for the development of initiatives to deal with these issues internationally. The UNCTAD Secretariat also took over the job of organizing and servicing negotiations for international commodity agreements, although these agreements, once in place, continued to have their own separate secretariats at their headquarters in London and elsewhere.

The creation and operation of UNCTAD has had a serious impact on the world-trade policy system and on other economic and development areas. UNCTAD succeeded in creating a new sense of unity and strength among developing countries, which are known as the 'Group of 77'; in the process, for better or worse, it injected a new element of North-South confrontation into almost every issue on the agenda.[8] This unity was never altogether firm, and divisions have emerged roughly among three groups: oil-exporting members of OPEC; middle-income countries such as South Korea, Brazil, Mexico, Singapore and the Philippines, often referred to as 'newly industrialized countries' (NICs), with expanding and diversified manufacturing industries; and the more numerous, poorer, least-developed countries. While the formal unity of the Group of 77 has been reasonably well preserved in UNCTAD, divergences of interest commonly emerge over particular issues.

UNCTAD has also had a profound impact on the ideological framework surrounding trade and other economic problems of developing countries. On the basis of research and analysis by the UNCTAD Secretariat, these problems were redefined, and new and controversial solutions to them were advanced. The role and activities of UNCTAD in trade areas were strengthened, in the mid-1970s, by the development of proposals in the United Nations General Assembly for a 'New International Economic Order' (NIEO), which was to be established by broad changes in the structure of the world economic system. Strategies for achieving these changes were adopted by the General Assembly in 1974 and 1975, although some industrialized countries, including Canada, expressed a number of reservations. These strategies covered a range of issues in areas of trade, international monetary arrangements, aid, and the transfer of technology, as well as reforms of international organizations in these areas. On the trade side, the proposals for a NIEO redefined many of the objectives of the Group of 77 in UNCTAD, giving a central place to problems of trade in primary commodities produced by less-developed countries.

The approach of the Group of 77 and the UNCTAD Secretariat to the trade elements of the NIEO reflected earlier questioning of the concepts and principles underlying the GATT system. Freedom of trade and non-discrimination, it was argued, lead to inequitable results, bringing greater benefits to industrialized countries than to less-developed countries. The free operation of market forces, combined with the role played by transnational corporations, results in low prices for primary commodities and low levels of export income for producing countries. Successive rounds of GATT negotiations have reduced barriers to trade among industrialized countries; but the less-developed countries, with their weaker bargaining power, have been unsuccessful in efforts to reduce barriers imposed by industrialized countries against their exports. These barriers discriminate against the processed forms of raw materials produced by less-developed countries, as well as against a range of their agricultural exports. High tariffs, combined with severe non-tariff barriers, continue to be imposed by industrialized countries in areas where less-developed countries have a competitive advantage; such areas include, for example, textiles, clothing, footwear and many light manufactures.[9]

The strategies of the Group of 77 in UNCTAD, well-supported by the UNCTAD Secretariat, have been aimed, in large part, until recently at least, at a number of objectives: first, securing preferential access for members' manufactured and processed products in the industrialized countries; and secondly, improving prices and other market conditions for primary commodities produced by less-developed countries. A third strategy has been aimed at controlling the operations of multinational corporations and restrictive business practices that adversely affect the interests of less-developed countries. Within UNCTAD, programs based on these strategies have generally been resisted or accepted with great reluctance by many of the industrialized countries, especially the United States. The industrialized countries have also, and more successfully, blocked initiatives aimed at undermining GATT as the central element in the trade system, or transforming UNCTAD into a world-trade organization along the lines of the ITO.

Over the past year or two, developing countries in UNCTAD have given more positive support to the principles underlying the multilateral trade system as reflected in GATT. This change in approach reflects growing concerns among developing countries about protectionist trade measures adopted by industrialized countries; some of these measures involve discrimination against manufactured goods exported by developing countries, especially under the Multifibre Arrangement (MFA). Recent UNCTAD studies and reports have called for the strengthening of the GATT rules and principles, rather than for their abandonment.[10]

UNCTAD Trade Activities

Since its creation in the mid-1960s, the main UNCTAD activities in trade areas have been the following.

Generalized System of Preferences (GSP)

This system, which was the result of initiatives in UNCTAD during the late 1960s, is described in more detail in Chapter 11, below. Briefly, it involves the granting by developed countries of tariff preferences to a range of products, mostly manufactured and semi-manufactured, when these are imported from developing countries. Although the GSP system was negotiated chiefly in UNCTAD, it was necessary for the industrialized countries to obtain from the GATT Contracting Parties approval for departing from the MFN rules, in order to extend tariff preferences to less-developed countries.

Integrated Program for Commodities

This program was developed within UNCTAD during the early 1970s. It has been aimed, in part, at the adoption of a longer list of international commodity agreements, covering primary products of special export interest to developing countries. It has also been aimed at the creation of an internationally financed Common Fund to assist the financing of buffer stocks which may be established under individual commodity agreements, and to finance a range of other projects aimed at improving the production and marketing of primary products exported by developing countries. As of late 1983, only two new commodity agreements (on natural rubber and jute) have been successfully negotiated and come into force under the UNCTAD program. While an agreement to establish a Common Fund has been signed, the Fund is far smaller than originally planned, and the agreement has not yet been ratified by a sufficient number of countries to come into force. The UNCTAD program for commodities is described in more detail in Chapter 11, below.

Restrictive Business Practices

Within UNCTAD, beginning in 1976, a code of "Equitable Principles and Rules for the Control of Restrictive Business Practices" was developed; it was adopted, after further negotiations, by a UN Conference in April 1980. This code is non-binding and is addressed both to business enterprises and to governments. In it, 'restrictive business practices' are defined as acts or behaviour of enterprises, which limit access to markets or otherwise unduly restrict competition, and which have or are likely to have adverse effects on international trade, particularly the trade and development of developing countries. The code covers both goods and services, and applies to state enterprises as well as to private firms, including multinational corporations. Since adherence to this code is voluntary, it contains no redress for violations of its rules, although it calls on signatory governments to take "appropriate steps" to meet their commitments to it. An intergovernmental group of experts within UNCTAD will monitor the operation of the code and consider proposals for its improvement and development. After five years of operation, the code will be reviewed by a second UN Conference. This new UN code on restrictive business practices makes considerably fewer demands on governments than did the provisions set out thirty-five years ago in the proposed Havana Charter. Nor is it as demanding as the series of OECD Recommendations adopted in 1967, 1973 and 1979, at least with respect to bilateral consultations and exchanges of information among governments on individual cases of restrictive business practices.[11]

Other UNCTAD Programs

Over the past year or two, the UNCTAD Secretariat and UNCTAD meetings have given increasing attention to protectionism and structural adjustment within the trade system, especially in the industrialized countries. Recently the UNCTAD Secretariat has also been actively promoting new concepts of 'collective self-reliance' and 'economic co-operation among developing countries'; these concepts involve the establishment of a new 'global' system of trade preferences among developing countries themselves, aimed at encouraging a greater flow of trade within the Third World.

Recent Developments

The worsening of the world economic situation over the past several years has involved stagnation of world markets for the exports of many developing countries, new protectionist trade measures by industrialized countries, and a general steep decline in world prices for primary commodities. There has also been a decline in the flow of aid funds and private financial resources to the Third World, combined with a dramatic increase in the burden of external debt for many less-developed countries.[12] These trends have led to continued criticism, within the Third World, of the structure and operation of the world-trade system. Recent developments in UNCTAD and GATT appear to have reinforced this criticism. There have been strong pressures for 'global negotiations' aimed, in part, at advancing the interests of less-developed countries through changes in the structure and operation of the trade system.

The Brandt Commission, in its 1980 report *North-South*, suggested a meeting of a group of world leaders to advance the cause of global co-operation along these lines; and in October 1981 the heads of government from twenty-two countries met for two days in Cancun, Mexico, with Prime Minister Trudeau of Canada and the President of Mexico serving as co-chairmen. This meeting failed to produce any consensus on a process of 'global negotiations,' largely because of US opposition, although it doubtless contributed generally to a better awareness of North-South issues in trade and economic areas.[13]

The GSP tariff preferences that were developed in UNCTAD and put into effect during the first half of the 1970s have provided only limited assistance, in practical terms, for the exports of less-developed countries. (See Chapter 11, below.) The UNCTAD program to raise and stabilize primary commodity prices, which was the centre-piece of UNCTAD during the last half of the 1970s, has also had limited results. (See Chapter 12, below.) The process of bargaining and confrontation in UNCTAD and in the United Nations has doubtless yielded changes in the way in which the international community addresses trade issues of concern to less-developed countries. Nevertheless, it is clear that the more powerful industrialized countries remain firmly opposed to giving UNCTAD or the United Nations any authority to control the operations of GATT, or to permitting UNCTAD to supplant GATT as the central element in the trade system.[14]

In GATT, the tariff reductions achieved as an outcome of the Tokyo Round will be implemented on an MFN basis, and thus will benefit the exports of less-developed countries. But these countries have complained that the industrialized countries have made few cuts on products of special interest to them, such as textiles, clothing and footwear, and that tariffs remain exceptionally high on these goods. Moreover, benefits arising from reductions in MFN tariff rates are offset, to some extent, by reductions in preferential margins enjoyed by developing countries under GSP schemes. The Tokyo Round also left almost intact 'escalating' tariff systems in most industrialized countries that provide high levels of effective protection for their processing and manufacturing industries. Nor were there significant changes in the highly protectionist import policies of many industrialized countries, especially in Western Europe, for a range of agricultural products, such as sugar, meat and grains, that are of export interest to less-developed countries.

Other concerns have been expressed about the application of the MFN rule on a 'conditional' basis, which is a feature of several of the codes dealing with non-tariff measures adopted as an outcome of the Tokyo Round. Less-developed countries can be denied benefits provided by these codes unless they become signatories and accept the obligations the codes impose; and only a few developing countries have so far signed the Tokyo Round codes. The Tokyo Round also developed the concept of 'graduation' of the more advanced of the developing countries, which is aimed at drawing these countries into fuller and more effective participation in the GATT system. However, the process of 'graduation' can lead to a denial of these countries' claims for special and more favourable treatment in GATT; and industrialized countries may deny these countries the same degree of preferential treatment under GSP schemes that is extended to other countries in the group. The Tokyo Round, in addition, did not lead to any significant liberalization of the restrictive import regimes which are maintained by all but a few of the less-developed countries, and which undoubtedly block the expansion of trade within the group. However, as noted elsewhere, the Round led to decisions by the GATT Contracting Parties, which further relax the rules governing exchanges of new trade preferences among less-developed countries, and these modifications may lead to some trade liberalization within the Third World. On balance, it seems evident that the Tokyo Round served to increase, rather than diminish, the dissatisfaction of less-developed countries with the operation of the GATT system.[15] This dissatisfaction has undoubtedly been reinforced by the arrangements under which the Multifibre Arrangement was extended in 1978 and 1982. As we noted in Chapter 8, above, the MFA has been changed in ways which permit industrialized countries to impose increasingly severe controls on imports of textiles and clothing from less-developed countries, particularly the larger suppliers.

Canadian Interests

Canadian policies relating to the trade interests of less-developed countries have been the subject of considerable discussion in recent years.[16] In the context of broader North-South relationships, Canada has been generally supportive of the interests of less-developed countries. As a leading exporter of a range of resource and food products, Canada shares the interests of less-developed exporters in strengthening international markets for primary products and reducing barriers to their trade. Canada and many developing countries also have a common interest in the reduction by the larger importing countries of tariffs and other import barriers against the processed forms of raw materials, since these barriers can stand in the way of the enlargement of processing industries in producer countries. On the import side, Canada has few tariff or other barriers against imports of raw materials and tropical agricultural products. But Canada has a long tradition of imposing tariff and non-tariff import measures designed to protect domestic manufacturing, as well as certain agricultural sectors. Canadian tariffs remain relatively high on many manufactured products exported by developing countries, and the lower GSP tariffs had had significant trade effects in only a few areas of trade. More serious still, over the past few years Canada has imposed increasingly severe quantitative restrictions on imports of 'low-cost' clothing, certain textiles and footwear, and these restrictions seriously damage the trade interests of many developing countries. Canadian restrictions in those areas, however, are generally no more severe than those of most other industrialized countries.

Canada's approach to UNCTAD activities in trade areas has been qualified by its underlying dedication to a liberal trade system governed by multilaterally agreed trade rules, as embodied in the GATT system. Moreover, as we noted above, UNCTAD activities have been highly politicized, and issues tend to be approached and settled through a process of confrontation and the exercise of power, a process that tends to shift decision making to larger countries. Within UNCTAD, Canada often is left to play an essentially defensive role or the role of facilitating compromises between polarized positions taken by other countries, and Canada's own interests can easily be squeezed out.

For the most part, major UNCTAD programs have been aimed at achieving objectives in trade areas that are not in line with basic and traditional Canadian trade-policy objectives. The thrust of the developing countries and the UNCTAD Secretariat has been directed more at the creation of new trade preferences than at the liberalization of world trade. UNCTAD programs in the area of primary commodities, moreover, have been narrowly focused on the interests of developing-country exporters. These programs have been pursued in a context of confrontation and ideological dispute, and this appears often to have stood in the way of reaching agreement on constructive new arrangements, rather than to have encouraged the development of new forms of international co-operation. One result of all this has been that producer interests in Canada have become mistrustful of UNCTAD as a framework for the negotiation of international agreements and of other arrangements for trading primary commodities.

Thus, while Canada has been actively involved in a whole range of UNCTAD activities, its approach in trade areas has tended to be defensive and even negative. Canada has not, moreover, played a significant role in the general management of the UNCTAD program, and there are only a few Canadians in the senior ranks of the UNCTAD Secretariat in Geneva.

Notes

1. For a general examination of the evolution of GATT and UNCTAD from the perspective of less-developed countries, see J.A. Finlayson and M.W. Zacher, "International Trade Institutions and the North/South Dialogue."

2. M. Perez-Guerrero, Secretary General of UNCTAD, *UNCTAD's Contribution to a Just and Durable Peace*, p. 1.

3. For a detailed examination of the role of less-developed countries in the post-war negotiations for the ITO and GATT, and for subsequent developments in GATT relating to less-developed countries, see K. Kock, *International Trade Policy and*

the GATT 1947–1967, Chapter IX. See also K.W. Dam, *The GATT: Law and International Economic Organization*, Chapter 14.

4. The panel consisted of Professors Haberler (USA), Tinbergen (Netherlands), Meade (Britain) and Campos (Brazil); their report is in GATT, *Trends in International Trade: Report by a Panel of Experts.*

5. The text of the GATT Action Programme is in GATT, *Basic Instruments and Selected Documents, Twelfth Supplement.*

6. The statement by the Minister of Trade and Commerce is set out in more detail in G.L. Reuber, *Canada's Interest in the Trade Problems of Less-Developed Countries*, pp. 5-7.

7. The United Nations Conference on Trade and Development has assembled six times: in Geneva (1964), New Delhi (1968), Santiago (1972), Nairobi (1976), Manilla (1979), and in Belgrade (1983). A detailed account of the negotiations leading to the first United Nations Conference on Trade and Development is in C.L. Robertson, "The Creation of UNCTAD" in R.W. Cox (ed.), *International Organization: World Politics.* For a comprehensive examination of the structure and operations of UNCTAD until the early 1970s, see B. Gosovic, *UNCTAD: Conflict and Compromise.* For a more recent analysis of UNCTAD, dealing particularly with its activities relating to trade in primary commodities, see R.L. Rothstein, *Global Bargaining: UNCTAD and the Quest for a New International Economic Order.* The UNCTAD *Monthly Bulletin*, contains information about current UNCTAD activities.

8. The 'Group of 77' emerged as a caucus of developing countries during preparations in the United Nations for the first UNCTAD Conference; its membership now greatly exceeds the original number of members. The industrialized countries have maintained a corresponding caucus known as 'Group B,' which makes use of OECD to co-ordinate positions on issues arising in UNCTAD. The socialist countries of Eastern Europe form a separate 'Group D.' UNCTAD activities are focused mainly on trade and development issues between the less-developed countries and the industrialized countries of Group B; The Group-D socialist countries are marginal actors.

9. The objectives of the New International Economic Order on the trade side are reflected in Chapters 9 and 11 of the report by the Independent Commission on International Development Issues, *North-South: A Program for Survival* (The Brandt Report). For a critical analysis of the trade aspects of the NIEO, see A. MacBean, *A Positive Approach to the International Economic Order, Part I: Trade and Structural Adjustment.*

10. See, for example, the analysis in UNCTAD, "Protectionism and Structural Adjustment in the World Economy"; also UNCTAD, "Report of the Trade and Development Board on the First Part of Its Twenty-Fourth Session."

11. *The Set of Multilaterally Agreed Equitable Principles and Rules for the Control of Restrictive Business Practices* was adopted by a United Nations Conference on Restrictive Business Practices in April 1980; the text is in *International Legal Materials* 19 (May 1980):813-23. (Washington, D.C.: American Society of International Law.) For an assessment of recent developments relating to restrictive business practices in UNCTAD, the United Nations and OECD, see T.L. Brewer, "International Regulation of Restrictive Business Practices."

12. See successive issues of *World Development Report* (Washington, D.C.: International Bank for Reconstruction and Development) for comprehensive reviews of trade and development issues of special concern to less-developed countries.

13. The Third World Foundation, *Third World Quarterly* 4 (July 1982), contains a series of articles and commentaries on the Cancun meeting. See also The Trilateral Commission, *Trialogue* 28 (Winter 1981/82), for commentaries on the meeting by Prime Minister Trudeau and others.

14. Finlayson and Zacher, "International Trade Institutions" pp. 762-65 contains a more detailed recent assessment of the role of GATT and UNCTAD in the trade system.

15. A generally negative analysis of the outcome of the Tokyo Round from the perspective of less-developed countries was issued by the UNCTAD Secretariat in 1980: see UNCTAD, Secretary-General, *Assessment of the Results of the Multilateral Trade Negotiations* TD/B/778 and TD/B/778/Addition 1. See also UNCTAD *Monthly Bulletin* (December 1981), for an evaluation of the impact on the trade system of the Tokyo Round negotiations and parallel developments in international trade relations. For a more positive assessment of the Tokyo Round from the perspective of less-developed countries, see B. Balassa, *The Tokyo Round and the Developing Countries.*

16. Among the studies in this area are Reuber, *Canada's Interest*; Economic Council of Canada, *For a Common Future: A Study of Canada's Relations with Developing Countries*; V. Corbo and O. Havrylyshyn, *Canada's Trade Relations with Developing Countries: The Evolution of Export and Import Structures and Barriers to Trade in Canada*; and M.A. Biggs, *The Challenge: Adjust or Protect?* The "Report of the Parliamentary Task Force on North-South Relations" contains, in Section III:E, an examination of Canadian interests in trade issues of concern to developing countries and recommendations by the Task Force with respect to Canadian policies in these areas. For the government's response, see Canada, Department of External Affairs, "Government Response to the Report of the Parliamentary Task Force on North-South Relations."

11

The Generalized System of Preferences (GSP)

S ince the early 1970s, the industrialized countries have extended to the group of less-developed countries tariff preferences covering most manufactured goods and some other products, within the framework of a Generalized System of Preferences (GSP), which was developed in the United Nations Conference on Trade and Development (UNCTAD) during the late 1960s. This system represents a departure from the 'no-new-preference' rule of GATT, which was embodied in the 1947 General Agreement. The success of these preferences in enlarging export opportunities for developing countries has been the subject of debate. Some products of prime interest to many developing countries, notably textiles, clothing and footwear, are generally excluded. Many industrialized countries, but so far not Canada, have quota limits on imports entering at the lower preferential rates. The group of newly industrialized and middle-income countries appears to have benefited most by the scheme. Canada introduced its GSP scheme in 1974.

Origins of GSP System

As we discussed in Chapter 3, above, the GATT rules adopted in 1947 generally prohibited the introduction of new preferences into the trade system. One of the exceptions to this rule, however, permitted the continuation of tariff preferences that had existed in 1939, notably those exchanged among Commonwealth countries and those that existed within the colonial systems of France, Belgium and the Netherlands. These European preferences were absorbed at a later date into the European Community's (EC) preferential arrangements with a group of 'associated states,' mainly in Africa. When Britain joined the Community in the early 1970s, these European preferences were further broadened to include some, but not all, of the less-developed countries and territories of the Commonwealth, under the Lomé Convention.

Thus, by the early 1970s, divisions had been sharpened between those less-developed countries which had preferential access to markets in industrialized countries and those that did not; the United States and Japan remained almost the only industrialized countries that did not extend preferential treatment to any less-developed countries; and the Latin American countries, along with a few others, remained excluded from preferential access to any of the industrialized countries. This exclusion of Latin American countries from preferential arrangements with industrialized countries led to growing pressures, during the 1960s, in GATT and in the newly established UNCTAD, for a broader system of preferences by industrialized countries from which all less-developed countries would benefit, and which would involve the granting of tariff preferences by the United States (USA).

In GATT, possibilities for the establishment of a broader system of tariff preferences for developing countries were discussed during 1963–64, in connection with the drafting of the Part IV Articles of the General Agreement, but no particular conclusions were reached. The industrialized countries were divided on the issue. The United States and Canada were generally opposed, partly for reasons of principle, and partly because new tariff preferences would increase import competition. Canada, in addition, had to consider the reaction of the less-developed countries of the Commonwealth, whose long-existing preferential access to the Canadian market would be eroded if they were to be shared by the whole group of developing countries. The United States was more sympathetic to an exchange of tariff preferences among the less-developed countries to Third World countries. The European Community, with its existing system of trade preferences for its associated African countries, was divided on proposals that would weaken this system by extending their preferences to other developing countries; and the associated African countries were also unenthusiastic about sharing with others their advantages in the European market.[1]

After the first UNCTAD Conference in 1964, the Latin American and some other developing countries exerted even stronger pressure for a new global system of preferences. Under pressure from the Latin American countries, the United States eventually abandoned its opposition, on the eve of the second UNCTAD Conference, held in New Delhi in 1968; but in follow-up negotiations it insisted that any new broader system should be limited to tariffs, should be temporary, should be based on voluntary adherence, and should be extended by all of the developed countries to all of the developing countries on a non-discriminatory basis. The USA also insisted that the new system should not include 'reverse preferences,' that is, preferences by a developing country for exports from particular industrialized countries. At the New Delhi Conference, a Generalized System of Preferences along these lines was agreed to in principle. In the Organisation for Economic Co-operation and Development (OECD), the industrialized countries further refined the ground rules on which such preferences would be extended and determined that individual industrialized countries would apply their schemes separately. In 1970 agreement was finally reached in UNCTAD on arrangements, acceptable on all sides, for a Generalized System of Preferences, and a Special Committee on Preferences was established to review the operation of the system on a continuing basis.[2]

Structure of GSP System

Between 1971 and 1976, some twenty developed countries implemented GSP schemes. Canada implemented its scheme in 1974, having waited until the intention of the United States to introduce a GSP scheme was clarified. The various schemes differ in some important details, but are broadly similar.

- Preferences are limited to tariffs and are generally focused on manufactured and semi-manufactured sectors, although shorter lists of agricultural products are included. Preferences are generally withheld from 'import-sensitive' product areas such as textiles, clothing, footwear and certain electronic products.

- Under some schemes, preferences result in duty-free treatment for the products involved; other schemes reduce most-favoured-nation (MFN) rates by varying amounts.

- Most countries, but so far not Canada, impose limits on amounts of particular imports from particular countries that can be admitted under GSP rates.

- While the GSP rates under separate schemes are similar for all developing countries to which they apply, the lists of beneficiary countries are somewhat different.

- All schemes incorporate 'rules of origin,' which differ somewhat, but are designed generally to limit preferences to goods actually produced in beneficiary countries and transported, without further manufacture, to the importing country.

- Preferences are not 'bound' and thus may be withdrawn or modified by importing countries without compensation or, indeed, without consulting beneficiary countries.

Since these new GSP schemes are inconsistent with MFN rules of the General Agreement, their implementation required a general waiver for the importing countries from Article I. In 1971 the GATT Contracting Parties granted this waiver for a ten-year period. Following the Tokyo Round, the Contracting Parties agreed, as part of the so-called 'Enabling Clause,' to extend the GSP scheme on a continuing basis.[3]

Canada's GSP Scheme

Canada's GSP scheme involves the addition to the Customs Tariff of a separate column of 'General Preferential Tariff' (GPT) rates.[4] In general, these GPT rates are equal to the MFN rates less one-third or to the British Preferential (BP) rate, whichever is lower, although some rates have recently been reduced to free. Canada's system thus may be regarded basically as an extension to all less-developed countries of the British Preferential rates that were already applied to imports from the less-developed countries of the Commonwealth. In terms of country coverage, it is one of the most extensive, applying in 1982 to 162 countries and territories, that is, to virtually all the countries that are recognized within the United Nations (UN) to have the status of less-developed countries. The United States (US) scheme is one of the most restrictive in this respect. Like others, the Canadian scheme withholds preferences from several import-sensitive areas; the list of exceptions includes most textiles and clothing products, most footwear,[5] certain electronic products, most food products, soaps, oils and drugs, and a list of miscellaneous consumer-type goods. Many raw products are tropical foods exported by developing countries are, in any case, free of duty. Duty-free entry is also accorded to 'handicraft products' from the GPT beneficiaries. As we noted above, there are so far no quantitative limits on goods that enter Canada under GPT rates. Many other countries, including the USA and the EC, impose such limits on the quantities of particular products that can be imported at preferential rates from particular countries; in some cases, these quantities are set at relatively low levels and are often changed, usually downwards.

In 1982 several changes were made to Canada's GPT system. For the first time, an element of 'graduation' was introduced, inasmuch as many goods became entitled to duty-free entry, but only if imported from a designated group of 'least-developed' countries. For these imports, a more liberal 'cumulative' concept of origin was introduced, enabling them to be partly processed in one least-developed country and finished in another. On the other hand, a potentially restrictive element was introduced, enabling the Canadian government, on the recommendation of the Tariff Board, to limit the quantity of a product imported under the GPT rate. (To date, no such tariff-rate quotas have been imposed.) In January 1983, the government introduced further amendments to the Customs Tariff, which will add some additional products to the list of those entitled to GPT rates.[6]

The actual impact of the GSP system on exports of developing countries has not been impressive. For Canada, developing countries provide a relatively small share of total imports. A study prepared for the Canadian Tariff Board in 1979 showed that imports from all developing countries represented about 10 to 11 per cent of total imports in the 1970s, and only 5 to 6 per cent if petroleum is excluded. In 1977 imports, including petroleum, from all developing countries, totalled about $4.4 billion; almost three-quarters of these imports entered duty free; of the remaining $1 billion worth, slightly less than one-half entered under GPT or BP preferential rates. This represented only slightly over 1 per cent of total Canadian imports.[7]

Moreover, most of the benefits of Canada's GPT preferences have gone to a relatively few more advanced and middle-income countries, such as South Korea, Hong Kong, Singapore, Malaysia and Brazil, despite the fact that some of the chief exports from these countries, that is, textiles, clothing and footwear, are excluded from GPT preferences and are, in addition, largely subject to quantitative limitations. A similar group of more advanced developing countries appear to be the main beneficiaries of the GSP schemes of other developed countries.

In many countries, although not yet in Canada, GSP schemes have tended to become less liberal over time, reflecting pressures by domestic producers in a period of economic recession. There is an inherent instability in the whole GSP system, as well as a more general trend by industrialized countries to limit quantities of imports permitted under the lower preferential rates, and to restrict full preferential treatment to the poorer, more backward countries whose exports are less threatening to domestic producers.

Impact of GSP

The limited impact of the GSP system is illustrated in Table 11-1, which shows that goods accorded preferential tariff treatment represent a very small proportion of total imports from developing countries, even of goods otherwise subject to duties.

While the GSP system has had only a limited effect in terms of world-trade liberalization, it will probably remain a more or less permanent feature of the world-trade system. From the perspectives of the developing countries generally, it may be regretted that some of the effort that was devoted in UNCTAD and elsewhere to creating the GSP system was not directed to greater efforts in GATT to obtain improved market access, on a permanent and MFN basis, for products of developing countries. Such a program in GATT would have gained considerable support from outside the developing-country grouping, and might have diffused the often unproductive North-South confrontations in UNCTAD on the subject of preferences.

Table 11-1:   Selected GSP Schemes, 1977[a]

(billions of US dollars)

Country	Total Imports from GSP Countries	MFN Dutiable Imports	Accorded GSP Preference
Canada	4.1	1.0	.4
USA	34.6	25.6	4.0
EC (1975)	57.6	13.6	2.2
Japan	38.8	31.4	2.3
Sweden	2.8	.6	.2
Switzerland	2.1	1.9	.4

Note
a. Source: G.H. Forrester and M.S. Islam, *The Generalized System of Preferences and the Canadian General Preferential Tariff, p. 7 and Appendix XI.*

Notes

1. A detailed account of early debates in GATT over the granting of tariff preferences to developing countries by industrialized countries is in G. Patterson, *Discrimination in International Trade: The Policy Issues 1945–1965*, pp. 343-84 and K.W. Dam, *The GATT: Law and International Economic Organization*, pp. 247-55.

2. See B. Gosovic, *UNCTAD: Conflict and Compromise*, pp. 65-92, for a detailed discussion of developments leading to the agreement reached in 1968 at UN-CTAD II in New Delhi, regarding the establishment of the GSP system and the follow-up negotiations in OECD and UNCTAD.

3. The text of the decision adopted in 1971 by the GATT Contracting Parties covering the Generalized System of Preferences is in GATT, *Basic Instruments and Selected Documents, Eighteenth Supplement*, p. 24. The text of the decision of 28 November 1979, regarding "Differential and More Favourable Treatment, Reciprocity and Fuller Participation of Developing Countries" which contains the "Enabling Clause" is in GATT, *Basic Instruments and Selected Documents, Twenty-sixth Supplement*, pp. 203-205.

4. Section 3.1 of the Customs Tariff governs the application of Canada's GPT rates, and the countries entitled to these rates are listed in an attached schedule. See G.H. Forrester and M.S. Islam, "The Generalized System of Preferences and the Canadian General Preferential Tariff." See also V. Corbo and O. Havrylyshyn, *Canada's Trade Relations with Developing Countries: The Evolution of Export and Import Structures and Barriers to Trade in Canada*, pp. 69-74, for analysis of the trade effects of Canada's GSP scheme.

5. There is no GPT reduction for imports of leather footwear into Canada. (The MFN

rate is being reduced from 24.7 per cent to 22.5 per cent as a result of the Tokyo Round negotiations.) For rubber footwear, the MFN rate is 20 per cent, and the BP rate is free; initially a GPT rate applied, also at the free level, but this rate was temporarily withdrawn in 1979. In July 1982, the Tariff Board, in a report to the Minister of Finance, recommended against the reinstatement of the GPT rate for rubber footwear; see *A Report by the Tariff Board: Reference 161 Relating to the Reinstatement of the General Preferential Tariff on Imports of Rubber Footwear.* There are GPT rates involving reductions from MFN rates for canvas shoes, downhill ski boots, and oriental sandals.

6. These changes were set out in Bill C-90, approved by the House of Commons on 16 November 1982, following an inquiry by the Tariff Board in accordance with Reference 158 from the Minister of Finance in July and August 1980.

7. Forrester and Islam, "The Generalized System," p. 24.

12

International Commodity Agreements

From the start, the multilateral trade system has provided a special frame-work of rules for the conclusion and operation of international commodity agreements among producer and consumer countries. These agreements are based on a general recognition that special difficulties exist for trade in primary products, leading to excessive instability of world prices and other market conditions. Within this framework, international commodity agreements aimed at the stabilization of world markets have been concluded for wheat, tin, sugar, coffee, cocoa, natural rubber and jute; other agreements are under discussion internationally. The structures of these agreements are similar in many ways, and most have embodied, for varying periods, 'economic provisions' which are designed to improve price stability. These provisions have included the creation of international buffer stocks, the use of export and import quotas, and long-term commitments to purchase or sell specified quantities of certain products within agreed price ranges.

The instability of world commodity markets has been of particular concern to developing countries within the trade system, especially those whose economies depend on the export of a single primary product or of only a few. Since the early 1950s, in the light of evidence of a downward trend in the prices of primary commodities relative to the prices of industrial and manufactured goods, developing countries have attempted to use commodity agreements, not only to stabilize, but also to raise, world prices for the primary products which they export. Within UNCTAD, since the mid-1960s, strong efforts have been made by developing countries to extend the range and scope of international commodity agreements, within a special UNCTAD Integrated Program for Commodities (IPC), as part of broader efforts to assist the economic development of the Third World.[1]

Within the trade system, there have been different and conflicting approaches, from the start, to the use of intergovernmental agreements aimed at influencing world prices of primary commodities and other conditions of trade. As a matter of principle, the United States (USA), Japan and West Germany have generally been negative towards such agreements, as representing distortions of free-market operations; in practice, however, these countries have become members of several such agreements. Canada has traditionally adopted a more neutral position with respect to international commodity agreements, although Canada's position involves an element of ambivalence. As a major world producer and exporter of a range of primary commodities, especially wheat, Canada has a major stake in the health of world commodity markets and a basic interest in co-operation with both producer and consumer countries in efforts to stabilize and improve the operation of world markets. Canada also has a tradition of a degree of government intervention in economic areas, including intervention in the marketing of Prairie wheat under the Canadian Wheat Board, dating from the 1930s and, more recently, under marketing boards established in the dairy, eggs, and poultry sectors. Thus Canada has participated actively in all post-war discussions and negotiations in the area of primary-commodity trade, demonstrating a recognition of the problems involved for developing-country producers. With the one exception of the current agreement for cocoa, Canada has become a member of all the commodity agreements with price-stabilization features that have been concluded; and in all of these agreements, apart from those pertaining to wheat, Canada has participated as an importer and a consumer country. On the other hand, Canada has resisted proposals for price-stabilization agreements for a number of commodities in which it has major exporter interests, such as copper, lead and zinc, and iron ore. Government departments concerned have evidently concluded that international commodity agreements for these products would not serve Canadian interests, and their attitude reflects the opposition of private sector producers to such arrangements.

Pre-War Commodity Agreements

The concept of international commodity agreements pre-dates the establishment of the multilateral trade system. While, for the most part, pre-war agreements took the form of cartels among private industries in producer countries, governments also participated in some of them. The governments of the leading tin-producing countries, for example, concluded a cartel-like agreement in the early 1930s, covering 90 per cent of world exports. With the participation of both producer countries and of importing countries, an international agreement covering sugar was concluded in 1937. Canada played a leading role in the conclusion of the first International Wheat Agreement, concluded in 1933 within the League of Nations framework. Both importing and exporting countries were members of this agreement which, in an effort to stabilize world prices, made provisions for limitations on production and exports. While this first International Wheat Agreement was in effect for only a brief period, it provided a model for future international commodity agreements within the post-war, multilateral, trade system.[2]

Commodity Agreements under ITO and GATT

During the negotiations for the Havana Charter, there was much discussion of the conditions under which international commodity agreements would be appropriate, the principles to govern their adoption, and the rules for their operation. The Charter devoted a separate Chapter VI to setting out in great detail the concepts and objectives of commodity agreements, their functions, and the principles to govern their negotiation and operation. The basic concepts involved were set out in Article 55 of the Havana Charter as follows:

> The Members recognize that the conditions under which some primary commodities are produced, exchanged, and consumed are such that international trade in these commodities may be affected by special difficulties such as the tendency towards persistent disequilibrium between production and consumption, the accumulation of burdensome stocks and pronounced fluctuations in prices. These special difficulties may have serious adverse effects on the interests of producers and consumers, as well as widespread repercussions jeopardizing the general policy of economic expansion. The Members recognize that such difficulties may, at times, necessitate special treatment of the international trade in such commodities through inter-governmental agreement.

One principal objective of the commodity agreements was stated in Article 57 as follows:

> . . . to prevent or moderate pronounced fluctuations in the price of a primary commodity with a view to achieving a reasonable degree of stability on a basis of such prices as are fair to consumers and provide a reasonable return to producers, having regard to the desirability of securing long-term equilibrium between the forces of supply and demand.

The Charter envisaged that international commodity agreements would take a variety of forms, with different objectives and functions, ranging from international 'study groups' to more elaborate agreements designed to stabilize world production, trade and prices. In all cases, adequate participation was required for both consuming and producing countries. The rules would have been particularly strict for agreements which involved the regulation of production or controls on exports or imports, or the regulation of prices. These were termed 'commodity control agreements,' and could be concluded only to deal with 'burdensome surpluses' which threatened serious hardship to producers, or where there was widespread unemployment or under-employment in the industry concerned. This type of agreement was also to be designed to assure adequate supplies at fair prices and could include measures designed to expand world consumption. Such 'control' agreements were envisaged as temporary and could not be concluded for periods of over five years.

Chapter VI of the Havana Charter, which deals with commodity agreements, has been described as 'a code within a code' and as 'a miniature charter in the field of primary commodities.'[3] Detailed rules and requirements were considered needed because trade in primary products would be treated as an exception from the normal rules of the new world-trading system. Such agreements would bring about a much higher level of involvement by governments in the control of trade, as well as the use of export quotas, import controls, and other measures that were otherwise prohibited or discouraged by the Charter.

Nothing along the lines of Chapter VI of the Havana Charter was included among the articles of GATT, apart from an exemption in sub-paragraph (*h*) of GATT Article XX, permitting member countries to depart from other GATT rules in order to comply with their obligations under an international commodity agreement; however the exemption applies only to an agreement "which conforms to the principles approved by the Economic and Social Council (ECOSOC) in its resolution 30(IV) of 28 March 1947."[4] This ECOSOC resolution expressed approval of Chapter VI of the Havana Charter and recommended that all members of the United nations adopt it as a general guide to the negotiation and operation of international commodity agreements. Thus, while Chapter VI of the Charter has never formally come into force, the concepts, principles and rules that it set out have been preserved, and have continued to provide a framework and guide for the negotiation and operation of commodity agreements.

In 1947 ECOSOC resolution 30(IV) also established an interim framework for the negotiation of commodity agreements within the United Nations (UN), in the form of an Interim Co-ordinating Committee for International Commodity Arrangements (ICCICA); this Committee was supported by the UN Secretariat, and remained in existence after the abandonment of the Havana Charter and the ITO. The Chairman of ICCICA was appointed by the GATT Contracting Parties after 1952. ICCICA provided a broad institutional framework within the UN system for those commodity agreements that were negotiated and renegotiated over a period of almost twenty years. Its work was supplemented after 1954 through the establishment of a United Nations Commission on International Commodity Trade (CICT), which concerned itself with broader issues of production and trade in primary commodities. In the mid-1960s, the functions of both these bodies were transferred to the newly created United Nations Conference on Trade and Development (UNCTAD), where a permanent Committee on Commodities was set up. A Committee on Commodity Problems of the Food and Agriculture Organization (FAO) has also made an important contribution to international consideration of problems affecting production and trade in primary agricultural products. It was settled during the Havana Conference, however, that FAO would not serve as a framework for the negotiation of international agreements, but rather provide advice and assistance to other international bodies and to member countries.

The encouragement, given under the Havana Charter and subsequently within GATT and UNCTAD, to intergovernmental commodity agreements which aim at controlling production and world prices, has never been extended to cartel-like agreements among producer countries alone, without the partic-ipation of consumer countries.[5] At the Havana negotiations, such agreements were regarded as cartels and as among the 'restrictive business practices' that could have adverse international economic and trade effects. While these and other forms of restrictive business practices would not, in themselves, have been prohibited by the Havana Charter, ITO members would have been obligated to take appropriate measures and to co-operate within the ITO and other international bodies to prevent those that had 'harmful effects.' As we have noted elsewhere in this study, international co-operation in dealing with restrictive business practices has subsequently developed, although slowly, within UNCTAD and the Organisation for Economic Co-operation and De-velopment (OECD).

Post-War Commodity Agreements

Since the Second World War, six international commodity agreements of the kind envisaged in Chapter VI of the Havana Charter, containing provisions aimed at price stabilization, have been concluded among producer and con-sumer countries. These cover wheat, tin, sugar, coffee, cocoa and natural rubber. A further agreement, covering jute and jute products, has been con-cluded, but it does not contain price-stabilization provisions; efforts are under way in UNCTAD to conclude agreements, without price provisions, to cover tropical timber and tea. For a few other products, including lead and zinc, international 'study group' arrangements have been made, some within FAO; others are under consideration, designed for such purposes as encouraging exchanges of information, research and development activities, market pro-motion and the improvement of productivity. An international agreement among olive-oil-producing countries has also existed for many years, but it is limited to exchanges of information among the member countries. Within GATT, other agreements, which govern specified marketing activities, have been concluded in fairly recent years, among exporters of certain dairy products and among exporters of bovine meat, for regular exchanges of production and marketing information. (See Chapter 13, below.)

The six international commodity agreements with price-stabilization features have come into effect at different times; the natural rubber agreement is the most recent. All have been 'temporary,' in the sense of requiring periodic negotiations for their extension; not all have been in force continuously, and the price-stabilization features of some have been interrupted for periods of time. All include both producer and consumer countries among their members, and all have established rather similar organizational structures, with permanent 'councils' and secretariats, most of which are located in London, although the Rubber Council is established in Kuala Lumpur. All of these agreements and arrangements have been concluded and operate within the multilateral trade system and form an important part of it, more or less as envisaged by the post-war architects of the system.

Provisions for Price Stabilization

The six international commodity agreements that have been concluded for wheat, tin, sugar, coffee, cocoa and natural rubber have had, as their major objective, the maintenance of world prices within agreed price ranges; however, they have employed different techniques to achieve their objective. These techniques have included:

- Contractual obligations assumed by producer and consumer countries. These involve, for example, commitments to sell certain quantities of goods and purchase certain quantities within agreed price ranges, or other conditions, such as limitations on trade with non-member countries;

- Agreement among members to the use of export quotas by producer countries in order to limit quantities of a product available on world markets in specified market conditions;

- The establishment of an internationally financed buffer stock, operated by a central body, which buys into and sells from the stockpile, under agreed circumstances, in order to influence world prices. (The stockpiles may be held 'nationally,' that is, in the producer countries.)

There has been much debate over the success of these agreements in achieving their objectives over recent years, especially that of establishing greater price stability in world markets. In general it would appear that while the agreements have had some success in improving co-operation between producer and consumer countries, and have achieved a higher degree of world-price stability than would have existed in their absence, they have been unable to contain the exceptionally strong upward and downward pressures on prices that have characterized world markets for primary commodities since the early 1970s. Under certain agreements, efforts to influence price movements have been abandoned for periods of time; the 'economic provisions' of some agreements have been suspended, although they have continued to function in other areas. In general, negotiations to keep the existing agreements in place, let alone to conclude new agreements covering other products, have been unusually difficult.

Techniques for price stabilization under the six international commodity agreements may be summarized as follows.[6]

Wheat

Since 1949, successive wheat agreements were designed to keep prices within agreed ranges, periodically renegotiated. They incorporated contractual obligations by exporting countries to make available specified quantities of wheat if world prices fell to agreed lower levels. Within this price band, there were no obligations either to sell or purchase. The wheat agreements contained no provisions for the establishment of international buffer stocks nor for the use of export quotas as price-stabilization techniques. However, during most periods, the major exporters, notably the United States and Canada, held large stocks off world markets in order to support world prices. In 1967 the Wheat Agreement was extended to cover other grains, and linked to a Food Aid Convention established within the FAO framework. The Convention's object was to provide food aid to needy developing countries, including the major wheat producers. Since 1971, with world prices at generally high levels, it has not been possible to agree on the price-stabilization features of the Wheat Agreement; that Agreement has been extended several times and has continued to function in other respects, mainly for continuing exchanges of production and market information among the members.

Tin

From 1954, successive International Tin Agreements have incorporated two techniques aimed at reducing world-price fluctuations. One technique is the maintenance of an international buffer stock financed at earlier periods by the producer countries. Sales are made from the buffer stock if world prices rise above agreed levels; purchases are made by it if prices fall to agreed lower limits. The second technique is the use of export controls by producer countries when prices fall below agreed levels, to back up the price-supporting purchases by the buffer-stock manager. For many years, the United States remained outside the Tin Agreement, but exerted a major influence on world prices by holding a very large strategic stockpile from which sales were periodically made in order to restrain upward price movements. In 1976 the United States became a member of the Tin Agreement. The Agreement was renewed in 1982, with Canada as a member.

Sugar

Much international trade in sugar takes place under bilateral preferential arrangements, leaving a relatively small part in the 'free market.' Since the first International Sugar Agreement was concluded in 1954, a main objective of successive Agreements has been to stabilize 'free market' prices within an agreed range, which has been periodically renegotiated. The producer countries have been assigned agreed export quotas; these are reduced in size when world prices fall to agreed floor levels and increased when prices rise to agreed ceilings. Consumer countries have accepted restraints with respect to purchases from non-members. The Sugar Agreement was suspended between 1962 and 1967, largely because of events in Cuba, and its price-stabilization features were non-operative between 1973 and 1977. Since 1977 the Sugar Agreement has incorporated both a buffer stock, financed by the producer countries and held 'nationally,' and agreed export quotas for producers. The operations of the Agreement have been weakened by the failure of the European Community (EC) to become a member. Negotiations took place in 1983 for an extension of the Agreement and will be continued in early 1984.

Coffee

From 1963, successive International Coffee Agreements have been based on a system of agreed quotas for exports from producer countries, which become operative when world prices fall to specified levels. There are no provisions for international buffer stocks or other price-stabilization measures.

Cocoa

The original 1972 Agreement and its successor, signed in 1975, used a combination of export quotas as well as an international buffer stock to maintain world prices between agreed floor and ceiling levels. An extension of the Agreement, signed in 1980, relies solely on a buffer stock to influence world prices. The buffer stock is financed by a tax imposed on exports. The 1980 Agreement is seriously weakened by the non-participation of the largest exporting country, Côte d'Ivoire, as well as of the largest importer, the United

States. In these circumstances and because of doubts about the effectiveness of its operations, Canada has not signed the 1980 Agreement.

Natural Rubber

The International Rubber Agreement, which came into force in 1980, is the most recent commodity agreement with price-stabilization features. The Agreement employs an international buffer stock as its sole means of stabilizing world prices. The buffer-stock manager buys and sells rubber from the buffer stock when world prices fall or rise to specified levels in relation to an agreed reference price, with the object of maintaining world prices at points between these levels. The buffer sock is financed by contributions from member countries, shared equally by the producer group and the consumer group.

The UNCTAD Integrated Program for Commodities

Within UNCTAD, the commodity-trade problems of developing countries were advanced mainly in terms of the instability of world prices for primary commodities; a perceived long-term deterioration of the terms of trade for exporters of primary commodities; short-falls of export earnings among developing-country exporters in recurring periods of low prices; and the dependence of economies of many developing countries on the export of a single commodity or a relatively few commodities. The developing countries called for new and comprehensive arrangements among governments, involving interventions in the free-market system, to stabilize and otherwise improve the conditions of trade in primary products for developing-country exporters; and these arrangements were pushed as a supplementary method of transferring assistance by developed countries to the Third World, to accelerate its economic development.

In the early 1970s, a combination of circumstances created a new surge of interest in commodity-trade issues. These included the sharp price rise for many primary commodities that took place in the early 1970s, followed by equally dramatic price declines; apprehensions over possible world shortages of certain non-renewable industrial materials; and, above all, the success of the Organization of Petroleum Exporting Countries (OPEC) in raising world oil prices and otherwise taking control of the world oil market. The OPEC example encouraged some exporters of other primary products to seek greater control of world markets by forming producer cartels or renegotiating arrangements with governments of importing countries. In major importing countries, there was, at the same time, an increasing appreciation of possibilities for reducing the inflationary impact of price increases for primary products under market-control arrangements with exporting countries.

In these circumstances of turbulent world commodity markets, the developing countries, in 1974, pushed through the General Assembly of the United Nations two resounding restatements of their economic and trade interests. These consisted of a "Declaration and a Program of Action on the Establishment of a New International Economic Order" (NIEO) and a "Charter of Economic Rights and Duties of States." In 1976, at UNCTAD IV in Nairobi, following these initiatives in the United Nations, the developing countries pressed through the adoption of an Integrated Program for Commodities (IPC) to be put into place within the UNCTAD framework.[7] The IPC was based on a further-reaching Declaration that had been drawn up in Manila, earlier in the year, at a meeting of the Group of 77. Many of the concepts involved, however, had come under discussion in earlier years.

The IPC pulled together a broad range of objectives of developing countries, relating to primary commodities. These objectives included price stabilization; improved export earnings for developing-country producers; improved market access, especially for processed forms of raw materials, in hope of increased processing of raw materials in developing countries; the encouragement of research and development; and an improvement in marketing, distribution and transport systems. The IPC covered an initial list of eighteen products exported by developing countries: bananas, bauxite, cocoa, coffee, copper, cotton and cotton yarns, hard fibres and their products, iron ore, jute and its products, manganese, meat, phosphates, rubber, sugar, tea, tropical timber, tin, and vegetable oils including olive oil and oil seeds. A wide variety of measures was called for under arrangements among producer and consumer countries, but the main elements of the IPC were the following two:

- The early conclusion or the continuation of commodity agreements covering ten 'core' commodities: cocoa, coffee, copper, sugar, cotton, jute, rubber, hard fibres, tea and tin

- The establishment of a $6 billion Common Fund to be financed internationally, to provide a central source of financing for buffer stocks, where these were required, under individual commodity agreements.

A series of discussions and negotiations has proceeded in UNCTAD since 1976, concerning the commodities included in the IPC. Progress has been slower than anticipated, and the results have been modest in terms of concluding new commodity agreements. As we noted above, only one additional product, natural rubber, has to date been brought under a formal intergovernmental agreement with price-stabilization features, and one other agreement, without these features, covering jute and jute products, has been concluded. Earlier agreements, however, have been renegotiated within the context of the IPC; these include agreements covering coffee (1976), sugar (1977), cocoa (1980), and tin (1976 and 1982). The previously existing International Wheat

Agreement, which is outside the IPC, was also extended in 1978–79, but without provisions covering prices.

There remain four 'core' commodities under the IPC, for which international agreements are not in place: copper, cotton, tea, and hard fibres. On the basis of UNCTAD discussions to date, there appear to be formidable difficulties in the way of establishing agreements to cover copper and cotton; for the other two 'core' products, prospects for concluding agreements are more promising. For the other eight products on the UNCTAD list, international discussions now appear to be aimed not at price-stabilization arrangements, but rather at measures to promote research and development, productivity improvements, export promotion, and further processing of the raw materials before export. The new agreement on jute is of this kind.[8]

It might be noted that discussions of primary-commodity issues do not always involve 'North-South' divisions Canada and Australia have major export interests in a number of products on the UNCTAD list, including copper, iron ore, oil seeds and vegetable oil, as well as other commodities not on this list, such as grains and nickel. Nor are the developing countries always united in UNCTAD discussions of commodity arrangements, especially arrangements which could involve increasing price levels; the resource-poor developing countries and some of the newly industrialized countries have major interests as importers, rather than as exporters.

Outside the UNCTAD program for commodities, but complementary to it, there are several international arrangements that are designed to deal with major problems of developing countries, arising from the instability of world markets for primary commodities. One arrangement has been developed within the International Monetary Fund (IMF), in the form of its Compensatory Financing Facility. Under this program, loans on favourable terms are available to any exporting country, to stabilize the availability of foreign exchange, in circumstances where its earnings from the export of primary commodities suffer a decline. Within UNCTAD, proposals have been advanced for a broader scheme of 'compensatory financing' designed to stabilize the export earnings of developing countries. The 'Stabex' program was established under the Lomé Convention between the European Community and a group of associated countries in Africa, the Pacific and the Caribbean (the APC countries); under the Stabex scheme, limited amounts of money, in the form of grants or interest-free loans, are available to exporting members which experience a decline in earnings from exports to the Community of a specified list of primary products.

The Common Fund

As we noted above, the UNCTAD Integrated Program for Commodities included proposals for the creation of a Common Fund, in the amount of $6 billion, which would serve as a central source of financing for buffer stocks under individual commodity agreements. After prolonged and acrimonious debate in UNCTAD, an agreement to establish a Common Fund was finally adopted in June 1980, but on a more modest scale and with rather different functions than originally proposed. The Common Fund, when it comes into force, will now consist of two separate elements.

• A First Account, with targeted capital of $400 million, contributed by member countries, to assist in financing buffer stocks established under individual commodity arrangements. These resources could be increased if existing or new commodity arrangements become formally associated with the Fund; otherwise, the Fund's relatively limited capital base will not be sufficient to allow it to finance, by itself, any substantial stockpile arrangements.

• A Second Account, with targeted resources of $350 million, provided largely by voluntary contributions, which would carry out technical assistance projects of special interest to the least-developed producers of primary commodities. It would provide funds for such purposes as improving structural conditions of commodity markets, research and development, and increasing production and marketing opportunities of primary commodities. A substantial part of this Second Account has now been pledged; and these funds could be used, when available, to finance the operation of the new international jute agreement and other agreements of this kind which may be concluded.

The Common Fund will represent a separate organization within the UN system, distinct from UNCTAD. The location of its headquarters has not yet been decided. However, the future of the Common Fund is uncertain. To come into force, the Agreement to create the Fund requires the signature and ratification of no fewer than ninety countries, representing contributions of two-thirds of the amount of the First Account. As of early 1983, only some forty countries had ratified. Despite the absence of commitments by the United States and many developing countries, Canada has signed and ratified the Common Fund Agreement.[9]

Canadian Interests

As we discussed above, Canada is a major world exporter of some of the commodities falling within the IPC and a substantial importer of others. As an exporter, Canada has shared a number of common interests with developing-country exporters, and has given support to many of the objectives of the UNCTAD program. At the same time, the Canadian view has continued to be that commodity arrangements should not distort the operation of normal market forces, but rather should be designed to improve the operation of international markets; that these agreements should increase the transparency of the operation of markets; and that they must accommodate the interests of both consumer and producer countries. Further, proposals for individual commodity arrangements should continue to be considered on their merits, on a commodity-by-commodity basis. Canada has resisted broader approaches involving multi-commodity arrangements which do not take into account the particular production and trade conditions surrounding individual primary commodities. Canada also generally resisted the concept, inherent in earlier UNCTAD approaches, of seeking to achieve transfers of resources from rich to poor countries through commodity-trade arrangements; in the Canadian view, such development assistance could be extended more effectively under IMF and other programs for compensatory financing. Similarly, Canada has joined many other countries in opposing proposals for indexing world commodity prices to prices for manufactured goods in world trade.

In line with these general policies, as we noted above, Canada has remained a participant in all of the existing commodity agreements as these were renegotiated for wheat, tin, coffee and sugar; Canada became a member of the 1980 International Rubber Agreement; and Canada was a member of the Cocoa Agreements of 1972 and 1976, but has not joined the 1980 Agreement. On the other hand, Canada has resisted proposals for including an agreement for copper and some other metals, on grounds that price stabilization for these products through buffer-stock or export-quota arrangements would not benefit producers and would be difficult to implement. For copper, Canada has supported international arrangements of the study-group kind, aimed at improving exchanges of market information and the transparency of market operations.[10]

Canada resisted earlier and more ambitious concepts for the Common Fund. Any such arrangement, in the Canadian view, ought to be linked closely to existing or future individual commodity arrangements, rather than to provide a large centralized pool of financing for stocking operations. Canada has supported the concept of the Fund's Second Account as a means of strengthening and bringing greater transparency to world markets for primary commodities of special interest to developing countries, and has made clear its readiness to contribute to the operation of the Second Account.

Notes

1. For general reviews of international commodity agreements in the post-war period, with accounts of the operations of individual agreements, see A.D. Law, *International Commodity Agreements: Setting, Performance, and Prospects* and C. Nappi, *Commodity Market Controls: A Historical Review*. An earlier examination of post-war commodity agreements, from a Canadian perspective, is in W.E. Haviland, *International Commodity Agreements*. A detailed recent analysis

of UNCTAD activities relating to commodity trade is in C.P. Brown, *The Political and Social Economy of Commodity Control*. A shorter analysis from a Canadian perspective is in the North-South Institute, *Primary Commodity Trade and Developing Countries*.

2. For a brief review of commodity-market controls during the inter-war period, see Nappi, *Commodity Market Controls*, Chapter 3. For an account of the first International Wheat Agreement, see C.F. Wilson, *Grain Marketing in Canada*, pp. 392-96.

3. A full account of the negotiation of ITO Chapter VI at the Havana Conference and its provisions is in W.A. Brown, *The United States and the Restoration of World Trade*, pp. 119-25, 217-22 and 525-40.

4. A discussion of the relationships between GATT and Chapter VI of the ITO Charter, and of GATT activities in the area of commodity agreements is in J.H. Jackson, *World Trade and the Law of GATT*, pp. 717-32.

5. Resolution 3202 (S-VI) regarding a Program of Action for a New International Economic Order, adopted by the Sixth Special Session of the UN General Assembly in May 1974, contained an endorsement of producers' associations or cartels; Canada and most other developed countries disagreed with this element and some other elements of the Program of Action. A similar endorsement of producers' associations was not contained in Resolution 93 (IV), adopted by UNCTAD IV in Nairobi in May 1976, which established the UNCTAD Integrated Program for Commodities. Over recent years, producers' associations or cartels among governments have been formed for a number of primary commodities including petroleum, copper, bauxite, iron ore, uranium and mercury; for an examination of some of these arrangements, see Nappi, *Commodity Market Controls*, Chapters 7-10.

6. The following sections relating to techniques for price stabilization are derived largely from Nappi, *Commodity Market Controls*, Chapters 4 and 5.

7. The "Declaration and Programme of Action" was the subject of General Assembly resolutions 3201 (S-VI) adopted by the Sixth Special Session on 1 May 1974; the Charter was the subject of resolution 3281 (XXIX), adopted by the General Assembly on 12 December 1974. The Integrated Programme for Commodities was the subject of resolution 93 (IV), adopted by the Fourth Session of the United Nations Conference on Trade and Development, held in Nairobi, on 30 May 1976; the test is in Brown, *The Political and Social Economy of Commodity Control*, pp. 272-78.

8. The UNCTAD *Bulletin* publishes current information about negotiations for the continuation of existing, international, commodity agreements and about discussions of possible arrangements for the other products on the IPC list. The UNCTAD *Bulletin* (November 1982) contains a note on the new International Agreement on Jute and Jute Products. The *Bulletin* (February-March 1983) contains a broader survey of UNCTAD activities relating to primary commodities.

9. The text of the "Agreement Establishing the Common Fund for Commodities" is in *International Legal Materials* 19 (July 1980): 896-937. For an analysis of the negotiations leading to the Agreement, see Brown, *The Political and Social*

Economy of Commodity Controls, Chapter 4. A short description of the Agreement is in UNCTAD *Bulletin* (September 1980).

10. See H. Labib and A. Ritter, "Stabilizing the International Copper Market: The Viability and Impacts of Alternate Market Management Arrangements," *Canadian Journal of Development Studies* 2 (No. 1, 1981), p. 109-13.

13

Trade in Agricultural Products

Trade in agricultural and fisheries products, especially those produced in the industrialized countries of the temperate zone, has never been brought securely within the rules and disciplines of the multilateral trade system; and in this area the GATT system is at its weakest. From the start, the GATT rules were less strict for agricultural products than for other products; even so, restrictions and distortions in this area of trade have spread far beyond the bounds permitted by the special dispensations from the normal GATT rules. Barriers and trade-distorting measures by governments in this area of trade include virtually the entire range of non-tariff barriers, export subsidies and tariffs, although with some exceptions tariffs are not a major barrier in world agricultural trade. While trade restrictions and other trade-distorting measures are widespread throughout the system, it has been the agricultural policies of the European Community (EC), the United States (USA) and Japan, affecting trade in temperate zone products, which have raised the most serious issues and have chiefly blocked efforts to liberalize world agricultural trade. Trade in many tropical agricultural products, such as coffee, tea, cocoa and bananas, is less fettered by restrictions, although high tariffs remain on processed products, such as cocoa preparations and soluble coffee; and some important exports by developing countries, such as meat, vegetable oils and sugar, are widely restricted by industrialized countries and by non-tariff measures. Many developing countries, themselves, generally maintain highly restrictive import regimes for agricultural products, both to protect local producers from outside competition and for balance-of-payments reasons.

Over the past two decades, the pattern of world agricultural trade has changed, with a shift towards basic products including wheat, feed grains, oil seeds and livestock products. Growth in the volume of world trade has outpaced growth in the volume of world production, but trade in the agricultural sector has grown less than has trade in industrial sectors. This slower rate of growth reflects, in part, an increase in trade barriers imposed by governments, especially on temperate-zone products. The European Community, Japan and the USA are the major world importers in this trade sector; the Soviet Union and China have emerged as major importers of grains; and a number of developing countries have increased in importance as import markets for food (some of which is supplied on aid terms), while they also remain major exporters of tropical agricultural products. For Canada, the largest export markets are the European Community, Japan and the United States; and the USA is the main source of Canadian imports. Canada's agricultural exports are quite narrowly based, with wheat and other grains, fisheries products, livestock products and alcoholic beverages representing the bulk of Canadian exports in this sector, and wheat alone representing over half the total.[1]

Canada has large interests in this area of trade, both as an exporter and as an importer. A traditional objective of Canadian trade policy has been to improve access to world markets for its exports of wheat, grains, fish and other products, and to enlarge opportunities for the export of other products in this sector that are competitive in world markets. At the same time, Canada itself has introduced increasingly restrictive import policies for some important agricultural products, notably dairy products, eggs, and certain meat and poultry products. Moreover, it has recently reinforced its long-standing and complex system of seasonal tariffs, which is designed to give additional protection to domestic fruit and vegetable producers during peak marketing periods.

While a modest degree of trade liberalization in the agricultural sector was achieved during the two most recent rounds of GATT tariff-and-trade negotiations, little progress was made towards the overall liberalization of world trade in this sector, and towards strengthening the disciplines of GATT over agricultural trade.

GATT Rules and Exceptions

As we noted earlier, in the post-war negotiations for a new multilateral trade system, several special and more lenient rules were written into the Havana Charter and into the General Agreement on Tariffs and Trade in regard to trade in agricultural products; these modifications were made largely at the insistence of the United States. One rule, set out in GATT Article XI (2) permits, under certain conditions, the imposition of quantitative restrictions on imports of agricultural and fisheries products, despite the general prohibition of the use of such restrictions. Another departure permits governments to subsidize exports of agricultural and other primary products, while export subsidies on industrial products are banned.[2]

These exceptions from the GATT rules, which are otherwise aimed at limiting the use of non-tariff barriers and minimizing governmental interference in the conduct of trade, had their roots in United States (US) legislation and programs adopted during the 1930s to protect farm prices and the income of farmers. These programs covered such basic products as wheat, sugar, cotton and rice, and had the effect of raising domestic prices for these products above world levels. Quantitative restrictions on imports were needed to prevent an inflow of lower-priced products from abroad. Moreover, these support programs involved efforts by the US government to limit the domestic production of the goods concerned, with the object of preventing the accumulation of surpluses, in such ways as providing incentives to farmers to reduce areas under cultivation or stimulating consumption (for example, under school-lunch and food-stamp programs). These programs also allowed the US government to pay subsidies on exports of the products concerned, in order to facilitate their disposal in other countries at lower world-market prices. In the post-war trade negotiations, the United States insisted that special exceptions be made to accommodate its own agricultural-support regime.

After prolonged debate, it was accepted that Article XI of the General Agreement, which set out the general prohibition on the use of quantitative import restrictions, should incorporate exceptions for agricultural and fisheries products, but only when import restrictions are

> . . . necessary to the enforcement of governmental measures which operate (i) to restrict the quantities of the like domestic product permitted to be marketed or produced . . . or (ii) to remove a temporary surplus of the like domestic product . . . by making the surplus available to certain groups of domestic consumers free of charge or at prices below the current market level. . . .

It was also provided that any such import restrictions should not "reduce the total of imports relative to the total of domestic production, as compared with the proportion which might reasonably be expected to rule between the two in the absence of restrictions." In essence, this exception to the general prohibition against import restrictions was tailor-made to fit US requirements.

The other main exception to the normal GATT rules that was made for agricultural products relates to the use of export subsidies. The Havana Charter generally prohibited the use of export subsidies, although in certain circumstances and subject to international consultations, export subsidies on agricultural and other primary products could be permitted. The comparable Article of the General Agreement (Article XVI) originally contained no such prohibition, but a Section B was added in the mid-1950s, prohibiting the use of export subsidies, but providing an exception for agricultural, fisheries and other primary products. For these products, export subsidies could be used, but should not give "more than an equitable share of world trade" to the product concerned. Again, the exception in the Havana Charter, which was later embodied in GATT Article XVI, was inserted largely at the insistence of the United States, to fit the requirements of its domestic legislation and agricultural-support programs.

These exceptions to the rules were not opposed by countries in Western Europe and elsewhere, which had their own programs designed to support their farming sectors, although at the time these countries were able to mask their barriers to agricultural imports as restrictive measures permitted for balance-of-payments reasons. Moreover, US exports of good and other products at subsidized prices were welcomed by many countries in a period of widespread food shortages.

These more lenient rules and exceptions for trade in agricultural products were, however, strongly opposed by Canada and other leading world exporters of primary products, which took the position that trade in agricultural products should be subject to the same rules as trade in other products. These exporters argued that it was unfair to exempt agricultural trade from the general prohibition of quantitative restrictions; that export subsidies for primary products gave an advantage to larger and richer countries, since smaller countries could not afford to subsidize their exports; and that departures from the normal rules should be permitted only in circumstances where special, intergovernmental, commodity agreements had been concluded under the new trade rules. The United States, however, insisted that exceptions and more lenient rules for agricultural trade were an essential condition for its participation in the new multilateral trade system.

Within a few years, even the exceptions written into GATT Article XI to permit import restrictions on agricultural products were inadequate to accommodate US trade measures in the agricultural sector. In the early 1950s, its agricultural support system was enlarged by Congress to include additional products, notably dairy products, but there were no accompanying provisions made for production controls. Since import restrictions to protect these new programs were contrary to the GATT rules, the United States sought a special waiver from its GATT obligations. This waiver was granted by the Contracting Parties in 1955, over the strenuous objections of the agricultural exporting countries, including Canada. This waiver for the United States, which has no terminal date, has remained a sore point ever since for major exporters of agricultural products, and has weakened the capacity of the United States to oppose other countries' use of restrictive trade measures in this area.[3] In the later 1950s, after a great deal of controversy, Germany was granted a waiver covering a range of restrictions on its imports of agricultural products; and Switzerland acceded to GATT a few years later with a special, and similarly controversial, exemption for its restrictions on agricultural imports. In 1958 the Haberler Report issued by GATT brought to light an astonishing array of restrictions and other barriers to world trade in agricultural products;[4] and these barriers were further exposed during detailed follow-up consultations by Committee II with the European Community, the United States and Japan. Committee II was established by the Contracting Parties as a means of exerting pressures on GATT-member countries for trade liberalization in this sector of world trade. Its consultations, however, did not lead to any significant reduction of trade barriers within the system.

Main Areas of Trade Restrictions

For the most part, restrictions in trade in temperate-zone agricultural products have been imposed by governments as integral parts of their domestic support programs, and they are designed to increase levels of food self-sufficiency, raise incomes of products, and stabilize or increase internal food prices. These trade measures involve not only direct quantitative controls or prohibitions on imports, but also state trading in various forms, subsidy programs for domestic production, and tariff systems designed to discriminate against imports of processed agricultural and food products. The following can give only a general and incomplete account of some of the main areas of restrictions within the trade system.[5]

European Economic Community

The creation of the European Economic Community in the late 1950s and the introduction of its Common Agricultural Policy (CAP) in the early 1960s added a new dimension to restrictions on world trade in agriculture. The Community, even before Britain's entry in 1973, constituted the world's largest importer of agricultural products, and was also a major exporter of many agricultural products. The CAP has been a central element and perhaps the main unifying force within the Community. It is aimed generally at raising levels of self-sufficiency and farm income within the member countries. The CAP involves a variety of market-intervention measures, designed broadly to maintain high and guaranteed prices to Community producers; to insulate Community producers from import competition by the use of a variety of import-control measures including, for major farm products, a system of variable levies (tariffs); and to subsidize exports to foreign markets of the surplus production that is generated by high domestic support prices, a consequential reduction of the consumption of food in the Community, and the absence of any controls on production.[6] The entry of Britain, Ireland and Denmark into the Community in 1973 and that of Greece in 1981 greatly extended the area of world trade affected by the CAP. The future enlargement of the Community to include Spain and Portugal would extend this area still further.

From the perspective of outside exporters, the operation of the CAP has resulted in a decline of a range of traditional exports to Europe, such as Canadian cheese, New Zealand butter, Australian meat and sugar, and a denial of opportunities to enlarge sales or to establish new markets; it has also increased competition in world markets from the subsidized exports of surpluses of Community products that are generated by high producer prices under the CAP and by consumer resistance to high food prices. Because of the major role of the European Community in world agricultural trade, both as an importer and as an exporter, its policies have not only introduced severe distortions into world production and trade patterns, but have also encouraged the maintenance and intensification of restrictive trade systems in other countries. Further, because of the great political and economic importance of the CAP to the unity of the EC, the CAP's provisions have been declared essentially 'non-negotiable,' thus imposing a major obstacle to efforts in GATT to liberalize world trade in this sector, and enlarging the already ample scope for disputes over agricultural trade issues within the trade system. Even within the Community, obstacles of various kinds remain to the free flow of agricultural products; and while free-trade agreements with neighbouring countries have removed barriers to trade in industrial and manufactured products, internal barriers remain on trade in agricultural and fisheries products.

Japan

Although Japan is a major food importer and depends on imports for much of its food, it maintains an agricultural system that aims at achieving as high a degree of self-sufficiency as possible. This system is protected by controls on imports, involving government procurement, high tariffs and quotas that impede the entry of foreign supplies of livestock products, dairy products, fruits, vegetables and processed foods. The difficulties of penetrating the Japanese market for food products are increased by internal distribution systems that are closely linked to domestic sources of supply.[7]

United States

The United States imposes quantitative barriers to imports in the important sectors of dairy products, meat and sugar. Tariffs on processed food products are relatively high and give even higher levels of 'effective protection' to domestic processing industries. Periodically, anti-dumping and countervailing duties are imposed or threatened on particular agricultural products, including certain Canadian exports, such as potatoes from the Maritime Provinces. While the United States plays a leading role in pressing for the reduction of barriers to agricultural trade within the GATT system, it has stoutly refused to give up its own broad and open-ended waiver in GATT.

Canada

The last two decades have seen a progressive escalation of government intervention in a number of important sectors of Canadian agriculture, aimed at increasing incomes of producers and stabilizing domestic markets and prices. The Canadian Wheat Board and the Canadian Dairy Commission operate as government monopolies, directly controlling imports of wheat, barley, oats and their products, and all dairy products. In effect, imports in these sectors of some products, such as butter and fluid milk, are blocked entirely, and there are quantitative restrictions on imports of cheese, combined with agreements with some exporters on minimum prices. Imports of margarine are prohibited. The supply-management programs that have been established for eggs, turkeys and chickens involve quantitative controls on imports. High tariffs also exist for many processed food products, and escalation is a feature of Canadian tariffs on many food products. Seasonal duties are also employed for many fresh fruits and vegetables in order to increase tariff protection for domestic producers during peak marketing periods. The operations of provincial liquor commissions represent a formidable body of controls on imports of alcoholic beverages and their pricing in the domestic market.[8]

Agriculture in the Kennedy Round and the Tokyo Round

In the two most recent rounds of GATT tariff-and-trade negotiations, the objective of trade liberalization in the agricultural sector was paralleled by efforts aimed at bringing agricultural trade more closely under the GATT rules and arrangements aimed at increasing the stability of international markets.[9]

In terms of trade liberalization, most of the participants in these negotiations, including Canada, agreed to reduce and bind a number of their tariffs in the agricultural and fisheries sector, and to enlarge a number of their import quotas. These changes added up to modest, but nevertheless significant, advances. In the Tokyo Round, Canada secured tariff concessions from the United States, Japan and the European Community, which covered well over $1 billion worth of 1978 exports of agricultural and fisheries products. It also agreed to make concessions in its own tariffs that would cover a somewhat smaller volume of imports. The United States, Japan and the Community made important tariff and quota concessions that will benefit Canadian exports of livestock products; exports of grains and oil seeds benefited from reductions in US and Japanese tariffs; and the United States reduced tariffs and other barriers against Canadian exports of potatoes, potato products and bakery products. Access to US, EC and Japanese markets for Canadian whisky was improved. Some improvement of access for Canadian fisheries products was secured in the US, EC and Japanese markets.

On the import side, Canadian tariff reductions mainly affected about $500 million worth of imports from the United States. Both countries eliminated their tariffs on pork products. Canada lowered tariff rates modestly on corn, tobacco, some bakery products, potatoes and a number of fisheries products.[10]

During the Tokyo Round, Canada also concluded with the European Community new arrangements, covering trade in cheese. Improved access for cheddar was obtained in the British and other Community markets, and the Community agreed to impose a system of minimum export prices on shipments of its subsidized cheese to Canada. Other Western European suppliers have subsequently agreed to impose a similar arrangement on their cheese exports to Canada. In a retreat from trade liberalization, Canada, in 1979, reduced its import quota for cheese from 50 million pounds to 45 million pounds annually.

Little progress was made at either of the two recent GATT tariff-and-trade negotiations towards reasserting the GATT rules and disciplines over agricultural trade or strengthening the GATT rules in this area. The fundamental reasons for this lack of progress were the unwillingness of GATT-member countries to address the impact on world trade of their domestic agricultural policies; the refusal of the European Community to discuss changes in its Common Agricultural Policy; and the refusal of the United States to abandon the broad waiver it obtained in 1954 to cover its import restrictions. During the Tokyo Round, it was proposed that a new framework should be established within GATT for continuing consultations and exchanges of information on the agricultural policies of member countries, with a view to avoiding trade conflicts and improving co-operation in this sector of trade. It was not possible, however, to reach agreement on setting up these new arrangements, largely because most countries, including Canada, opposed accepting any substantial international discipline over their domestic agricultural policies. Nevertheless, since the conclusion of the Tokyo Round, informal discussions among governments of the main countries concerned have been held on an irregular basis in GATT and the Organisation for Economic Co-operation and Development (OECD); these discussions have covered the impact of the participating countries' agricultural policies on world trade. As an outcome of the 1982 GATT Ministerial Meeting, discussed in Chapter 17, below, a new GATT Committee on Agriculture was created. This Committee is to carry out, by 1984, a comprehensive review of trade measures affecting agricultural products and a study of the effectiveness of subsidies affecting agricultural trade.

A special study is also to be made of trade problems for fish and fisheries products.

In recent years and especially after the conclusion of the Tokyo Round, there has been a surge of challenges, under the dispute-settlement procedures in GATT, to specific agricultural trade measures introduced by a number of countries, especially the European Community, United States and Japan. In 1980, of thirteen trade measures before GATT dispute panels, all but three involved agricultural trade measures. Two of these trade measures involved Canadian complaints and were resolved in favour of Canada. As a result, the European Community opened to Canadian exports a restrictive tariff quota on high-grade beef, hitherto open only to the United States; and the United States terminated a prohibition on imports of tuna fish from Canada that had been imposed in the non-trade context of a dispute over fishing rights in west-coast boundary waters. The recent trend towards using GATT dispute-settlement procedures to attack and control restrictive measures in the area of agricultural and fisheries trade may be seen as a new attempt by exporters to reassert the GATT rules and disciplines in an area where the system has traditionally been weakest.

The negotiations of the Kennedy Round and the Tokyo Round included several efforts to stabilize prices and otherwise to control international markets for wheat, certain dairy products, and meat. As described in Chapter 17, below, it was not possible during the Tokyo Round, to reach agreement on the continuation of the price-stabilization elements of the International Wheat Agreement, although that Agreement continues to function in other respects; the associated Food Aid Convention also continues in place. Earlier arrangements were renegotiated to provide for continuing consultations among exporters of certain dairy products. The new arrangements contained provisions which establish minimum export prices for certain milk powders, milk fat and certain types of cheese. Canada has stood outside the minimum-price arrangements for milk powder, which would have impeded Canadian sales of surplus milk powder in Mexico and the Caribbean area. A GATT arrangement establishing continuing consultations among exporters and importers of bovine meat was also put in place, but this arrangement does not contain any provisions to regulate prices and is aimed mainly at regular exchanges of market information.[11]

Notes

1. See T.K. Warley, *Agriculture in an Interdependent World: U.S. and Canadian Perspectives,* for an analysis of Canada's role in world agricultural production and trade; a more recent survey is in "Canadian Agricultural Trade: Its Current and Future Performance," *Agronews* (Supplement, November 1982). See also B.W. Wilkinson, *Canada in a Changing World Economy,* pp. 97-100. For rele-

vant statistical material, see successive issues of Canada, Department of Agriculture, *Canada's Trade in Agricultural Products.*

2. See W.A. Brown, *The United States and the Restoration of World Trade*, pp. 115-19, 193-94 and 214-26, for an account of the negotiations in Geneva and Havana in 1947–48, with respect to special rules for trade in agricultural products; see also K.W. Dam, *The GATT: Law and International Economic Organization*, Chapter 15.

3. For an account of the US waiver, see J.H. Jackson, *World Trade and the Law of GATT*, pp. 733-37.

4. GATT, *Trends in International Trade: Report by a Panel of Experts.* The group consisted of Haberler (USA), Campos (Brazil), Meade (United Kingdom) and Tinbergen (Netherlands).

5. A more detailed analysis of some of the main barriers to world trade in agricultural products is in Warley, *Agriculture in an Interdependent World*, Chapter 5.

6. The objectives, structure and operation of the Common Agricultural Policy are described in Office for Official Publications of the European Communities, *The Agricultural Policy of the European Community.* See also B. Nadeau, "L'Entrée de la Grand-Bretagne dans le marché commun et les exportations agricoles du Canada à ce pays."

7. For a comprehensive examination of Canadian agricultural exports to Japan and Japanese import policies, see K.A.J. Hay and M.O. Lovatt, *Canadian Food for Japan.*

8. A detailed analysis of government intervention in Canadian agriculture is in J.D. Forbes, D.R. Hughes and T.K. Warley, *Economic Intervention and Regulation in Canadian Agriculture.*

9. E. Preeg, *Traders and Diplomats* contains a detailed examination of negotiations in the Kennedy Round in the agricultural sector. The negotiations in this sector during the Tokyo Round are reviewed in GATT, Director-General, *The Tokyo Round of Multilateral Trade Negotiations* and GATT, Director-General, *Supplementary Report.*

10. For the results of the Tokyo Round affecting Canadian trade in agricultural and fisheries products, see Canada, Office of the Coordinator for Multilateral Trade Negotiations, *Multilateral Trade Negotiations 1973–1979*, pp. 95-100, and "Multilateral Trade Negotiations 1979: Canadian Participation," News Release, dated 11 July 1979.

11. GATT *Basic Instruments and Selected Documents, Twenty-sixth Supplement*, contains the texts of the International Dairy Arrangement, and its Protocols covering certain milk powders, milk fat and certain cheeses, as well as the Arrangement Regarding Bovine Meat. For an account of negotiations leading to these arrangements, see GATT, Director-General, *The Tokyo Round of Multilateral Trade Negotiations* and GATT, Director-General, *Supplementary Report.*

14

State Trading and the Multilateral System

S tate trading has presented two rather distinct sets of issues in the GATT system. One relates to the participation in the trade system of countries with relatively complete state-trading, centrally planned economies. The other relates to the international trade activities of state-owned or -controlled enterprises in countries that have private-market systems. The relevant rules of the General Agreement, in Article XVII, deal largely with the latter set of issues, although in practice these issues have not occupied a prominent place on the GATT agenda. The participation of the state-trading countries in GATT, on the other hand, has for many years raised a range of difficult issues on which the General Agreement is almost silent. The inadequacy of GATT in this regard is explained partly by the historical circumstances surrounding the 1946–48 negotiations of the Havana Charter and the General Agreement on Tariff and Trade, and partly by the difficulties of fitting into the GATT system countries where decisions on production, prices, imports and exports are determined, not in the market place, but by governments. Underlying the GATT system is the assumption that trade is conducted by private traders who are free to export and import on the basis of commercial considerations, and who are not restricted by government controls, except for a customs tariff and those few other controls on trade which are permitted and controlled by GATT rules.[1]

In the mid-1960s, Mitchell Sharp, then Minister of Trade and Commerce, summarized as follows the difficult and complex issues surrounding the participation of state-trading countries in the trade system. In an introduction to a symposium on East-West trade sponsored by the Canadian Institute for International Affairs, Mr. Sharp asked:

> How in a negotiation do you strike a fair balance between the import opportunities available in a market economy and the access which a planned economy accords? How do you protect your domestic producer from disruptive selling from countries where costs may not be the determinant of prices? How do you protect your exporter of basic materials from the impact of irregular offerings from Communist countries which both through price and volume could have considerable impact on world prices? Can a multilateral system of access to these countries be elaborated which would be an improvement over the present network of bilateral agreements which limit competition amongst Western countries for these markets? Can techniques be worked out to provide within planned economies for greater competition between imports from Western countries and those from other bloc countries? And what about competition between imports from market economies and planned production within the Communist countries themselves?[2]

Despite problems of this kind, Canada's approach has been positive to trade with the Soviet Union, China and other countries with centrally planned, state-controlled, economic and trade systems, and relatively free from the political controversy about trading with communist countries that has prevailed in the United States, especially within Congress. In his statement quoted above, Mr. Sharp expressed Canada's approach as follows: ". . . both from the point of view of political relations and the economic gains available through trade, I am convinced that the effort should be made to develop trade between East and West and to bring this group of countries to an increasing extent within the community of trading nations."

GATT now provides a framework, however imperfect, for Canada's trade relations with Yugoslavia, Czechoslovakia, Poland, Hungary and Romania, as well as Cuba. With certain of these countries, bilateral trade agreements are also in place. Canada's trade with the Soviet Union, China and Bulgaria takes place within bilateral agreements; and a trade agreement has now been signed with the German Democratic Republic, after negotiations that extended over a period of several years.[3]

State-Trading Countries in GATT

During the Second World War, the Soviet Union showed a positive interest in the creation of a multilateral world-trade system, but in 1947 it turned against the planned International Trade Organization (ITO) and portrayed it, along with the Bretton Woods organizations, as an instrument of United States (US) domination. Moreover, the Soviet Union did not attend the Geneva and Havana Conferences of 1947–48. While Czechoslovakia was one of the founding members of GATT, and while Poland and Hungary were represented at the Havana Conference, these countries did not, at the time, have state-trading systems. Thus there was little constructive debate, during the formative years of the post-war trade system, concerning problems arising from the participation of state-trading countries.

During the initial discussions of the Havana Charter, a provision was considered which was designed to provide that wholly state-trading countries would make a fair exchange for the advantages they would gain from membership in the ITO. This provision would have required such countries, in exchange for tariff and other benefits granted by other members, to "undertake to import in the aggregate over a period products of the other members valued at not less than an amount to be agreed upon." This provision, which was in the US "Suggested Charter" for the ITO, was abandoned when it became clear that the Soviet Union was unlikely to attend the Havana Conference. However, a similar approach to reciprocity through some form of global import commitments by state-trading countries re-emerged at later stages, when Poland and other Eastern European countries applied to join GATT.

East-West trade during the early post-war years was insignificant as a result of the extension of Soviet control over the East European countries, the policies of economic self-sufficiency followed within the Soviet bloc, and controls by many Western countries on exports of strategic and other goods to the Soviet bloc.[4] During the mid-1950s, following the death of Stalin and the reduction of cold war tensions, the climate for East-West trade improved. The Soviet Union and the East European countries turned towards policies aimed at fostering their industrial development through foreign trade. They formed among themselves the Council for Mutual Economic Assistance (CEMA, alternatively referred to as 'COMECON') for the purpose of co-ordinating their economic planning and encouraging trade among themselves; and they sought to expand their exports to Western countries as a means of financing imports of needed technology and producer goods. Further, in certain East European countries, there began a process of decentralization and control over economic and trade activities that was carried furthest by Yugoslavia after it broke away from Soviet control in 1948.

In the mid-1950s, the Soviet Union itself launched a surprising initiative in the United Nations, in support of ratification of the Havana Charter or, alternatively, the establishment of a new and broader world-trade organization within the United Nations (UN) system. This initiative was evidently designed to discredit GATT and to capitalize on growing criticisms by developing countries of the international economic and trade order. These Soviet moves were resisted by the Western countries, including Canada, and gained little support from developing countries, which were more interested in separate plans that led, in 1964, to the creation of the United Nations Conference on Trade and Development (UNCTAD).

As we noted above, Czechoslovakia was a founding member of GATT, and it continued as a GATT member after it was absorbed into the Soviet bloc in 1948. In 1951 the United States severed its GATT relationship with Czechoslovakia, following the adoption by Congress of legislation requiring, in effect, the termination of most-favoured-nation (MFN) treatment for imports from communist-dominated countries. While no other GATT countries followed suit, many Western European countries, but not Canada, have, in practice, imposed discriminatory controls on some of their imports from Czechoslovakia and otherwise withheld full GATT treatment from that country.

Of the other East European countries, Yugoslavia, Poland, Romania and Hungary became GATT members over a period years, but under different terms and conditions.[5] Yugoslavia was granted observer status in 1950; it formed an 'association' with GATT in 1958; it became a provisional member in 1962; and it was finally admitted as a full member in 1966, during the Kennedy Round. Its admission as a full member on the same terms as other GATT countries reflected, in part, the degree of decontrol and decentralization of economic and trade activities in Yugoslavia. It was generally accepted that this process would enable Yugoslavia to function within GATT more or less as a market-economy country, with state trading an exceptional practice, no central control over price setting, and no central government control over imports and exports, apart from balance-of-payments restrictions administered in accordance with normal GATT rules. By contrast, Poland, Romania and Hungary, whose economic and trading systems are somewhat different, but closer to state-trading models, were admitted to full GATT membership during the early 1970s. Their admission, however, was under separate protocols that depart in a number of ways from the normal terms of accession, and that limit, in various ways, their GATT relationships with other member countries.

For these East European countries, foreign trade represents a much higher proportion of the gross national product (GNP) than it does for the Soviet Union; and their trade with non-bloc countries, while smaller in volume than their trade within the CEMA group, represents a substantial part of their total trade. For Poland and Hungary, in particular, exports to Western European countries are important. One of their main objectives in joining the GATT system was to seek to reduce non-tariff obstacles to their exports that were maintained by members of the European Community (EC). Another objective was to obtain more secure MFN-tariff treatment from Western countries. Some countries, like Canada and many Western European countries, already extended MFN-tariff treatment to East European countries, but under bilateral agreements which sometimes involved those countries' commitments to purchase agreed quantities of imports from the favouring country or to grant other trade concessions. GATT membership has assisted the East European countries concerned to resist making such special commitments and to secure MFN-tariff treatment from the United States.

As we have noted above, a major issue in the negotiations for the accession to GATT of Yugoslavia, Poland, Hungary and Romania was how to ensure some degree of reciprocity from them in exchange for MFN-tariff treatment and other benefits of the GATT system. For Poland, the solution finally reached involved that country's assumption of an obligation to increase, by an agreed percentage, the value of its imports from GATT members as a group, over fixed time periods. Romania resisted making any similar commitment, partly on the basis of its claim to be a developing country; but it agreed to accept a somewhat loosely formulated obligation to increase its imports from GATT members at a rate corresponding to the growth of its total imports. The terms of Hungary's accession in 1973 followed a degree of decontrol and decentralization of its foreign-trade system and the introduction of a customs tariff; and it acceded to GATT on much the same basis as other GATT countries, despite some scepticism on the part of many existing members, including Canada, about the validity of its tariff system.

Other difficult issues relate to the pricing of exports of state-trading countries, the valuation of their exports for customs purposes, and the question of dumping practices. In regard to dumping, it is recognized in an interpretative note to Article VI of the General Agreement that the regular rules governing the use of anti-dumping duties do not necessarily have to be followed in the event of dumping by state-trading countries; and that "a strict comparison with domestic prices" in those countries may not provide an appropriate basis for determining the existence and extent of dumping. This interpretation of Article VI parallels special rules that Canada sometimes applies to imports from state-trading countries under its system for valuing goods for customs purposes and as a basis for applying anti-dumping duties. In a number of cases, imported goods from state-trading countries have been valued arbitrarily by 'Ministerial prescription,' rather than on the basis of their price in the country of export; these goods are normally evaluated by comparison with a like or similar product imported into Canada from a third country.[6]

Concerns were also raised about the adequacy of the regular GATT safeguard rules in Article XIX of the General Agreement, to cover imports from state-trading countries. The outcome was the insertion into the accession protocols of Poland, Romania and Hungary, of provisions enabling other GATT members to impose restrictions, on a discriminatory basis, on imports from these countries, in circumstances where their exports cause or threaten injury to domestic producers in the importing country. Canada has not made use of discriminatory safeguard measures of this kind against individual East European GATT members. However, Canada has concluded several bilateral agreements with them covering their exports of certain textile and clothing products, under the provisions of the Multifibre Arrangement (MFA).

The accession of Poland, Romania and Hungary to GATT involved arrangements for periodic consultations with the GATT Contracting Parties to review the operation of their accession protocols. These consultations have provided continuing opportunities for other GATT members to press the East European members to bring their trading systems more closely into line with the GATT system. The results have not been impressive, since any substantive progress in this direction would involve fundamental changes in the economic and trade systems of those members. The three countries concerned, for their part, have used the consultations as a means of pressing for the removal of discriminatory quantitative restrictions against certain of their exports, mainly by EC and Nordic countries. In these efforts, the three state-trading countries have been generally supported by other GATT countries, including Canada and the United States, which view these EC restrictions as representing a kind of bilateralism that is potentially damaging to their own trade interests.

Thus five East European countries were accepted into the GATT system during the 1960s and 1970s, by a pragmatic process of negotiations that did not contribute very much to the development of the rules governing the participation of centrally planned, state-controlled countries. Except perhaps for Yugoslavia, the East Europeans have tended to be regarded and treated in GATT as second-class members while, at the same time, other GATT countries have tended to be sceptical of the trade-policy advantages they have obtained from these countries in exchange for MFN-tariff treatment and other GATT rights extended to them. The weakness of the multilateral framework for trade relations between market-economy countries and state-trading countries has tended to support the continuation of a parallel network of bilateral trade agreements with these countries, particularly between them and the Western European countries. It is thus not clear whether the participation of the East European countries in GATT could provide a meaningful precedent for the eventual membership in that body of larger state-trading countries such as China or the Soviet Union.

As we noted earlier, Canada's approach to the participation of the East European countries in GATT has been generally positive. GATT membership for these countries has been viewed as a means of reducing excessive bilateralism in their trade relations, especially with their western European neighbours, which could have adverse effects on Canada's trade interests in Europe. Membership in GATT could be expected to encourage the evolution of more open economic and trade systems in those countries, within the framework of GATT rules and practices; and it might also serve, in the longer run, to loosen the economic and political dominance of the Soviet Union over these GATT members. The membership of those East European countries is also consistent with general Canadian support for the evolution of GATT as a broader trade body. Further, Canadian support for the participation of the East European countries in GATT has been viewed as a means of fostering improved and closer bilateral relationships with countries that are of growing interest as markets for a range of Canadian exports.

East-West Trade and the Economic Commission for Europe

Outside the framework of GATT, Canada maintains an association in trade areas with the Soviet Union and the East European countries within the United Nations Economic Commission for Europe (ECE), which Canada joined as a full member in 1973, after many years of active participation as an observer. The ECE was created in 1947 as one of the first 'regional economic commissions' within the United Nations system; similar regional commissions have been established for other areas, generally for the purpose of fostering economic and trade co-operation among countries of the geographic region concerned.[7] ECE membership covers all of the countries of Eastern Europe, including the Soviet Union, as well as all of the countries of Western Europe, the United States and Canada.

From the start, the trade activities of the ECE have focused largely on East-West trade. A good deal of useful work has been done in the ECE, with the intent of overcoming practical problems involved in trade between the market-economy member countries and the state-trading countries of Eastern Europe. The ECE has provided a framework for continuing contracts at the technical level among government officials and, to some extent, industry representatives. Within ECE a number of useful and practical arrangements have been developed to facilitate the growth of East-West trade, including arrangements to simplify and harmonize trade documents and procedures, to facilitate transportation of goods within the area, to encourage the harmonization of industrial standards, and to assist the arbitration of commercial disputes. In addition, the ECE has provided, over the years, a unique and useful output of statistical and other information and of research reports dealing with economic developments in the Eastern and Western member countries.[8] With its focus on practical measures to enlarge opportunities for East-West trade, ECE has generally operated in harmony with the underlying objectives of the GATT system. Moreover, many of the technical arrangements made within ECE, with respect, for example, to the transportation of goods and to standards for trade in lumber, have benefited Canadian trade interests in the broader European area.

State Trading in Market-Economy Countries

The foreign-trade operations of government-owned or -controlled enterprises or state monopolies in market-economy countries represent an important and a growing sector of world trade: perhaps 10 to 15 per cent of the total trade of

GATT-member countries with market systems is conducted by such enterprises, although the proportion varies greatly among different countries.[9] State trading is widespread in food grains, petroleum, iron and coal. Most of Canada's large exports of grains are controlled by the Canadian Wheat Board, which also controls Canadian imports in this sector; and elements of state trading are also an important feature of Canadian trade in uranium, petroleum, fish, dairy products and a number of other agricultural products, and alcoholic beverages. Procurement of goods and services by governments for their own use also represents an important and expanding sector of world trade.

The GATT rules contain no obligation to abandon or reduce state trading in international commerce. Rather, they are aimed at discouraging the use of state-trading operations for protective purposes, by seeking to impose the same rules as apply to private trade. The central provisions of Article XVII of the General Agreement thus require that state-owned enterprises shall, in their trading activities, "act in a manner consistent with the general principles of non-discriminatory treatment prescribed in this Agreement," and that these enterprises shall "make any such purchases or sales solely in accordance with commercial considerations. . . ."[10]

The rules governing state trading in the General Agreement do not cover the procurement by governments of goods and services for their own use. With respect to these operations, Article XVII requires only that imports from other GATT members shall be given "fair and equitable treatment." During the Tokyo Round, more elaborate and precise rules governing procurement of goods by governments were drawn up and adopted by a group of GATT members, including Canada. (See Chapter 15, below.)

In practice, the GATT rules governing state trading in market-economy countries have generated relatively little interest, at least in recent years. The absence of debate in this area may arise from a general reluctance to come to grips with the difficult issues arising from state-trading activities. In 1955, during a major review of GATT, Article XVII was extended to require the regular submission by member countries of information about their state-trading activities, but these reports have also tended to be treated as routine and have given rise to little debate.

Notes

1. For a full legal and technical analysis of the problems raised by the participation in GATT of countries with centrally planned economies, see K.W. Dam, *The GATT: Law and International Economic Organization*, Chapter 18 and M.M. Kostecki, *East-West Trade and the GATT System*.

2. Mitchell Sharp, "Introduction," pp. xv-xvi in P.E. Uren (ed.), *East-West Trade*. The trade agreement with the German Democratic Republic was reported in the Toronto *Globe and Mail* (12 September 1983), p. B14.

3. Since the mid-1970s, the Institute of Soviet and East European Studies, Carleton University, Ottawa, has published a number of research reports in an "East-West Commercial Relations Series," including several studies of Canadian commercial relations with these countries; see, for example, C.H. McMillan, *Canada's Post-war Economic Relations with the U.S.S.R.: An Appraisal.* An earlier study of Canadian trade with East European countries is in I.M. Drummond, *Canada's Trade with the Communist Countries of Eastern Europe.*

4. Since the early 1950s, the member countries of the North Atlantic Treaty Organization (NATO) and Japan have co-operated in implementing controls on exports of certain strategic goods to the Soviet-bloc countries, within an informal Coordinating Committee for Multilateral Export Controls (COCOM). The activities of COCOM are surrounded by secrecy, still less widely publicized; for a brief account, see C.M. Friesen, *The Political Economy of East-West Trade*, pp. 21-22; see also *Business Eastern Europe* 11 (22 January 1982).

5. The participation of Czechoslovakia in GATT, and the processes by which Yugoslavia, Poland, Romania and Hungary became members of the General Agreement are discussed fully in Kostecki, *East-West Trade.*

6. Section 39 of the Canadian Customs Act provides that the value for duty shall be determined 'in such manner as the Minister of National Revenue prescribes" in "unusual circumstances" or when the value for duty cannot be determined under the regular provisions of the Customs Act. The selection of a third country for price comparison is at the discretion of Canada's Department of Revenue, and this practice can give rise to controversy. In 1981, for example, imports from the United States were chosen as a basis for valuing leather footwear from four East European countries. (Canada, Department of Revenue, "Interim Memorandum D34-38," 6 July 1981.) The Department of Revenue has evidently ruled that imports of hydraulic turbines from the Soviet Union should be valued on the basis of Japanese prices for similar equipment, and dumping duties would be imposed, on this basis, on imports from the Soviet Union.

7. The New Zealand Ministry of Foreign Affairs publishes annually a useful and comprehensive guide to the United Nations organizations and their functions in *United Nations Handbook.* Canada is a member of the regional economic commissions for Europe and for Latin America.

8. A detailed account of ECE activities is contained in United Nations, *Three Decades of the United Nations Economic Commission for Europe.* See also G. Myrdal, "Twenty Years of the United Nations Economic Commission for Europe."

9. Kostecki, *East-West Trade* contains a useful discussion of state trading in market-economy countries.

10. The provisions of Article XVII are more complex than indicated in this brief summary; moreover, rules relating to state trading exist in other articles of the General Agreement. For a full discussion, see J.H. Jackson, *World Trade and the Law of GATT*, pp. 329-61.

15

The Tokyo Round of Multilateral Trade Negotiations, 1973–1979

The Tokyo Round, also known as 'The Multilateral Trade Negotiations' (MTN), occupied centre stage in the international trade system during the 1970s. The outcome of these lengthy negotiations in Geneva represented an advance in trade liberalization comparable to that achieved by the 1947 negotiations in Geneva that established the GATT system, or by the 1963–67 Kennedy Round. The resulting cuts in the tariffs of the developed countries that apply to industrial products will average about 35 per cent, and the average level of these tariffs will be reduced to the 5-8 per cent range. Equally or even more important, the Tokyo Round resulted in the conclusion of a number of new international codes and other agreements governing the use of non-tariff measures, leading to a significant extension and elaboration of international trade law. The concurrent negotiations on non-tariff measures distinguished the Tokyo Round from earlier rounds of GATT negotiations, which were largely concerned with tariff reductions. In terms of trade liberalization, the overall consequences of these new non-tariff codes and arrangements is less clear: while some of them involve new commitments by governments to follow more liberal trade policies, others represent the codification of existing trade policies of the participating countries, policies that are not always aimed at trade liberalization.[1]

For Canada, the Tokyo Round was a major event in the development of its commercial policy, both from a domestic and from an international perspective. The outcome will reduce many tariffs in traditional export markets for a broad range of Canadian industrial and agricultural products, and will result in a significant further liberalization of Canada-United States (USA) bilateral trade. Several important changes in United State (US) trade policy were achieved, which had long been sought by Canada. The MTN will lead to a significant reduction in tariff protection over the broad range of Canada's imports, and this development should help to increase the overall competitiveness of Canadian industry in international markets. However, in Canada, as in many other countries, tariff protection will remain almost untouched in a number of import-sensitive manufacturing sectors, and quantitative controls remain on several important categories of imports, notably clothing, textiles, footwear and a range of agricultural products.

One major effect of the MTN, throughout the decade of the 1970s, was to dampen pressure for trade protection arising in many countries as a result of high inflation, slow economic growth, balance-of-payments difficulties, and alarming increases in unemployment. During the 1970s, the negotiations in Geneva served as a brake on a retreat into trade protection that might otherwise have taken place throughout the trading world. In the following years, however, pressures for import protection re-emerged in many countries, including Canada, in response to declining economic growth and rising unemployment.

Preparations for the Tokyo Round

When the Kennedy Round was concluded in 1967, no new multilateral trade negotiations on a comparable scale were foreseen for some time to come. Nevertheless, within the GATT, a program of preparatory work for a further round of negotiations was soon opened, and this program was actively supported by Canada. These preparations focused largely on non-tariff measures that restricted or distorted trade, reflecting a growing recognition that governments were increasingly following policies of intervention in the organization and direction of economic affairs, which indirectly or directly had trade effects. Furthermore, the reduction of tariffs achieved by the Kennedy Round had the effect of increasing the visibility of non-tariff trade barriers to trade. It was generally assumed that the next round of negotiations would be concerned with non-tariff trade barriers as much as with tariffs. GATT's preparatory program accordingly included the drawing up of detailed lists of non-tariff measures affecting trade, and the drafting of possible, new, international codes of conduct relating to the use of several non-tariff measures. Some of this preparatory work was also done in the Organisation for Economic Co-operation and Development (OECD), on government procurement policies, for example.

Meanwhile, the structure of power relationships within the trade system continued to evolve during the late 1960s and early 1970s, in ways which affected Canada's role and influence within the system. The position of dominance in the world economy held for so long by the United States had come to be shared with the European Community (EC) and Japan. The Community was in the process of enlargement to include Britain, Denmark and Ireland, and was establishing new preferential relationships with other countries of Western Europe and the Mediterranean area. The developing countries were evolving greater unity and strength within the trade system, displayed not only in the United Nations Conference on Trade and Development (UNCTAD) but in GATT as well. Within such new patterns in the world-trade structure, the role of Canada and other middle-sized trading countries was inevitably modified and, to a degree, diminished.

While preparations in Geneva for a further round of multilateral trade negotiations were quietly under way, severe strains were building up in the world-trade and -payments systems, especially in the United States. An over-valued US dollar, along with increased foreign competition for a number of important domestic industries, led to an increase of complaints about 'unfair' competition from imports; and new pressures emerged in Congress for restrictive trade legislation. Similar pressures built up in some other countries. The GATT Director-General warned, in 1970, that "protectionist influences . . . are today making themselves felt more strongly than at any time since the 1930s."[2]

The series of measures announced by President Nixon in August 1971 to strengthen the US balance-of-payments included the imposition of a 10 per cent surcharge on about one-half of US imports. These measures also included new means to subsidize exports: tax advantages were granted to firms, based on their export performance, under the Domestic International Sales Corporation (DISC) program. These measures were widely regarded as a serious threat to the multilateral trade system, and brought the United States into collision with other trading countries, including Canada. Indeed, as the largest trading partner of the United States, Canada was probably more damaged by these US trade measures than any other country.

The monetary settlement concluded in the autumn of 1971, which led to the devaluation of the US dollar in comparison to other major currencies (the Smithsonian Agreement)[3] led to the United States' termination of the 10 per cent import surcharge, but on condition that the European Community, Japan and Canada would engage in 'urgent negotiations' on outstanding trade issues. Subsequent US discussions with the Community and Japan resulted in bilateral undertakings, announced in February 1972, to initiate jointly "a new round of multilateral and comprehensive negotiations in GATT beginning in 1973"; the proposed negotiations would cover "all elements of trade, including measures which impede or distort agricultural, raw materials and industrial trade." Other countries would be invited to join in the negotiations.[4]

In negotiations with Canada over the winter of 1971–72, US officials displayed an unusual toughness, but ran into an equally tough refusal on the part of the Canadian government to accept that Canada was in any way responsible for US balance-of-payments problems, or that Canada's current bilateral trade surplus was in any way 'unfair.'[5] But Canadian concern about the attitude of US officials in ensuing bilateral negotiations deepened Canadian preoccupations about excessive vulnerability in trade relations with the United States. These preoccupations underlay the formulation, in the autumn of 1972, of the so-called 'Third Option' strategy for Canada, announced by Mitchell Sharp, then the Secretary of State for External Affairs.[6] This strategy was aimed, in part, at enlarging and diversifying Canada's trade with other countries. In discussing the Third Option concept, Mr. Sharp dismissed any suggestion that the liberal world-trade system was responsible for the imbalance in Canada's trade relationship with the United States; indeed, he expressed the view that a less liberal world-trade system would have led to even stronger links between the US and the Canadian markets. He also said that despite irritants in bilateral trade relations, the two countries had a very strong common interest in promoting improvements in the international trade and payments system.

Thus Canada readily joined other developed countries in endorsing a decision by the GATT Council in March 1972, in support of the proposed new round of multilateral trade negotiations, and declared its readiness to participate in those negotiations. Canadian support for the proposal was restated by the Minister of Industry, Trade and Commerce at a ministerial-level GATT meeting in Tokyo in September 1973, which formally launched the Tokyo Round.

The "Tokyo Declaration"

The "Tokyo Declaration" set out the design of the new round, which was to be broader and more ambitious than any trade negotiations held since 1948.[7] It was agreed that the negotiations would be open to non-GATT countries, as well as to GATT members. Following the precedent set by the 1964–67 Kennedy Round, tariff negotiations would not proceed on an item-by-item basis, but would be aimed at linear across-the-board reductions, in accordance with "appropriate formulae of as general application as possible." With respect to non-tariff measures, the objective would be to reduce or eliminate them, "or, where this is not appropriate, to reduce or eliminate their trade restricting or distorting effects, and to bring such measures under more effective international discipline." The Declaration stated that negotiations on agricultural trade "should take account of the special characteristics and problems in this sector"; this somewhat imprecise prescription reflected sharp differences of view, especially between the European Community and the United States, about how negotiations should proceed in this sensitive sector. Tropical products would be considered "a special and priority sector." While the negotiations would be conducted on the traditional basis "of the principles of mutual advantage, mutual commitment and overall reciprocity," it was agreed that the industrialized countries would not expect full reciprocity from developing countries; in general, developing countries would be accorded "special and more favourable treatment." Of special importance to Canada was agreement that the negotiations would examine "possibilities for the co-ordinated reduction or elimination of all barriers to trade in selected sectors," even though this sector approach would be regarded as "a complementary technique."[8] Optimistically, the Tokyo Round was planned for completion in 1975; in the event, the negotiations continued until the spring of 1979.

In the Canadian Parliament, leaders of all parties joined the government in welcoming the proposed negotiations. The Minister of Industry, Trade and Commerce stressed the importance of the proposed sector negotiations. In a speech in Toronto, in late September 1973, he stated, "This holds tremendous potential for Canada, especially with our abundance of resources and the government's policy that, where competitive, these resources be processed in Canada prior to export."[9]

To assist in the negotiations, the Government established more elaborate arrangements than during past negotiations for consultations with provincial governments, industry and other interested groups. A Canadian Trade and Tariffs Committee, chaired by L.E. Couillard, a former senior official of the Department of External Affairs, was set up in 1973, in order to consult with interested business, labour and other elements in the private sector. In 1977 the government appointed former Ambassador J.H. Warren as Canadian Co-ordinator for Trade Negotiations, and a special Cabinet Committee was established to oversee the negotiations chaired by Alan MacEachen, the Deputy Prime Minister.[10] A team of negotiators, headed by Ambassador Rodney De C. Grey, was stationed in Geneva from 1975.

Progress of Negotiations

The beginning of serious negotiations in Geneva was held up by delays in the United States' enactment of trade legislation governing its participation, which was not adopted until January 1975. The Trade Reform Act of 1975, when it was finally adopted, was fairly liberal, although a number of protectionist features were added during its passage through Congress.[11] From Canada's point of view, it was disappointing that the President's authority to reduce US customs duties was limited to 60 per cent, except for duties below the 5 per cent level, which could be bargained down to zero in the negotiations.

In Geneva, negotiations were stalled for a long time, partly by differences between the United States and the European Community on procedures for negotiations in the sector of agricultural trade. Further difficulties surrounded efforts to agree on a formula for tariff cutting on a linear basis. Alternative formulae were suggested by the United States, the European Community, Japan and Switzerland; and eventually, in late 1977, the Swiss formula was accepted as a 'working hypothesis' for the negotiations. By this formula, average tariff levels in the industrial sector would be cut by 30-40 per cent, with a greater reduction in higher rates than in lower rates. According to an August 1977 report by the Chairman of the Canadian Trade and Tariff Committee, none of these formulae for tariff cutting were regarded in Ottawa as offering Canada a balanced or equitable tariff-negotiating framework. It was noted that most of Canada's dutiable industrial exports faced relatively low tariffs in major world markets, while Canada's customs duties on industrial imports were relatively high; thus reductions in Canadian tariffs would be proportionately larger than the reduction of tariffs facing Canadian exports.[12] In January 1978, the Canadian government announced the basis on which Canada would participate in the ensuing negotiations. It was stated that Canada's acceptance of the Swiss formula would depend, among other things, on the substantial elimination or reduction of many of the relatively low tariffs facing Canada's industrial exports; the elimination, reduction or bringing under effective control certain non-tariff measures; and a greater liberalization of tariff and non-tariff barriers in the key resource-based sectors (non-ferrous metals and forest products) of Canada's export trade.[13]

A complex series of bilateral and plurilateral negotiations took place in Geneva during 1978 and into 1979, covering variations in the tariff-cutting formula to be applied by individual countries, exceptions of specified products from the formula cuts, the staging of the tariff cuts, and other matters. At the same time, negotiations on non-tariff measures were accelerated, with the object of concluding supplementary codes that would clarify or elaborate GATT rules in these areas. These non-tariff measures included subsidies and countervailing duties, technical barriers to trade (standards), customs valuation, government procurement, and import-licencing procedures.

The Tokyo Round was formally concluded in July 1979. A brief summary of the outcome follows.

Tariff Reductions

In global terms, the results of the tariff cutting in the Tokyo Round were impressive. For industrial products, the average depth of cuts and resulting, average, tariff levels for leading developed countries, including Canada, will be as appears in Table 15-1 when they are fully implemented in 1987.

The post-Tokyo Round tariffs of the major trading countries will also be harmonized to a greater extent than in the past. The overall impact of the tariff reductions should not, however, be over-emphasized. The cuts are being made in stages, annually, until 1987. Relatively high tariffs will remain for certain products in most countries, including Canada. The tariff systems of most countries, moreover, will continue to embody a significant degree of 'escalation,' as indicated in Table 15-1, giving high levels of effective protection to domestic processing industries. These protective tariff barriers will continue to face the processed forms of Canada's resource-based industries in major world markets, especially in western Europe and Japan. Tariffs will also continue to have a special significance where preferences exist, as within the complex of preferential trade arrangements surrounding the European Community.

Table 15-1:   Post-MTN Average Tariffs on Industrial Products[a]

Country	Depth of Cut[b]	Raw Materials	Semi Manufacturers	Finished Manufacturers
USA	31	0.2	3.0	5.7
Canada	38	0.5	8.3	8.3
Japan	49	0.5	4.6	6.0
EC	29	0.2	4.2	6.9
Sweden	28	0.0	3.3	4.9

Notes
a. Source: GATT, Director-General, *The Tokyo Round of Multilateral Trade Negotiations, Supplementary Report* (January 1980).
b. Depth of cut is for all industrial products; depth of cut and average post-MTN rates are weighted on the basis of actual customs collections.

The Canadian government, in its July 1979 report on the Tokyo Round, expressed general satisfaction with the outcome of the tariff negotiations, noting that tariffs would be cut for a wide range of Canadian exports to its main trading partners, particularly the United States. The report stated that when the MTN cuts are fully implemented, a much larger part of Canada-USA bilateral trade will be liberalized on both sides; close to 80 per cent of Canada's exports to the USA will enter duty free, and over 90 per cent will enter under rates of 5 per cent or lower. On the Canadian side, about 65 per cent of imports from the United States will be duty free.[14]

Agricultural Trade

The special problems relating to the liberalization of trade in agricultural and fisheries products have been discussed earlier, in Chapter 13. During the Tokyo Round, these products were generally excluded from the linear across-the-board technique that was used as a basis for negotiations in the industrial sector; and negotiations for reductions of tariffs on agricultural and fisheries products, to the extent these took place, were generally on an item-by-item basis, for the most part between pairs of countries. While important areas of agricultural trade, such as grains and sugar, were essentially excluded from the negotiations, significant cuts in tariffs were made on a range of other agricultural imports by many countries, including Canada. However no fundamental changes were made by the European Community in its Common Agricultural Policy, and its variable import levies will continue to cover Canada's exports of wheat and some other products. An important concession was obtained for Canadian exports of aged cheddar cheese to the EC, and following the negotiations, Canada succeeded in obtaining a share of a sizeable tariff quota for high-quality beef, which was opened by the Community as a result of the Tokyo Round.[15]

Negotiations on wheat and other grains were transferred from the Tokyo Round to negotiations taking place in London for an extension of the International Wheat Agreement; as we noted in Chapter 13, the Agreement was extended without any provisions relating to the regulation of prices.

Negotiations on trade in meat led to the conclusion of a new commodity-type "Arrangement Regarding Bovine Meat," within the GATT framework, among meat exporters, including Canada. This Arrangement is of a consultative nature, with no price provisions, but an International Meat Council was established to keep world markets for meat under review, and the Council has the authority to propose to governments "possible remedial solutions" to problems of world trade in bovine meat.[16]

Negotiations in the area of dairy products led to the extension, with some changes, of existing commodity-type arrangements in this area among the leading exporters, including Canada. Under the "International Arrangements on Dairy Products," an International Dairy Products Council will function along the lines of the Meat Council, and will have the authority to propose to governments "possible remedial solutions" to problems of trade in dairy products. Unlike the meat arrangement, however, provisions were included for establishing minimum export prices for the products concerned. These price arrangements are set out in three protocols covering milk powders, milk fat, and certain cheeses.[17] As we noted in Chapter 13, Canada has not signed the Protocol relating to milk powders.

Sector Approach

Despite strong efforts by Canadian negotiators, the 'sector approach' was not accepted as a basis for reducing tariff and non-tariff measures together, in certain identified sectors such as non-ferrous metals and forest products. The major importers viewed the approach as a threat to their own processing industries. Countries that have preferential access to the European Community also resisted the erosion of their preferences. The developing countries, which might have been expected to support a sector approach, showed a lack of interest or introduced complicating issues linked to their broader demands for special and more favourable treatment in GATT. The final report of the Canadian Government on the negotiations noted it had not been possible to achieve the Canadian objective of eliminating or reducing US, EC and Japanese tariffs over the whole range of non-ferrous metals and semi-fabricated products, although a number of tariff reductions in this area were achieved; it also recorded that significant tariff concessions in the forest-products sector were obtained from the USA, the EC and Japan. Because of the resistance of major importing countries to reducing their tariff and other barriers to processed forms of major Canadian resource products, Canadian negotiators indicated that Canada would not be able to accept new obligations with respect to export restrictions and charges in addition to those already set out in GATT, as proposed by importing countries. In his 1979 report on the Tokyo Round, the Director-General of GATT noted:

> Canada continues to consider that the negotiating technique advanced in its sector proposals would be an effective one for future negotiations, particularly those involving the range of measures affecting trade in resource-based products.[18]

The United States advanced a variation of the sector approach, aimed at eliminating or harmonizing all tariffs and other barriers for selected industrial areas such as steel or aircraft: that is, following a 'horizontal' approach rather than the 'vertical' approach proposed by Canada. This horizontal approach was the basis of the agreement reached on trade in civil aircraft, noted below.

Codes on Non-Tariff Barriers

Five new 'codes' were adopted, as a result of the Tokyo Round, which have the effect of extending and clarifying a number of existing GATT rules governing the use of non-tariff barriers to trade and, in certain cases, laying down new rules.[19] The new codes, in brief, cover the following matters:

- *Subsidies and Countervailing Duties.* This code reaffirms the rule in GATT Article VI that countervailing duties can be imposed on subsidized imports only when there is evidence that these imports are causing or threatening "material injury" to an established domestic industry, or will retard "materially" the establishment of a domestic industry. The code also includes a new illustrative list of export-subsidy measures which are prohibited under GATT Article XVI, and extends the prohibition to cover minerals, in addition to manufactured products. The adoption of this code led the United States to bring its legislation governing countervailing duties into conformity with GATT rules, thus meeting a long-standing objective of Canada and many other countries. Related changes were also made to the 1967 GATT Code on Anti-dump-

ing Duties, to bring it into line with the new Code on Subsidies and
Countervailing Duties.

- *Customs Valuation.*   This code aims at international standardization of
  methods of valuing imports for customs purposes. Its adoption will
  involve some substantial changes in Canadian and US legislation and
  practices in this area. Canada undertook to implement the code by 1
  January 1985, provided it could negotiate upward changes in Canadian
  tariff rates where the adoption of the new system would result in a
  significant decrease in the level of protection afforded domestic producers
  under the existing system.[20]

- *Import Licensing.*   This code lays down a number of rules to be
  followed in the administration of import-licensing systems, where these
  exist; these rules are designed to reduce any unnecessary restrictive
  effects arising from the operation of these systems. A number of countries are considered to administer their import-licensing systems in
  unduly restrictive ways: for example, by employing complicated procedures relating to applications for import permits or deliberately delaying
  the issue of permits.

- *Technical Barriers to Trade (Standards).*   Under this code, signatory
  countries undertake to administer in accordance with agreed rules their
  regulations for product standards, including testing and certification
  requirements, so as to minimize unnecessary restrictive effects on imported goods. The code is also aimed at further development of common
  standards on an international basis and the adoption of these standards
  by national governments.

- *Government Procurement.*   This code sets new international rules in an
  important and growing area of international trade. It is aimed at reducing
  discrimination against imports by government bodies in their purchases
  of goods and related services, which is a widespread practice in many
  countries. Compliance with this code will require changes in legislation
  and practices in many countries, and could result in significant liberalization of world trade. While the coverage of the new code is somewhat
  limited, further negotiations are to be held with the intent of enlarging
  the range of goods the code covers, and possibly extending the code to
  cover certain services.

Committees of signatory countries are set up under all of these codes to
supervise their operation, and detailed provisions are included for the settlement of disputes. Like the 1967 Anti-dumping Code and the Multifibre
Arrangement, these codes are not integral parts of the General Agreement, nor
do they amend the Agreement, but they will operate within the GATT system.
The codes are binding only on their signatories, which include most of the

industrialized countries and a considerable number of the less-developed countries have signed as members.

The codes thus represent a further extension of 'conditional' most-favoured-nation (MFN) treatment within the GATT system, in contrast to the 'unconditional' MFN principle that is embodied in the General Agreement itself. Generally, these 'conditional' MFN features relate to procedural elements, such as consultations and dispute settlement among the signatories. In the code relating to subsidies/countervailing duties and the code on government procurement, however, the 'conditional' MFN feature applies to substantive elements of the codes.[21]

Canada has signed all of the codes. Taken together, the new Tokyo Round codes represent a significant enlargement and strengthening of the GATT system; and these new trade rules could lead to new trade liberalization, depending on how they are implemented in practice by signatory countries. As we shall see further, below, the Canadian government has embarked on a comprehensive revision of the legislative and administrative elements of Canada's import regime, largely on the basis of the new GATT codes. This process should be completed by the mid-1980s and is likely to lead to some far-reaching changes.[22]

Proposals for a Safeguards Code

It was also proposed that a new 'safeguards' code should be concluded during the MTN, but negotiations for establishing this code were unsuccessful. One of the main obstacles was the issue of 'selectivity': that is, whether restrictive import measures imposed under GATT Article XIX against imports causing injury to a domestic industry can be applied, on a selective basis, against only one or a few countries, instead of on a non-discriminatory basis against all sources of imports of the product concerned, as Article XIX has traditionally required. The European Community held out for new rules to permit the selective use of safeguards, but was opposed by the developing countries, which were supported by Japan and, to some extent, by the United States and Canada. Other unresolved issues include a re-definition of the circumstances under which safeguards can be used and proposals to tighten international surveillance over safeguard measures. Negotiations on a possible safeguards code are continuing in a special GATT committee established for this purpose.[23]

Agreement on Trade in Civil Aircraft

An agreement was concluded among a group of developed countries with important interests in trade in civil aircraft, including Canada, the USA, Japan, the European Community, Sweden and Switzerland. This code required the elimination, as of 1 January 1980, of all tariffs and import quotas on civil aircraft, engines, parts and certain related equipment, as well as on the services of related overhauls and repairs. The agreement also contains provisions governing a range of other governmental measures related to trade in this area, such as technical regulations and government assistance to the industry. The Canadian government has stated that the agreement will not stand in the way of its programs to provide financial assistance to the aircraft industry, or efforts to include 'offset' arrangements requiring the participation of Canadian industry in the production of aircraft built abroad under major contracts. As we have noted above, this agreement represents a variation of the 'sector approach' to trade liberalization in an area of advanced industrial technology. However, several important producers of aircraft and parts, such as Brazil, have not signed the agreement.

The 'Framework' Decisions

Important negotiations took place during the Tokyo Round on a number of issues relating to the operation of the GATT system, which were grouped under the heading of "Framework for the Conduct of International Trade." The outcome of these negotiations included several elements. One was the adoption by the Contracting Parties, following the Tokyo Round, of a so-called 'enabling clause,' which generally authorizes GATT-member countries to accord "differential and more favourable treatment" to developing countries, without giving such treatment to other GATT members. This decision also extended the Generalized System of Preferences on a continuing basis. (See Chapter 10, above.) It authorized preferential treatment for developing countries under the new Tokyo Round codes and agreements; it authorized, for the first time, "regional or global arrangements" among less-developed countries, involving exchanges of preferences under both tariff and non-tariff measures; and it authorized GATT members to give more favourable treatment to the poorer, least-developed countries than to other developing countries. This enabling clause restated earlier understandings that industrialized countries do not expect reciprocity in tariff and trade negotiations from less-developed countries, especially the least-developed; and it also included a somewhat ambiguous statement regarding the 'graduation' of the more-advanced developing countries, a process aimed at bringing these countries more fully under the regular GATT rules and forgoing preferential treatment.[24]

Under another of the framework decisions, procedures for GATT examinations of trade-restrictive measures taken for balance-of-payments reasons were strengthened; and recognition was given to the fact that certain countries may use surcharges and other measures, as well as quantitative restrictions, to restrict imports, as a means of dealing with balance-of-payments problems.[25]

Another framework decision will strengthen GATT procedures for consultation and the resolution of trade disputes. In addition, new rules were adopted covering the establishment, composition and work of panels of experts established by GATT to help settle disputes.[26]

Implementation of Tokyo Round Results

Following the conclusion of the Tokyo Round, the United States enacted new legislation, the Trade Agreements Act of 1979, which had as one of its major purposes the amendment of various existing US laws and practices to bring them into line with the agreements reached during the MTN. One important change, from a Canadian perspective, was the requirement of a 'material injury test' for the application of countervailing duties to dutiable imports, as well as to non-dutiable imports; previously the imposition of countervailing duties on dutiable imports did not require determination of injury to a domestic industry as arising from subsidized imports. However, even under the new legislation, the United States applies the injury test generally only to countries that have signed the new Tokyo Round code on subsidies/countervailing duties. The US legislation governing the use of anti-dumping duties was also amended, to require a test of 'material injury' rather than simple 'injury,' thus bringing it closer into conformity with GATT rules. Moreover, new procedures were established for inquiries resulting from requests by domestic producers for the imposition of countervailing duties, anti-dumping duties, and other special import measures. Under related new legislation, there was also a substantial reorganization of responsibilities within the US Administration in the area of trade policy.[27]

The Canadian government initially indicated that Canada could meet its basic obligations under the new Tokyo Round codes with few changes in existing legislation, although changes in various trade-policy practices will be required and, as we have noted above, adherence to the code on customs valuation will require amendments to the Customs Act. However, the Minister of Finance issued a "Discussion Paper" in July 1980, in which it was stated that a number of changes in Canadian import legislation would be required if Canada is to take full advantage of its rights under the GATT, including the rights provided for under the new MTN agreements on non-tariff measures. This discussion paper, titled "Proposals on Import Policy," proposed the enactment of a new Special Import Measures Act to replace the current Anti-dumping Act and the section of the Customs Tariff that now deals with countervailing duties. The proposed legislation would make a number of substantive changes in Canada's anti-dumping and countervailing duty systems. Other proposed legislative changes would include:

- Amending the Customs Tariff in order to facilitate the imposition of surtaxes on imports which are causing or threatening serious injury to domestic producers.

- Providing clearer authority for the government to impose controls on imports in order to deal with balance-of-payments difficulties.

- Authorizing the government to impose restrictive measures on imports in response to actions by foreign governments which either affect Canadian trade in goods and services or impair Canada's rights under trade agreements.[28]

These proposals for new legislation on import policy were the subject of prolonged hearings by a Sub-committee of the House of Commons Standing Committee on Finance, Trade and Economic Affairs. In its report, issued in June 1982, the Sub-committee endorsed most of the proposals contained in the discussion paper of July 1980. It also recommended that new procedures should be adopted for a review by the Tariff Board of decisions by the Anti-dumping Tribunal when requested by consumer advocates; and it suggested an in-depth review of the relationships among the current import agencies, that is, the Tariff Board, Anti-dumping Tribunal, Textile and Clothing Board, and Department of National Revenue (Customs and Excise).[29] The new legislation was submitted to Parliament in Bill C-8 and adopted in June 1984.

Notes

1. For the main issues and developments during the Tokyo Round, see two studies by S. Golt: *The GATT Negotiations 1973–1975: A Guide to the Issues* (1974) and *The GATT Negotiations 1973–1979: The Closing Stage.* An account of developments during the negotiations and their outcome is in GATT, Director-General, *The Tokyo Round of Multilateral Trade Negotiations,* and GATT, Director-General, *Supplementary Report.* Following the conclusion of the negotiations, the Canadian government issued, on 11 July 1979, a News Release titled "Multilateral Trade Negotiations 1979: Canadian Participation," with detailed supporting material.

2. See GATT, *Activities in 1970.*

3. For an account of the Smithsonian Agreement, see A.F.W. Plumptre, *Three Decades of Decision: Canada and the World Monetary System, 1944–75,* Chapter 10.

4. For an account of the agreement reached with the European Community and Japan, see US Department of State, *Bulletin* (3 April 1972). Strong support for a new round of trade negotiations was given in OECD, *Policy Perspectives for International Trade and Economic Relations,* a report by a 'high level group' that had been formed by the Secretary-General. This report also contains an examination of major trade and trade-related issues in the early 1970s. For further analysis

of world economic and trade problems in the early 1970s, see Trade Policy Research Centre, Advisory Group, *Towards an Open World Economy.*

5. For a Canadian government reaction to the US trade measures of August 1971, see Minister of Industry, Trade and Commerce, "Notes for a Luncheon Address" to the Canada-California Symposium, San Francisco, 29 October 1971. See also Canadian Institute of International Affairs, *International Canada* 3 (March 1972), pp. 45-47, for summaries of statements on Canada-USA relations in March 1972 by the Prime Minister and by the Minister of Industry, Trade and Commerce.

6. The 'Third Option' strategy was presented by the Secretary of State for External Affairs in an article entitled "Canada-U.S. Relations: Options for the Future," *International Perspectives* (Autumn 1972 Special Issue).

7. The text of the "Tokyo Declaration" is in GATT, *Basic Instruments and Selected Documents, Twentieth Supplement*, pp. 19-22 and also in GATT, Director-General, *The Tokyo Round of Multilateral Trade Negotiations*, Annex B; the Tokyo Declaration was tabled in the House of Commons on 17 September 1973. The speech by the Canadian Minister of Industry, Trade and Commerce at the Tokyo ministerial meeting was issued in Department of Industry, Trade and Commerce, *News Release* (12 September 1973).

8. See "Tokyo Declaration," note 7, above. For a discussion of the sector approach in negotiations during the Tokyo Round, and the importance attached by Canada to sector negotiations, especially for non-ferrous metals and forest products, see C. Pestiau, *The Sector Approach to Trade Negotiations: Canadian and U.S. Interests.*

9. For reaction in Parliament to the opening of the Tokyo Round, see Canada, Parliament, House of Commons, *Debates* (17 September 1973), pp. 6613-14. The speech by the Minister of Industry, Trade and Commerce in Toronto on 24 September 1973, is reported in Canadian Institute of International Affairs, *International Canada* 4 (September 1973), pp. 236-37.

10. The Canadian Trade and Tariffs Committee issued, in August 1977, a comprehensive *Review of Developments in the GATT Multilateral Trade Negotiations in Geneva*, for the purpose of informing interested parties in the private sector about the progress of the negotiations. From 1977, the Office of the Coordinator for Multilateral Trade Negotiations issued a series of press releases relating the development of the negotiations. For a study of the process of consultations and decision-making within the Canadian government during the Tokyo Round, see G.R. Winham, "Bureaucratic Politics and Canadian Trade Negotiation."

11. The text of the US Trade Act of 1974 (Public Law 93-618) is reproduced in *International Legal Materials* 14 (January 1975): 181-230.

12. Canadian Trade and Tariffs Committee, *Review of Developments in the GATT Multilateral Trade Negotiations in Geneva*, pp. 20-24.

13. Canadian Institute of International Affairs, *International Canada*, 9 (January 1978), pp. 8-10.

14. See note 1, above. The Canadian government's report on the negotiations contains detailed information on tariff reductions to be made by Canada's main trading partners, as well as the agreed cuts in Canadian tariffs.

15. Canada obtained access to the Community's tariff quota for high-quality beef only by invoking the dispute-settlement procedures of GATT, which led to a determination by a dispute panel in Canada's favour; see GATT, *Activities in 1981*, pp. 43-44.

16. The text of the "Arrangement Regarding Bovine Meat" is in GATT, *Basic Instruments and Selected Documents, Twenty-sixth Supplement.*

17. The texts of the "International Arrangements on Dairy Products" and the related protocols are also in GATT, *Basic Instruments and Selected Documents, Twenty-sixth Supplement.*

18. For an account of efforts to pursue the 'sector approach' during the Tokyo Round, see GATT, Director-General, *The Tokyo Round of Multilateral Trade Negotiations*, pp. 88-89.

19. For accounts of the negotiation of these codes and of their provisions, see the reports of the Director-General of GATT referred to in Note 1, above; comments by the Canadian government are in the report referred to in Note 1. The texts of the codes are in GATT, *Basic Instruments and Selected Documents, Twenty-sixth Supplement*. The codes, together with other results of the Tokyo Round, are discussed in a series of papers by various authors in Georgetown University Law Centre, "Symposium on the Multilateral Trade Agreements."

20. In a letter dated 29 August 1980, the Minister of Finance directed the Tariff Board to consider whether draft legislation it had prepared "could provide a suitable basis for valuing Canadian imports in accordance with the agreement" and the impact that implementation of such legislation would have on tariff protection (Reference 159). See Reports by the Tariff Board, Reference 159; *The GATT Agreement on Customs Valuation, Part 1: Proposed Amendments to the Customs Act*, (1981), and *Part 2: Tariff Adjustments* (1983). The proposed amendments are in Bill C-6, introduced in January 1984.

21. For a discussion of the 'conditional' MFN elements of the Tokyo Round codes in the context of US trade legislation, see G.C. Hufbauer, J.S. Erb and H.P. Starr, "The GATT Codes and the Unconditional Most-Favored-Nation Principle."

22. For a discussion of prospective changes in Canada's import regime, see Canada, Department of External Affairs, *Canadian Trade Policy for the 1980s: A Discussion Paper*, pp. 29-31.

23. For a discussion of efforts during the Tokyo Round to modify the GATT safeguards system, see GATT, Director-General, *The Tokyo Round of Multilateral Trade Negotiations*, pp. 90-95.

24. GATT, *Basic Instruments and Selected Documents, Twenty-sixth Supplement* pp. 203-205 contains the Decision of the Contracting Parties of 28 November 1979 entitled "Differential and More Favourable Treatment, Reciprocity, and Fuller Participation of Developing Countries." For a discussion of the concept of 'graduation,' see I. Frank, "The 'Graduation' Issue for the LDCs."

25. Decision of GATT Contracting Parties of 28 November 1979, "Declaration on Trade Measures Taken for Balance-of-Payments Purposes" is in GATT, *Basic Instruments and Selected Documents, Twenty-sixth Supplement*, pp. 205-209.

26. Decision of 28 November 1979, "Notification, Consultation, Dispute Settlement

and Surveillance," is in GATT, *Basic Instruments and Selected Documents, Twenty-sixth Supplement*, pp. 210-18.

27. For a detailed analysis of new US trade legislation and procedures from a Canadian perspective, see R. de C. Grey, *United States Trade Policy Legislation: A Canadian View*. The US Trade Agreements Act of 1979 (Public Law 96-39) is reproduced, with certain omissions, in *International Legal Materials* 18 September 1979): pp. 1256-1368.

28. Canada, Department of Finance, *Proposals on Import Policy: A Discussion Paper Proposing Changes to Canadian Import Legislation*. See note 22 above.

29. Canada, Parliament, House of Commons, Standing Committee on Finance, Trade and Economic Affairs, Subcommittee on Import Policy *Report on the Special Import Measures Act*.

16

The Rise in Protectionism

The post-war process of trade liberalization continued into the late 1970s, within the Tokyo Round of multilateral trade negotiations, resulting in agreement, among most industrialized countries, to make further and substantial cuts in most of their tariffs, in stages, by 1987, and to elaborate GATT rules governing a number of non-tariff barriers to trade. But during the later 1970s, many of the world's main trading countries also introduced new measures, mostly of a non-tariff kind, to restrict or distort their international trade, or they intensified existing restrictive measures. This process is often called 'the new protectionism,' partly to distinguish the new or intensified restrictions from earlier restrictive elements in the system, and partly because of changes in the nature and purposes of the newer protectionist measures.[1]

The distinction between 'new' and 'old' protectionism is not always clear, nor perhaps useful. Nor is it easy to measure the extent to which protectionism within the system has increased over recent years, and to balance the evident spread of non-tariff restrictive measures against the tariff reductions that are under way. But it is clear that unlike tariffs, which, under GATT rules, are mostly bound against increase and applied on a most-favoured-nation (MFN) or Generalized System of Preferences (GSP) basis, non-tariff measures can be introduced by governments relatively easily and, if necessary, outside GATT rules, and can more easily be applied on a bilateral basis, as well.

'New Protectionism'

The spread of protectionism within the world-trade system occurred over a decade that has been marked by great turbulence in the world economy, high levels of inflation and, during most years, slow economic growth and a decline in productivity in many industries.[2] In the later 1970s, economic growth was at a rate averaging about one-half that experienced in the 1950s and 1960s, and it was still lower in the early 1980s: about 1 per cent for the industrialized countries as a group. This slow-down in economic growth, accompanied by an unemployment rate that increased to crisis levels in many industrialized countries, placed heavy pressures on governments to assist domestic producers, to adopt measures to protect them against competing imports, and to promote their exports by the use of subsidies and in other ways. In 1983, while the United States (US) economy began to recover, stimulating a parallel recovery in Canada, the recession continued in Western Europe; and unemployment continued at very high levels in Western Europe, the United States (USA), Canada and elsewhere, generating continuing severe pressures for protectionist trade measures.

Another cause of trade protection has been the greater instability and uncertainty of the world monetary system after the abandonment of relatively fixed exchange rates in the early 1970s. Deficits in international balances, exchange-rate problems, large-scale international movements of funds, and the severe debt burden of many developing countries have led to protectionist trade measures and discouraged the liberalization of import policies. Moreover, the governments of most industrialized countries have adopted tight monetary policies at home, involving high interest rates, for the purpose of reducing inflation and defending the external value of their currencies. These policies, by depressing domestic economic activity and increased unemployment, have provoked further pressures from domestic producers and labour groups for protectionist trade measures.

A further source of protectionist trade measures is attributed to a 'backlog of adjustment' by established industries in many industrialized countries to changing patterns of world production and trade. The past decade has seen dramatic international shifts in comparative advantage among industries; these shifts have involved not only new competition from expanding standard technology and labour-intensive industries in developing countries, but also new competition from advanced technology industries in Japan and elsewhere. Some established industries in importing countries have been able to adjust to this new competition by restructuring, rationalizing and modernizing their operation; others are faced with the prospect of curtailing their operations or phasing them out. But established industries that are unable or unprepared to adjust to new international competition commonly call on their governments to protect them from rising imports, and to assist them with subsidies and other help, in order to maintain their production and employment.

Many of the protectionist trade measures in support of industries facing severe adjustment problems are thus aimed, not only at newer and strong sources of competition in 'low-cost' developing countries, but also at advanced and highly efficient industries in Japan and other Asian countries. For example, Canada and other countries have placed controls on imports of footwear, and these controls are aimed, not only at 'low-cost' exporting countries, but also at lower-wage footwear industries in Italy, Spain and Eastern European countries. The United States has imposed new barriers to imports of steel from the European Community (EC), Japan, Canada and other countries. Imports of automobiles from Japan into the United States, the European Community and Canada are limited under bilateral arrangements with Japan, and Australia restricts imports of automobiles on a global basis. Members of the EC restrict imports of television and radio sets from certain Asian countries, and the USA also applied restrictions on imports of these products, at least until recently.

Most industrialized countries have introduced a variety of 'adjustment programs' designed to assist established industries, firms and workers to adjust to changes in technology, as well as to changes in patterns of international production and trade. In some cases, however, these adjustment programs are 'defensive' in their purpose and are designed to subsidize continued production and employment in established, high-cost, less-efficient industries, rather than to encourage the shift of resources from areas of lower productivity into those of higher productivity; these programs commonly involve continued protectionist measures against imports, and may not contribute to the abandonment of the protectionist measures. Such 'defensive' adjustment programs are, in effect, a form of disguised protectionism, and they serve to slow, rather than to facilitate, the process of adjustment to changes in international competition.[3]

The increase in protectionist trade measures in recent years has also been attributed, in large part, to a general growth in the level of intervention in economic areas by the governments of most industrialized countries. For more than a decade, governments have been enlarging their role far beyond traditional responsibility for monetary and fiscal management and for general trade policy. They have embarked on an array of industrial strategies and regulatory programs affecting many sectors of industry and agriculture, including the activities of individual firms and producers, which often embody elements that restrict or distort external trade. These strategies and programs are put in place to serve a variety of objectives. Some objectives are longer-term, to encourage regional development, maintain farm population, control foreign investment, and encourage advanced research and development. Other programs, which can incorporate severely restrictive or trade-distorting elements, are often designed to meet short-term and narrowly defined objectives. Most represent responses to pressures for assistance by particular groups of producers or workers, or even by individual firms. Others are introduced to protect invest-ments made earlier by governments, to reduce levels of budget expenditures, or for other financial reasons.

The extension of governmental intervention involving trade measures has been accompanied by a growing politicization of trade policy.[4] In this process, the influence at political levels of industrial and agricultural groups seeking protective trade measures is commonly much greater than the influence of less-well-organized groups such as consumers. And the GATT rules have become less of a constraint on the adoption of protectionist trade measures than they were at earlier periods; protests against protectionist measures based on respect for the GATT rules, are often rejected as 'boy-scoutism.' The fear of retaliatory action by other countries may, of course, act as a powerful constraint on the adoption of protectionist trade measures. But such retaliation, if imposed, can simply add further protective measures to the trade system and invite counter-retaliation.

The new protectionism does not necessarily involve the imposition at the border of direct controls of a non-tariff kind against imports. In many cases, purely domestic programs in support of favoured industrial sectors or firms can have equivalent effects of restricting or distorting international trade. Whatever the form of protective restrictions, the new protectionism has introduced new elements of instability and unpredictability into international trade, in contrast to traditional protectionist systems based on known and relatively stable customs tariffs.

It becomes increasingly evident that governments of the leading GATT members, including Canada, are coming to regard their trade policies as simply one element of, and subservient to, their industrial, agricultural and other domestic strategies, which often have narrowly defined and short-term objectives. This shift in approach to trade policy by the major trading countries, if pursued, will have the most serious consequences for the multilateral trade system that has been built on the GATT principles. There is a growing risk that the main GATT countries will turn away from the pursuit of broader global objectives, such as those of extending the open world-trade system, reinforcing non-discrimination in the system, strengthening the rule of law in international trade, and assisting through trade measures the economic growth of the developing countries. Closely harnessing trade policy to the pursuit of domestic industrial, and other, economic strategies threatens a reversion to the kind of beggar-thy-neighbour policies that led to the disintegration of world trade in the 1930s. And in such a world, middle-sized countries with large trade interests, such as Canada, would be particularly exposed to damage.

Extent of Protectionism

It is impossible to measure with any accuracy the extent of protectionism within the trade system, or its spread.[5] One weakness of GATT is that it lacks an effective system for the surveillance of protectionist trade measures by member countries, or even for the notification by members that such measures are being imposed; the only exceptions are for those measures imposed under the formal safeguard provisions of Article XIX and the Multifibre Arrangement (MFA). New codes and understandings adopted as a result of the Tokyo Round will strengthen the GATT system somewhat in this regard.[6] But a recognized feature of contemporary protectionism is the scale of the restrictions that exist under bilateral agreements concluded outside the framework of the GATT rules or the rules of the MFA, in the form of voluntary export restraints, orderly marketing arrangements, and other measures imposed unilaterally by importing countries. A GATT Secretariat study made in 1982 estimated that whereas less than $2 billion-worth of trade was restricted on the basis of Article XIX rules, some $20 billion-worth of world trade was restricted by voluntary export restraints, orderly marketing arrangements, and other measures put in place outside the GATT rules; these estimates do not include the large volume of world trade in textiles and clothing, which is restricted within the framework of the Multifibre Arrangement, nor trade in agricultural products that is controlled on the basis of GATT rules or governments' interpretations of those rules.[7]

Without attempting to measure the volume of trade affected, we may categorize the main areas of protectionism within the trade system as follows:[8]

- Restrictions on imports of agricultural products, mostly temperate zone products, by many industrialized countries, including Canada. The products include beef and veal, dairy products, wheat, eggs, sugar, oil seeds and vegetable oils, and many others.

- Controls on imports of textile and clothing products by the industrialized countries, including Canada, especially those under bilateral agreements concluded within the Multifibre Arrangement with developing countries and state-trading countries in Eastern Europe.

- Controls on imports of footwear into the European Community, Canada, Australia and Japan, aimed mainly at 'low-cost' developing countries and, to some extent, against Italy and Spain.

- Restrictions imposed mainly by European Community countries and also, until recently at least, by the United States, on imports of television sets and other electronic equipment from Japan, Korea and Taiwan.

- Countervailing duties, anti-dumping duties, and quantitative restrictions by the United States on imports of steel, especially from the European Community (although some Canadian exports are also restricted), and controls by the Community and Australia on imports of steel from a number of countries, including Japan.

• Controls on imports of automobiles from Japan by the United States, the European Community and Canada, under bilateral export-restraint agreements with Japan, and Australia's restrictions on imports of automobiles.

• High tariffs maintained by many industrialized countries, including the United States and Canada, on imports of textiles, clothing, footwear and a variety of consumer-type goods.

• Tariffs on the processed forms of raw materials by many countries, especially Japan and the European Community, that give high levels of 'effective protection' to their domestic processing industries.

• Comprehensive and severe import restrictions maintained by many developing countries for balance-of-payments reasons, which serve also to protect domestic producers.

• The trade and economic system of state-trading countries.

There is evidence of an increase of the use of 'contingency-protection' measures in the United States, the European Community and Canada; these measures include anti-dumping duties, countervailing duties, and 'safeguard' import measures against an upsurge of imports on the basis of GATT Article XIX. The use of such measures reflects, in part, the more legalistic and complex set of GATT rules that emerged from the Tokyo Round, which have been translated into new trade legislation, procedures and policies, especially in the United States.[9] The Canadian government, for its part, has made somewhat parallel changes in Canada's import legislation and practices, designed to bring these closer into line with the GATT rules and with the import systems of the United States and other countries. These changes will substantially enlarge the scope for controlling imports into Canada for protectionist as well as for other purposes.[10]

The increase in protectionism within the trade system in recent years should probably not be over-emphasized. While new barriers have been introduced in some important sectors of world trade during the past decade, there has not so far been any general retreat into protectionism. Large volumes of international trade flow free of restrictions and tariffs, or subject to progressively lower tariff barriers. At the GATT Ministerial Meeting in November 1982, it was agreed that the member countries would "resist protectionist pressures in the formulation and implementation of national trade policy and in proposing legislation"; there was no agreement, however, for a standstill on protectionist trade measures, or for a roll-back of such measures. (See Chapter 17, below.) At successive Summit Meetings, leaders of the major trading countries, including Canada, have stated their determination to resist protectionist trade policies and their firm support for the GATT multilateral trade system.[11] Nevertheless, there is clearly a danger that the future trade policies of the larger trading countries, and of Canada also, could be aimed, in time to come, more at the further international regulation of protective trade measures than at their reduction or elimination.

Notes

1. The post-war process of trade liberalization and the growth of protectionism in the mid-1970s are examined in R. Blackhurst, N. Marian and J. Tumlir, *Trade Liberalization, Protectionism, and Interdependence*. A good description and analysis of 'new protectionism' is in B. Balassa, "World Trade and the International Economy: Trends, Prospects and Policies," in *World Trade:Constraints and Opportunities in the 1980s*. (This study also appeared in the *Journal of World Trade Law* [September 1978] under the title "The New Protectionism and the International Economy.")

2. Successive annual issues of *International Trade*, published by the General Agreement on Tariffs and Trade, Geneva, contain detailed surveys of developments in the world economy and in world trade.

3. For an analysis of adjustment problems in Canada and government policies in this area, see C. Pearson and G. Salembier, *Trade, Employment, and Adjustment*. C.R. Frank, *Foreign Trade and Domestic Aid*, contains a description and analysis of adjustment programs in the United States; a section on Canadian programs is on pp. 129-33. See also M. Wolf, *Adjustment Policies and Problems in Developed Countries*.

4. For a discussion of the increasing politicization of trade policy, see D.R. Nelson, *The Political Structure of the New Protectionism*. The growing responsiveness of governments to pressures for protectionist trade policies is also examined in M.B. Krauss, *The New Protectionism: The Welfare State and International Trade*. An examination of the role of special interest groups in the formulation of trade policy in Canada is included in D.R. Protheroe, *Imports and Politics: Trade Decision-Making in Canada, 1968–1979*, Chapter 3.

5. A recent comprehensive survey of protectionist trade measures by the major industrialized countries is in Commonwealth Secretariat, *Protectionism: Threat to International Order. The Impact on Developing Countries*, Chapter 3. For an earlier survey of protectionist trade measures introduced during the mid-1970s by the United States, the European Community and Canada, see B. Nowzad, *The Rise in Protectionism*.

6. See GATT, *Basic Instruments and Selected Documents, Twenty-sixth Supplement*, pp. 210-18 for the text of the Decision adopted by the Contracting Parties on 28 November 1979, on an "Understanding Regarding Notification, Consultation, Dispute Settlement and Surveillance." This Understanding includes an obligation on GATT members to notify the Contracting Parties when adopting "trade measures affecting the operation of the General Agreement." Notification is to be in advance, if possible, and otherwise immediately after the adoption of such a measure. The General Agreement itself contains several obligations with respect to the notification of trade measures: for example, safeguard measures taken under Article XIX; the agreements on non-tariff measures adopted at the Tokyo Round, as well as the Multifibre Arrangement, contain separate commit-

ments regarding the notification of measures adopted on the basis of these instruments.

7. "GATT Looks at Spread of Trade Curbs," Toronto *Globe and Mail* (12 October 1982).

8. The restrictions and other trade barriers listed here are based, in part, on Commonwealth Secretariat, *Protectionism: Threat to International Order*, Chapter 3. See note 5, above.

9. For a description and analysis of the recent changes in US trade legislation and implications for Canada, see R. de C. Grey, *United States Trade Policy Legislation: A Canadian View*. F. Lazar, *The New Protectionism: Non-Tariff Barriers and Their Effects on Canada* also contains an examination of contingency-protection measures in the United States.

10. See Canada, Department of Finance, *Proposals on Import Policy: A Discussion Paper Proposing Changes to Canadian Import Legislation*; Canada, Parliament, House of Commons, Standing Committee on Finance, Trade and Economic Affairs, Subcommittee on Import Policy, *Report on the Special Import Measures Act*; Canada, Laws, Statutes, etc., Bill C-8 (An Act respecting the imposition of anti-dumping and countervailing duties, to amend the Currency and Exchange Act, the Customs Tariff and the Export and Import Permits Act and to repeal the Anti-dumping Act), introduced in the House of Commons for first reading on 17 January 1984 and adopted on 26 June 1984.

11. The Communiqué issued after the Williamsburg, Virginia, summit conference in May 1983 stated: "We commit ourselves to halting protectionism, and as recovery proceeds to reverse it by dismantling trade barriers."

17

The Multilateral System: Appraisal and Outlook

The multilateral system of world trade, which has existed since the Second World War, and which is centred on the General Agreement on Tariffs and Trade, represents a great advance in international co-operation from the network of bilateral and often discriminatory trade arrangements of the inter-war period. The system has provided a relatively high degree of stability and predictability in world trade and trade relationships among the main trading countries. Within it, through a process of negotiations among members of the GATT, an impressive reduction of tariffs and other barriers to trade in goods has been achieved; and the industrialized countries have made some further reductions in tariffs on imports from developing countries. The trade rules of the original General Agreement remain intact and have exerted a continuing discipline over the trade policies of member countries in many, though not all, areas. These rules have been strengthened and extended in certain ways over the years, especially by the supplementary codes governing a variety of non-tariff measures and other matters, which were adopted by many GATT members as a result of the Tokyo Round. Outside GATT, guidelines for trade policy in a number of areas have been adopted by the broader membership of the United Nations Conference on Trade and Development (UNCTAD), and by the industrialized countries in the Organisation for Economic Co-operation and Development (OECD); and members of the several international commodity agreements have agreed to special rules aimed at stabilizing world prices and other market conditions for the primary products concerned.

The International Monetary Fund (IMF) has deterred, with varying degrees of effectiveness, the manipulation by governments of their exchange rates in order to improve their trade balances; and by providing loans and other assistance to governments to help them meet temporary balance-of-payments difficulties, the IMF has lessened the inclination of governments to impose import controls to deal with external payments problems. Longer-term loans and other assistance provided by the International Bank for Reconstruction and Development (World Bank) have helped developing countries to develop their economies and participate in the world trading system.

The multilateral system also has fostered an almost continuous process of consultations on trade developments and policies at meetings arranged within GATT, UNCTAD, OECD and other international organizations, at quadrilateral meetings held periodically by the United States, The European Community (EC), Japan and Canada,[1] and at the annual summit meetings. Within GATT, special facilities for the resolution of trade disputes among member countries are being used more often and more effectively than in past years, and these have helped to reduce both frictions within the system and recourse to retaliation and counter-retaliation.

The international institutions that have been established to support and administer the General Agreement and other elements of the multilateral trade system have made an important contribution to its operation. As an institution, GATT is highly respected; and long ago it evolved to the stage where it resembles, in most respects, other specialized agencies within the United Nations system. However, GATT has never enjoyed the firm institutional base and financial, personnel and other resources of the kind provided to the IMF, the World Bank, UNCTAD or OECD, nor does it have the capacity to match the output of research and analysis of those organizations.

Despite the successes of the multilateral trade system, severe strains have emerged within it, especially since the mid-1970s. Some of the reasons for these strains were discussed in the last chapter. They have been caused in part, but not entirely, by depressed conditions in the world economy, shrinking demand in world markets, and critically high levels of unemployment in many countries. But other weaknesses have existed in the system for many years. While tariffs have been greatly reduced, especially by the industrialized countries, they still remain high in certain areas, such as textiles, clothing, footwear, many chemical products, and a variety of consumer goods. The tariff systems of most industrialized countries continue to incorporate elements of escalation according to the degree of processing, which can provide high levels of 'effective protection' to domestic processing industries. Many less-developed countries maintain high tariffs as integral parts of import policies designed to foster domestic manufacturing industries or agricultural production. Moreover, as tariffs have come down, the trade-protecting or trade-distorting effects of non-tariff barriers have become more evident. International trade in some important, temperate zone, agricultural products has all along been exempt from normal GATT rules; and restrictions and distortions have increased over the past decade in this area of trade. Within the framework of the Multifibre Arrangement (MFA), there has been a proliferation of restrictive controls, especially since the mid-1970s, on exports of textiles and clothing from developing countries and state-trading countries. One of the most disturbing developments in the system, however, has been the recent spread of bilateral arrangements, concluded by the governments of the largest trading countries, to restrain international trade in major sectors such as steel and automobiles. Other threats to the open world-trade system governed by traditional GATT rules have emerged as governments have sought more aggressively to use their trade policies as integral parts of domestic strategies to foster the development of targeted industries.

The spread of protectionism and bilateralism within the system has taken place despite repeated declarations by political leaders in many international forums of their intentions to resist protectionism and maintain the integrity of the multilateral system, and the threat exists that protectionism will increase further. There is evidence of an erosion of the prestige and authority of GATT, and growing concern that the system is becoming less relevant to the current trade-policy agenda.

While many GATT members may be implementing policies and practices which violate the letter or spirit of GATT, none are evidently prepared to risk the consequences of the collapse of the multilateral system. Indeed, there has been a surge of interest, both inside and outside governments of the many GATT members, in the analysis of the deficiencies of the system and in proposals for its reform in the light of current and prospective trade-policy issues. Below is a list of some of the improvements to the system that have been suggested over the past few years from one quarter or another. Some of these suggestions, in fact, are now being pursued in GATT or in capitals of GATT-member countries, largely as an outcome of the GATT ministerial meetings held in Geneva in November 1982 (which is the subject of the following section).[2]

- A further round of GATT tariff-and-trade negotiations should be held during the last half of the 1980s, to stave off a further retreat into protectionism, and to restore momentum towards a more open and rule-oriented multilateral trade system.

- The GATT rules and the supplementary Tokyo Round codes dealing with non-tariff measures should be further extended and strengthened.

- The proposed understanding on the use of GATT safeguard provisions, discussion of which began during the Tokyo Round, should be adopted without further delay.

- Restrictions on trade in 'low-cost' textiles and clothing under the Multifibre Arrangement should be brought under the normal GATT safeguard provisions as these may be applied under the proposed new understanding on safeguards, and the Multifibre Arrangement should be phased out.

- Bilateral arrangements, outside GATT, to restrain international trade in steel, automobiles and other products, should also be brought under the normal GATT safeguard provisions as these may be interpreted under the proposed new understanding.

- GATT codes or guidelines should be developed to cover trade in certain sectors of services that are traded internationally.

- Special problems of trade in products of advanced technology industries should be examined, with a view to determining the desirability and feasibility of adopting GATT codes or guidelines in this area of trade.

- The GATT rules governing trade in agricultural products should be improved and adapted to deal with current trade-policy problems in this area.

- Special arrangements among member countries, affecting trade in fisheries products should be brought within the purview of GATT.

- New GATT rules should be adopted to provide for a closer review of the formulation and operation of regional trade arrangements and other preferential arrangements. These rules would enable non-members of these arrangements to seek redress, in the event that their trade interests were adversely affected.

- The rules governing the participation of state-trading countries in GATT should be elaborated and strengthened, as should the rules governing the foreign trade operations of state-owned or -controlled enterprises in market-economy countries.

- GATT rules and procedures for the resolution of trade disputes should be further strengthened.

- Government policies on foreign investment which affect international trade should be brought within the purview of GATT.

- Trade problems arising from restrictive business practices and related government policies should be brought within the purview of GATT.

- GATT procedures should be improved for the examination of structural adjustment policies developed by member countries to respond to changing conditions of world production and trade, and possibilities should be explored for developing GATT guidelines relating to these policies.

- Negotiations should be initiated with the intent of bringing the newly industrialized countries more fully into the GATT system and encouraging them to accept the normal GATT rules and disciplines, while continuing to provide special and more favourable treatment for the poorer less-developed countries.

- GATT rules should be adapted to accommodate, under agreed conditions, special trade arrangements concluded among groups or pairs of member countries, to deal with problems of unique or special interest to them, without prejudicing the rights and interests of other member countries.

- Arrangements in GATT for more regular high-level consultations among the main trading countries and for the general management of GATT activities should be strengthened.

- The GATT secretariat should be strengthened and given increased independent authority to monitor and conduct surveillance of trade policies of member countries and to research evolving trade-policy issues.

- More effective institutional links should be established between GATT and the IMF, and between GATT and the World Bank.

- In the light of progress in achieving improvements along the lines noted above, some of the activities relating to international trade, now carried on in UNCTAD and in the OECD, should be transferred to GATT.

As the number of unresolved trade-policy issues grew during the early 1980s, a consensus emerged that the 1982 annual meeting of the GATT Contracting Parties should be held at the ministerial level, in an effort to arrest a retreat into protectionism and strengthen the authority of GATT. After almost a year of preparatory work, the trade Ministers from the member countries assembled in Geneva in November 1982, for the first time since 1973. The meeting was designed, in part, to address a number of specific issues left over from the Tokyo Round, including renewed efforts to reduce barriers and other distortions in trade in the agricultural sector, and to conclude an understanding on the use of safeguard measures under GATT Article XIX. Moreover, several member countries wished to use the occasion to advance initiatives of special interest to them; these initiatives were aimed at future liberalization of trade in particular sectors, and at extending or elaborating the GATT rules in particular areas. The United States was pressing for an extension of GATT rules into the area of trade in services, and for an examination of problems of trade in high-technology products.

Because of the prevailing and difficult world economic conditions, it was not generally expected that the meeting could roll back protectionist trade measures already in place or agree on any form of standstill on additional protection in the system. However, as noted in Chapter 16, above, the Ministers did agree to make determined efforts to "resist protectionist pressures in the formulation and implementation of national trade policy"; they also agreed to refrain from taking or maintaining any measures inconsistent with GATT and to make determined efforts to avoid measures which would limit or distort international trade.

It was hoped that the Ministers would be able to resolve the long-disputed issues surrounding proposals for a new understanding on the use of safeguard measures. However, the ministerial meeting failed to reach agreement on these proposals, again, mainly because of opposition to the continued efforts by the European Community to legitimize the application of safeguard measures on a 'selective' basis against individual exporting countries, rather than on a most-favoured-nation (MFN) basis, as Article XIX requires. The Ministers agreed that further efforts would be made to have such a code drawn up and adopted within a year, but a year later, agreement was still not in sight.

Several other results of the ministerial meeting were of special interest from a Canadian perspective. A new GATT Committee on Agriculture was created, which is to carry out, before the end of 1984, a comprehensive review of trade measures affecting agricultural products, as well as the effectiveness of GATT rules on subsidies in this sector, especially export subsidies. A special study is being made of problems of trade in three natural resource sectors: non-ferrous metals and minerals, forestry products, and fish and fisheries products; the study will cover trade in the basic, semi-processed and processed forms of these products. The Ministers agreed that the widespread problem of escalation of tariffs according to degree of manufacture should be given 'prompt attention,' with a view to making progress towards the elimination or reduction of such escalation where it inhibits international trade. And a special study is to be made, by the end of 1984, of the economic effects of restrictions on trade in textiles and clothing, especially those maintained under the Multi-fibre Arrangement; it is to include exploration of possibilities for phasing out restrictions under the MFA and bringing this sector of trade back under normal GATT rules.

Other elements of the GATT program approved by the Ministers include a further review of existing quantitative restrictions and other non-tariff measures within the trade system, with the objective of eliminating measures that are not in conformity with GATT rules. Possibilities are being explored for further liberalization of trade in tropical products, and the results of this exploration will be reviewed before the end of 1984. A review is being made of the operation of the codes and other arrangements that were adopted as an outcome of the Tokyo Round, aimed, in part, at identifying obstacles to their acceptance by more GATT-member countries. Possibilities are being examined for new GATT rules to deal with trade in 'counterfeit goods,' meeting a long-standing United States (US) objective, and for GATT action in connection with goods that are exported by member countries, but are not permitted, for health or other reasons, to be sold at home.

The United States was unable to make much progress with its proposal to extend GATT rules into the area of trade in services, partly because of the opposition of less-developed countries and partly, also, because the groundwork was still lacking for pursuing specific proposals for new rules. The subject is to be considered again in 1984, on the basis of further exchanges of views among the countries with interest in the issue. The proposed extension of GATT rules to cover trade in services presents a new challenge to the GATT system and to its capacity to adapt to broad changes in the structure of international trade and economic activity.

The communiqué issued by the Ministerial Meeting contained an elaborate statement of good intentions by the industrialized countries in the matter of responding to the requirements of Part IV of the General Agreement, of extending 'differential and more favourable treatment' to less-developed countries, and of lowering tariffs and non-tariff barriers against their exports. However, no specific undertakings were given; nor did the communiqué refer to the controversial issue of the 'graduation' of the newly industrialized countries.

Clearly, such positive results as were achieved at the ministerial meeting largely took the form of initiating a series of studies of possibilities for future progress towards liberalizing trade in a few selected sectors and strengthening the trade rules in several particular areas. The meeting thus represented essentially a holding operation at a time of severe difficulty for the world economic and trade system; and it remains to be seen whether the studies and other initiatives approved by the meeting will bear fruitful results.[3]

It seems clear that some further initiative will be needed within GATT to build on the program launched at the 1982 GATT Ministerial Meeting, to dismantle the protectionist trade measures which have been erected over the past decade and resume momentum towards a liberal world trade system, and to strengthen the legal and institutional elements of the GATT system. Whether and when such a new initiative will emerge is unclear. There have been recent indications of interest in planning for a further and possibly major round of GATT tariff-and-trade negotiations, during the last half of the 1980s. At the May 1983 Summit Meeting in Williamsburg, Virginia, it was agreed "to continue consultations on proposals for a new negotiating round in the GATT." More recently, it has been reported that the subject of a further round of GATT negotiations was discussed during 'quadrilateral' meetings of trade Ministers from the United States, the European Community, Japan and Canada; the meetings took place in Ottawa in September 1983, and in Florida in February 1984. It has also been reported that Prime Minister Nakasone of Japan has called openly for a new round of GATT trade negotiations in order "to consolidate the free trading system and to inject renewed confidence in the world economy," and that this initiative was endorsed by President Reagan and also by Prime Minister Trudeau during their visits to Tokyo in the autumn of 1983.[4]

Canadian Interests

From the start, Canada has given strong and generally consistent support to the multilateral trade system, and has participated actively in its operation, especially in GATT. Canada has almost consistently advocated the maintenance and progressive strengthening of the GATT trade rules, with a minimum of exceptions, backed up by effective procedures for obtaining compliance with the rules. Canada has also emphasized the underlying concept of GATT as embodying an exchange of rights and obligations; it considers that within GATT, its adherence to the trade rules imposes obligations on other countries to observe them similarly, except where derogations have been agreed to by the countries concerned and approved by other member countries. Canada's role in the system reflects not only its large and diverse interests as a world trading country, but also a recognition that the system provides a better framework than a system of bilateral relationships for managing Canadian trade-policy interests internationally, and especially its relationships with the larger countries which are its main trading partners.

One principal function of the GATT rules, from a Canadian perspective, is to restrain and discipline the trade policies and practices of the United States and the other larger countries which are its main trading partners. These restraints and disciplines can be exerted more effectively within a multilateral system of rules, where alignments with other countries can usually be found, than within bilateral relationships where Canada would almost always be a junior partner with correspondingly smaller bargaining leverage. In bilateral relationships with smaller countries, Canada's influence over their trade policies and practices would also tend to be overshadowed by the influence that the larger trading countries can exert on them in pursuit of their own trade interests.

Within the complex of international agreements and institutions which comprise the trade system, Canada can participate in the almost continuous process of consultations and exchanges of views on developments in international trade, evolving world-trade issues, and the trade policies of the world's trading countries. As a matter of policy, Canada has asserted its right, which has generally been acknowledged, to a seat at the table at all international meetings of any significance. The leading role which, in earlier years, the United States has played in the broad management of the trade system has come to be shared to a larger degree with the European Community and Japan; and the organized group of less-developed countries has occupied a special place of influence in the system over recent years. These changes have modified, but not necessarily diminished, the influence of Canada and other middle-sized countries with substantial trade interests. On almost any issue, Canada is able to align itself with one or another grouping of countries that share similar interests, thus enabling Canada to press its own interests with greater chances of success than it could in one-to-one relationships, especially with its larger trade partners, and to hold on to a fair share of the management of the world-trade policy agenda. The GATT system, in particular, allows the middle-sized and smaller countries to exert their influence and pursue their special interests because it represents an exchange, on a contractual basis, of specific trade-policy rights and obligations among all its members, and provides the mechanisms for each member to defend its rights.

The GATT rules are generally in line with the objectives of Canadian trade policies and, to a large extent, with traditional Canadian trade practice. They have permitted the continuation of the exchange of trade preferences with other Commonwealth countries, although these preferences are now greatly diminished. Canada has been able to retain traditional policies of protection for secondary manufacturing and also to add new protection for domestic agriculture, in line with enlarged programs for supply management. GATT rules have permitted the continuation of Canada's long-established anti-dumping system and, until they are changed in the next year or so, of traditional valuation-for-duty practices. The GATT safeguard provisions are available and have been used on a number of occasions to implement special measures of protection against disruptive imports; and for over two decades, the GATT system has provided additional ways to control imports of 'low-cost' textiles and clothing products. Nor have GATT rules prevented Canada, in recent years, from following the United States and the European Community in concluding arrangements with Japan to limit exports of automobiles to Canada. In some respects, and from the perspective of Canada's overall economic interests and consumer interests, the GATT rules may, indeed, appear to be unduly tolerant of protectionist Canadian trade policies. In fact, the GATT rules provide even greater flexibility than Canadian trade legislation has allowed; and the new import legislation recently enacted by Parliament is designed, in part, to authorize the government to take fuller advantage of the GATT rules governing controls on imports.

For the reasons outlined above, Canada has generally favoured a strong GATT and resisted proposals that could transfer GATT functions to other international bodies such as UNCTAD or OECD, or which could erode the authority and role of GATT in the broader system. It would appear to be in Canada's interest to give even stronger support in the future to the enlargement of the role of GATT as an institution; it could do so, for example, by strengthening its resources for information gathering in trade-policy areas, research and analysis.

Canada has greatly benefited from the far greater degree of openness of world trade that has been achieved within the GATT system. One major gain has been the substantial reduction of US tariffs on Canadian exports and the protection offered by GATT rules against increases in US tariffs. As noted in an earlier chapter, if the tariff-free exports of automobiles to the United States are included, close to 80 per cent of Canadian exports to the USA will be duty free when the Tokyo Round results are fully in effect, and over 90 per cent will enter at tariffs of 5 per cent or less. Nevertheless, US tariffs will continue to be significant obstacles to certain Canadian exports, and the US anti-dumping and countervailing duty systems can be used to harass Canadian exporters and create serious uncertainties for bilateral trade. Moreover, there are various measures in place in both countries that have adverse effects on the development of bilateral trade, and perhaps bear more heavily on each other's interests than on countries elsewhere in the world.

In recent years Canada has made special efforts in GATT to achieve the liberalization of tariff and non-tariff barriers to world trade in several important resource sectors of trade, which include forest products and non-ferrous metals, and cover the natural, processed and finished forms of such products. During the Tokyo Round, Canada advanced the sectoral approach to negotiations in order to deal with trade barriers in these areas. Sectoral free-trade arrangements of this kind would involve the elimination of escalating tariffs that can give high levels of 'effective protection' to the processed and finished forms of the raw products. Canada has linked advances towards such arrangements with its participation in any efforts to strengthen GATT rules governing export quotas and taxes.

On the import side, Canada has made a respectable contribution to the liberalization of world trade; this contribution includes reductions in its import tariffs, agreed to during the Kennedy Round and the Tokyo Round, and the introduction of its General Preferential Tariff in the mid-1970s, covering a range of imports from less-developed countries. However, Canada's tariffs have been reduced only marginally, if at all, in a number of important sectors of special interest to Canadian consumers, including textiles, clothing and footwear. More serious, Canada, in recent years, has introduced new quantitative controls or intensified existing controls over imports of textiles, clothing and footwear, as well as over imports of a growing number of agricultural products; and Canada has followed other countries in limiting its imports of Japanese automobiles. Except for the latter arrangement, Canadian controls have been introduced under GATT rules. These intensified quantitative controls on imports reflect, in part, stronger domestic pressures from Canadian producers and labour unions for import protection, but they are also a response to similar and, in some cases, more severe, protectionist measures adopted by larger trading countries, particularly the United States and the European Community. On balance, Canada's import policies are probably no more restrictive, and possibly more liberal, than those of most of the other industrialized countries.

In overall terms, the multilateral trade system has served well the interests of Canada, as a middle-sized country which has large and diverse trade interests, but whose main trade partners are larger countries; and the GATT system, in particular, has offered a wide range of opportunities to advance and defend Canada's trade-policy interests. As we have seen, the GATT system has come under some severe strains in recent years, and the weakness in the system have become more evident. There is now a clear need for new co-operative efforts to restore confidence in GATT, to resume progress towards a more open world-trade system, and to adapt the system to deal more effectively and equitably with the trade issues of the 1980s. Canada should play an active part in promoting and carrying forward these efforts. Canada's stake in the continued strength of GATT is sufficiently large to require that the effective operation and progressive improvement of the system should, in itself, be viewed as a prime objective of Canada's trade policy, and that Canadian trade policy should not be viewed narrowly as simply an extension of shifting, domestic, economic strategies. Further, while opportunities will continue to arise to advance Canadian trade interests on a bilateral basis, especially with the United States, care should be taken to develop these opportunities in ways that do not erode the strength and authority of the multilateral rules and, especially, the GATT system.

Notes

1. These quadrilateral meetings of trade Ministers from Canada, the European Community, Japan and the United States have taken place three or four times annually over the past several years. There are no formal arrangements governing their frequency or location, and the meetings are marked by an absence of formality and publicity. The two most recent meetings, attended by the Canadian Minister for International Trade, the Honourable Gerald Regan, were held in Ottawa in September 1983 and in Florida in February 1984.

2. A survey of long-run economic and political trends which threaten the multilateral trade system is in C.M. Aho and T.O. Bayard, "The 1980s: Twilight of the Open Trading System?". For an analysis of strains in the GATT system and prescriptions for improvements in the system, see M. Camps and W. Diebold, *The New Multilateralism: Can the World Trading System be Saved?* An analysis of current issues in world trade and proposals for dealing with these issues within the multilateral trade system are set out in C.F. Bergsten and W.R. Cline, *Trade Policy in the 1980s*. Other proposals for improvements in the multilateral trade system are contained in G.K. Helleiner *et al.*, *Towards a New Bretton Woods: Challenges for the World Financial and Trading System*. A more comprehensive analysis of issues within the world-trade system is in C.F. Bergsten and W.R. Cline (ed.), *Trade Policy in the 1980s*, which consists of a collection of papers prepared for a conference held in June 1982 by the Institute for International Economics.

3. The Communiqué issued at the end of the November 1982 GATT Ministerial Meeting is in GATT, *Focus* (December 1982), and also in GATT, *Basic Instruments and Selected Documents, Twenty-ninth Supplement.*

4. *New York Times* (11 November 1983), p. 1, and statements reported to have been issued by the Japanese authorities in Tokyo during visits by President Reagan and Prime Minister Trudeau in November 1983.

18

From the Tokyo Round to the Uruguay Round and Beyond

The Tokyo Round of multilateral trade negotiations under the General Agreement on Tariffs and Trade (GATT) took place between 1973 and 1979. The negotiations were broader and more comprehensive than any since GATT was established in 1947-48, and they shaped the evolution of the international trade system over the following decade. The Tokyo Round achieved an impressive eight-year program of tariff reductions (mainly by the industrialized countries) on a most-favoured-nation basis, further liberalizing large sections of world trade. These reductions were substantial: they brought the average level of the tariffs of the industrialized countries well below 10 per cent. The negotiations also resulted in an elaboration and extension of the GATT rules in a number of areas, aimed both at codifying existing trade policy practices as well as at trade liberalization. In this regard the Tokyo Round was concerned as much with the management of trade flows as with the reduction of trade barriers.

However, the negotiations left in place some relatively high tariffs in certain sectors, including textiles, clothing, footwear and some chemical products. The Round was also unable to reduce many tariffs on the processed forms of agricultural and resource products, under "escalating" tariff systems that are designed to protect processing industries in importing countries. More generally, the Tokyo Round negotiations were unsuccessful in reducing distortions in world agricultural trade. There was also little movement in rolling back the numerous quantitative controls on world trade, often imposed outside

GATT under bilateral "voluntary" agreements, and bringing these restrictions under the GATT rules that govern the use of "safeguard" import measures. The negotiations also left in place the network of bilateral controls under the Multifibre Arrangement (MFA) that limits exports of textiles and clothing from "low-cost" suppliers.

The Tokyo Round made no major changes in GATT as an institution, although it made some improvements in GATT procedures for the resolution of trade disputes and introduced a period of more intensive use of these procedures. The Round also reaffirmed and extended GATT arrangements for special and differential treatment in favour of developing countries, maintained existing arrangements for exports from developing countries, and adopted new provisions for the exchange of trade preferences among developing countries.

The direction and content of the Tokyo Round negotiations were determined in large part, but not entirely, by the world's three major economic powers—the United States, the European Community and Japan. Canada participated closely in the negotiations, and made a full contribution in terms of reductions in its own tariffs and helping to design the ancillary codes and agreements that emerged. The developing countries played a more active role in the Tokyo Round than in previous GATT negotiations. Although many were concerned with protecting their special position in the GATT, a number of developing countries were active in particular areas of the negotiations, including tropical and agricultural products, safeguards, subsidies, government procurement and institutional arrangements. However, the negotiations left intact highly restrictive trade systems maintained by many developing countries.[1]

The negotiations took place during a period of turbulence in the world economy. They were followed by a period of widespread and serious recession in North America and Western Europe marked by increased unemployment in many countries, a sharp decline in many commodity prices, continued inflation, record-breaking interest rates, and wide fluctuations in exchange rates. Critical problems emerged for heavily-indebted developing countries in Latin America, Africa and elsewhere, which continue to face formidable difficulty in servicing their international debts. There has since been further shifts in patterns of world production and trade, due to the relative decline in the role of the United States in the world economy and the emergence of new sources of international competition in Japan and the newly-industrialized countries (NICs) in Asia and Latin America.

The depressed conditions in the world economy in the post-Tokyo Round period spawned new pressures on governments for interventions to support and protect domestic industries. This led to a further proliferation of protectionist trade measures, often imposed on a bilateral basis outside the GATT, and an erosion of confidence in the principles and rules of GATT. Serious frictions emerged among the main trading countries, especially in the areas of trade in agricultural products, automobiles and steel. In the early 1980s, many GATT observers expressed serious apprehensions about a decline in the credibility of GATT and the future of the system of cooperation in international trade, based on the GATT, that had developed during the post-war period.[2]

In these difficult circumstances, a special meeting of the trade Ministers of the GATT Contracting Parties was held in Geneva in 1982. Not surprisingly, the results were disappointing in terms of dealing with the serious and urgent problems of world trade, holding back the "new protectionism" that had emerged in the trade system, making progress on the unfinished business left over from the Tokyo Round, or restoring confidence in the GATT. However, the 1982 Ministerial meeting launched a program of studies and activities which, after a four year period of gestation, gave birth to the Uruguay Round of trade negotiations. The Uruguay Round of multilateral trade negotiations was launched formally in September 1986 at a meeting of trade Ministers in Punta del Este, Uruguay, with an agenda that had the potential to become one of the most important events in the history of GATT since its inception in 1947–48.

GATT Work Program

As noted above, the work program established by the 1982 GATT Ministerial meeting largely provided the momentum during the 1982–1985 period. This program covered, among other things, agricultural trade, quantitative restrictions and other non-tariff measures, the use of safeguards import measures, textiles and clothing trade, and dispute settlement procedures. This work, in all of which Canada actively participated, served to clarify outstanding issues and explore new areas for GATT activity. It also provided a foundation for preparations for the new Uruguay Round in 1986. The main elements of this work program and progress made were as follows.[3]

Trade in Agricultural Products

A committee on trade in agriculture presented a report in 1984 that set the tone for ongoing debate within GATT, the Organization for Economic Cooperation and Development (OECD) and elsewhere, and laid out a framework for subsequent Uruguay Round negotiations in this area. In brief, the committee's report recommended the following: that all quantitative restrictions and other related measures should be brought under strengthened GATT rules and disciplines, including restrictions maintained under waivers and the operations of state trading enterprises; that rules and disciplines for agricultural trade should be elaborated to cover restraint arrangements, variable levies, unbound tariffs and minimum price arrangements; and that all subsidies, including those on exports, should be brought under strengthened GATT rules. The report also recommended the adoption of improved procedures to minimize adverse effects of sanitary and phytosanitary regulations on trade in agriculture; there was also the suggestion that the domestic policies and measures affecting agricultural trade should be subject to regular review and examination in GATT.

Quantitative Restrictions and Other Non-Tariff Measures

Some of the most useful work commissioned by the 1982 Ministerial meeting was a review by a group of GATT countries of existing quantitative restrictions and other non-tariff measures, and the conformity of these measures with GATT rules. The objective of the review was to bring these measures into conformity with GATT and achieve greater trade liberalization. The group focused mainly on quantitative restrictions and other non-tariff measures affecting trade in industrial products, other than those imposed on textiles and clothing which were regularly reviewed under the Multifibre Arrangement. It obtained lists of such measures both from countries maintaining them and countries whose exports were affected by them. The lists were long, and the group, with the help of the Secretariat, laboured over a three year period to refine and improve the list, country by country and product by product, raising a good deal of controversy in the process. By 1986, a data base had been prepared on quantitative restrictions and other non-tariff measures maintained on trade among GATT member countries, along with an analysis of the justification for such measures under GATT rules, and an inventory of non-tariff measures on industrial products. The analysis suggested that little progress had been made over this three year period in the overall reduction of these numerous barriers to trade; it also illustrated the range of quantitative restrictions, justified for balance-of-payments reasons or developmental purposes, that were maintained by developing countries.

Safeguards

The Tokyo Round negotiations had been unsuccessful in clarifying and strengthening the GATT rules that govern the use of safeguard import measures, and bringing under the GATT rules the restrictive measures that had been applied, outside GATT, in the trade of ships, automobiles, steel and some other products. The 1982 Ministerial meeting requested the GATT Council to draw up "a comprehensive understanding on safeguards", and over the next two years a series of consultations were held with member countries in an attempt to reach such an understanding.

However, a 1984 report by the chairman of the Council demonstrated that divergent views continued to exist on the issues involved. It was generally recognized that the use of safeguards should be limited to situations where imports caused or threatened serious injury to domestic producers, and that safeguard measures should be temporary and progressively liberalized. It was also recognized that exporting countries should retain the right to retaliate against safeguard measures affecting their trade, although this right could not be effectively exercised in practice by developing countries. However, retaliatory measures should be avoided because of their disruptive effects on trade.

At the same time, the report suggested that longstanding differences continued to exist on whether safeguard measures should be global in their application or might be applied on a selective basis to exporting countries. There was also a lack of agreement on phasing out and prohibiting the so-called "grey area" arrangements that had been put in place outside the GATT rules, rather than in conformity with the provisions of Article XIX; no further progress was made either on the notification and surveillance of "grey area" measures.

Trade in Textiles and Clothing

At the 1982 Ministerial meeting it was agreed that the Contracting Parties should examine ways of bringing about further liberalization in the textiles and clothing sector, including possibilities for bringing this trade back under normal GATT rules. In effect, this meant the abandonment of the Multifibre Arrangement and the controls under it on exports from "low-cost" countries. In May 1984, the GATT Council established a working party to carry out this study. The working party met twelve times in 1984–85. Although it failed to develop any common views on the liberalization of world trade in textiles and clothing, the work of this group increased pressure for the eventual termination of the Multifibre Arrangement.

Dispute Settlement Procedures

The 1982 Ministerial meeting did not call for any major changes in the GATT procedures for dispute settlement, but made a number of improvements in the operation of these procedures. At its annual meeting in November 1984 the Contracting Parties pointed to the need for clear understandings on the timeframes for agreement in the following areas: dispute settlement processes under the General Agreement and the Tokyo Round codes; the process by which the recommendations of dispute panels were approved; and follow-up action by member countries in response to decisions in GATT on disputes. However, no agreement was reached by the Contracting Parties on these basic issues. The only improvement made to the process was to establish a roster of non-governmental experts to serve on GATT dispute panels, who would be nominated by individual member countries. The GATT Director General was authorized to draw on this roster for panelists, especially in the event of deadlocks over the composition of panels.

Trade in Natural Resource Products

The 1982 Ministerial meeting launched a study of particular importance to Canada and other exporters of non-ferrous metals and minerals, forestry products and fish and fisheries products. Problems of trade in these products were examined by a special working party over a two year period (1984–1986). It was found that trade in all three sectors was restricted by tariffs and a variety of non-tariff measures, and that tariffs of many importing countries "escalated" according to degree of processing, giving high levels of "effective protection" to their domestic processing industries. Trade barriers in the fisheries sector were especially numerous and mostly designed to encourage processing in importing countries. Trade was further complicated by limits on access to fisheries areas and changes in jurisdiction over these areas, as well as by bilateral agreements that linked access to markets to access to fisheries. The conclusion of the working party in 1986 was that in all three sectors trade liberalization could best be achieved through a process of multilateral negotiations, which by then were planned to take place.

Adoption of the Harmonized Tariff System

One major advance in the GATT system in the 1980s was the adoption by many GATT member countries of the Harmonized System (HS) of tariff classification, which had been developed by the Customs Cooperation Council in Brussels. Following the 1982 Ministerial meeting, a GATT committee on tariffs coordinated the complex arrangements involved in the adoption of the new system. Its objectives were: to provide greater uniformity and simplicity among the tariffs of member countries; and to facilitate the conduct of trade and the analysis of trade data. It was agreed that conversion to the new system should not involve any changes in existing levels of protection, and it was recognized that the conversion would in some cases require negotiations with exporting countries.

Since the new Harmonized System entered into force at the beginning of 1988, 64 out of 101 GATT members, including Canada and the United States, have adopted this system of customs nomenclature. This represents more than 95 percent of GATT trade.[4] Moreover, the tariff classification of the Harmonized System is used extensively in the rules of origin in the Canada-U.S. Free Trade Agreement.

The adoption of the new system involved the development by the GATT Secretariat of the Integrated Data Base (IDB) containing details of the tariffs and non-tariff measures of a number of main trading countries, including Canada. The purpose of the data base is to act as an information source in the negotiations in the tariff and non-tariff measures during the Uruguay Round. Over 36 countries (with the EC countries represented as one member) have indicated their intention of participating in the system. These countries represent over 94 percent of total trade of GATT contracting parties.[5]

Other Elements of 1982 Work Program

Pursuant to the Ministerial meetings in 1982, and in response to pressure by the United States, a number of countries, including Canada, undertook a series of reviews of submissions on trade in services. These reviews served to bring out the complex issues involved in negotiations for GATT rules in this area of trade. A special working party in a series of meetings in 1982–83 continued an analysis of the links between structural adjustment and trade policy.

In 1985, the GATT Committee on Trade and Development carried out a series of consultations with individual member countries, including Canada. These consultations examined the operation of their respective trade policies with developing countries and reviewed action taken by individual developed countries to provide duty-free treatment for exports from the "least developed" countries. Canada now provides duty-free access for most products from 41 least developed countries, with some exclusions for "sensitive" products such as textiles, clothing and footwear.

The Leutwiler Report

In 1983, the GATT Director General invited seven "eminent persons" to study and report on problems facing the international trade system. Chaired by Fritz Leutwiler of Switzerland, this group presented a report in 1985 that contained a perceptive analysis of the problems facing the GATT system and a set of far-reaching proposals for the reform of the system. The group made fifteen recommendations, a number of which found their way later on the Uruguay Round agenda. Among their recommendations:

- We support the launching of a new round of GATT negotiations, provided they are directed toward the primary goal of strengthening the multilateral trading system and further opening world markets.

- A timetable and procedures should be established to bring into conformity with GATT rules voluntary export restraints, orderly marketing agreements, discriminatory import restrictions, and other trade policy measures of both developed and developing countries which are inconsistent with the obligations of contracting parties under the GATT.

- At the international level, trade policy and the functioning of the trading system should be made more open. Countries should be subject to regular oversight of surveillance of their policies and actions, about which the GATT Secretariat should collect and publish information.

- When emergency "safeguard" protection for particular industries is needed, it should be provided only in accordance with the rules: it should not discriminate between different suppliers, should be time-limited, should be linked to adjustment assistance, and should be subject to continuing surveillance.

- Rules on subsidies need to be revised, clarified and made more effective. When subsidies are permitted they should be granted only after full and detailed scrutiny.

- Developing countries receive special treatment in the GATT rules. But such special treatment is of limited value. Far greater emphasis should be placed on permitting and encouraging developing countries to take advantage of their competitive strengths, and on integrating them more fully into the trading system, with all the appropriate rights and responsibilities that this entails.

- Trade in textiles and clothing should be fully subject to the ordinary rules of the GATT.

- To ensure continuous high-level attention to problems in international trade policy, and to encourage prompt negotiation of solutions to them, a permanent Ministerial-level body should be established in GATT.

- The health and even the maintenance of the trading system, and the stability of the financial system, are linked to a satisfactory resolution of the world debt problem, adequate flows of development finance, better international coordination of macroeconomic policies, and greater consistency between trade and financial policies.[6]

Regional Trade Arrangements

During the 1980s, a number of new regional trade arrangements were formed among GATT members, including the 1989 Canada-United States Free Trade Agreement (FTA). While these arrangements will achieve a significant liberalization of world trade, they represent a further reduction in the amount of world trade that is conducted on a most-favoured-nation basis.

In 1983, a GATT working party concluded its examination of the accession in 1979 of Greece to the European Community. As in the case of many other regional trade arrangements, no consensus could be reached on whether the terms of accession are compatible with GATT rules. Similarly, after two years of study, members of a GATT working party examining the terms of accession of Spain and Portugal in 1986 to the Community could not agree on the consistency of the Treaty with the GATT. The EC argued that, as a result of their accession, Spain and Portugal would be affecting substantial tariff reductions and liberalizing other regulations of commerce, thus opening their markets to the benefits of all contracting parties. On the other hand, the United States argued that the inconsistency of the terms of the Community's latest enlargement with Article XXIV:5 was clear: the trade restrictions, both tariff and non-tariff, imposed at the time of the enlargement were on the whole higher and more restrictive than the general incidence of such barriers prior to Spain and Portugal's accession to the Community. The United States also did not share the interpretation given by the EC of its other obligations under Article XXIV.[7] The United States was also concerned about the adverse effects on its exports of certain agricultural products to the new member countries.

In October 1988, the chairman of the working party reported that, because of divergent views, the report could only summarize the views expressed during the discussion. Many delegations supported the adoption of the report, but some, such as the United States, expressed disappointment that no consensus had been reached.

The free trade agreement concluded between the United States and Israel was examined by a GATT working party in early 1987, but no consensus was achieved on its compatibility with GATT rules. The 1983 Australia-New Zealand Closer Economic Relations Trade Agreement, which superseded an earlier free trade agreement, encountered fewer difficulties during its examination by GATT; in mid-1988 further liberalization of trade was achieved under this agreement and its scope was extended to, among other things, services. It is noteworthy that Australia and New Zealand have eliminated their anti-dumping laws for bilateral trade after the five-year review of the 1983 arrangement.

In the mid-1980s, both Canada and the United States introduced special arrangements to assist the exports of Caribbean countries, which required the approval of the GATT Contracting Parties. In 1984, the United States obtained a waiver from GATT to cover its Caribbean Basin Initiative, by which the United States accords duty-free treatment to most imports from a group of Caribbean and Central American countries. In 1986, Canada obtained a waiver from GATT to implement its Caribcan arrangement, whereby imports of most products from the Commonwealth Caribbean countries were allowed to enter Canada free of duty.

Following the entry into force of the Canada-United States Free Trade Agreement on 1 January 1989, the GATT Council agreed at its February meeting to establish a working party to examine the compatibility of this agreement with GATT provisions, particularly Article XXIV. As of June 1991, the working party had not concluded its examination. In the same month, negotiations began on a trilateral free trade arrangement among Canada, the United States and Mexico.[8]

Operation of the Tokyo Round Agreements

Since 1980, a new and important feature of GATT activities has been the operation of the various supplementary codes and agreements that were established by the Tokyo Round. Most of these codes and agreements were designed to clarify and elaborate important provisions of the General Agreement; others created new rules in areas not covered by the General Agreement. Each has a committee of its members that meets regularly to oversee its operation, monitor measures taken by participating countries that are covered by its provisions, and help settle disputes among the participants. These arrangements are self-standing agreements, separate from the General Agreement and the membership of these codes differs significantly from GATT membership.

Membership in the Uruguay Round codes, as of 31 December 1989, is as follows:

• Subsidies/Countervail—24 members

• Anti-dumping—25 members

• Technical Barriers—39 members

• Government Procurement—12 members

• Import Licencing—27 members

• Customs Valuation—28 members

• Civil Aircraft—22 members

• Dairy Arrangements—16 members

• Bovine Meat Arrangements—27 members*

Participation by the developed countries in these ancillary codes and agreements is almost universal. There is limited participation by developing countries, although they have sought to encourage, through the establishment

---

* The European Community is the single member of these codes, while the E.C. member states remain contracting parties to the GATT.

of committees, broader membership. Canada is a member of all of the Tokyo Round codes and agreements except the Dairy Arrangement.

The Uruguay Round includes a review of these Tokyo Round codes and agreements, and could result in significant changes in the provisions of some of them. Indeed, Agreement on Trade in Civil Aircraft was amended in 1985 to extend its coverage to further categories of products; and the Code on Government Procurement was amended in 1988 to lower the threshold of government purchases that are covered by it, and to cover leasing contracts.

In October 1990, agreement was reached on a comprehensive revision of the Tokyo Round Agreement on Technical Barriers to Trade and on improvements to the agreements on import licensing and customs valuation. These results will remain provisional pending the final outcome of the Uruguay Round.[9]

The Multifibre Arrangement

In 1986 the Multifibre Arrangement (MFA) was extended for a period of five years by its 43 members; this was the third extension of the MFA. The MFA now covers a broad range of textile and clothing products, including those made of cotton, artificial fibres, wool, silk and certain vegetable fibres, and blends of them. Over the years the MFA has become progressively more restrictive; within its framework most of the developed countries have concluded bilateral arrangements with low-cost developing country suppliers to restrict their exports. The operation of the MFA is overseen by the GATT Textiles Committee, on which all its members are represented.

The Textiles Surveillance Body (TSB) monitors and supervises the detailed implementation of the MFA. In January 1990, the membership of the TSB was enlarged by two to ten members. For 1991, the TSB consisted of the following parties: Canada, the EC, Finland, Hungary (for the first six months, thereafter a member country of the ITCB), Japan, Korea, Peru, Thailand, Turkey and the United States. Canada rotates membership with the Nordic countries to give the membership a balanced representation.

The Uruguay Round is the first time that the textiles and clothing sector has been specifically included in multilateral trade negotiations. At the mid-term review, there was a commitment to engage in substantive negotiations. However, there was no consensus on how to reach an agreement: some of the developing countries (exporters) sought a commitment with a clear timetable and phase-out program, while developed countries (importers) were looking for linkages between liberalization and progress in other areas such as intellectual property.

Proposals were subsequently tabled by Canada, the United States, the EC, Japan, a group of developing countries, members of the ITCB, Switzerland, and the Nordic countries. There were proposals on a quota expansion scheme, global quotas, tariff equivalents, and a tariff quota.

No agreement, however, was reached in Brussels in December 1990. Certain bilateral agreement have been renewed with improved access provisions (Austria, Sweden) and many existing agreements were modified (Canada, the EC, and the United States). In several cases, the modifications were required for the introduction of the Harmonized System (the EC and the United States). In other cases, new restrictions were added.

There has been some movement toward greater liberalization: the EC has liberalized some restrictions on imports from several central and East European countries; Norway has liberalized some provisions in its agreements; Finland has replaced a few restraint agreements with consultations; and Sweden has announced it will implement its earlier decision to eliminate MFA restrictions as of 1 August 1991.[11]

Presently, however, there is a great deal of uncertainty. Current MFA agreements are scheduled to expire on 1 August 1991; the failure to conclude the Uruguay Round before this date introduces a major element of uncertainty in the regulation of trade in the textile and clothing sectors.

Dispute Settlement in the 1980s

The use of independent panels in GATT to examine and assist the settlement of disputes has become more frequent over the past decade, especially to deal with disputes among the United States, the European Community (EC), Japan and Canada. Between 1979 and 1988 over fifty disputes were referred to the GATT Council and some twenty-five of these disputes were dealt with under the panel process or are under consideration for the panel process. The others were settled by consultations between the parties in one way or another. In 1987 alone, sixteen disputes were brought before the GATT Council.

The year 1988 was itself a milestone with respect to the GATT dispute settlement system. The year saw the establishment by the Council of an unprecedented number of panels: thirteen dispute settlement panels were established—almost double the 1987 total, which itself was a record.[12] All but one of the panels related to agricultural products.

Canada was involved in twelve of these panel processes during 1979–1988. In eight of the cases Canada was the complainant either alone or in company with other countries. Four cases involved measures taken by the United States, three involved measures by Japan, and two cases involved measures by the European Community. The other four cases involved measures by the European Community. With respect to four cases involving complaints against Canada, two were by the United States, one by the European Community and one by South Africa. Nine of these twelve disputes involving Canada were resolved by the GATT process; in two recent cases Canada has announced action it will take in response to panel reports; and a further case involving a Canadian complaint against Japan is being examined by a panel.

The operation of the GATT dispute settlement process in the 1980s indicates that it is working reasonably successfully, and that it has become a major and much used feature of the GATT system. Most of the unsuccessful cases fall into two categories: disputes over agricultural trade, where the GATT rules are less precise and compliance with them is uneven; and disputes that are essentially political, such as Nicaragua's complaint against the U.S. trade embargo. In the 1970s, the process bogged down in disputes over the Domestic International Sales Corporation (DISC) program in the United States and the tax practices affecting exports followed by France, Belgium and the Netherlands. These cases essentially involved the operation of tax policies, as distinct from trade policies.

The problems with the DISC cases and more recent experience in the 1980s have demonstrated some weaknesses in the GATT dispute settlement process. For example, a party to a dispute can block the process by denying a consensus decision by the GATT Council to appoint a panel, or to adopt a panel report. Without blocking the process, a party to a dispute may simply decline to carry out the agreed Council recommendations and take its chances on retaliation by the injured party. The developing countries have long complained that in practical terms the GATT dispute resolution process cannot be used to deal with their complaints because of their dependence on trade with larger, more powerful trading partners. Moreover, the process can sometimes lead to bilateral settlements of disputes that leave intact measures that may not be compatible with GATT rules.

These and other weaknesses in the GATT dispute resolution process are well recognized. In the preliminary stages of the Uruguay Round it was acknowledged that this important element of the GATT system needed strengthening and reform, and a variety of proposals have been introduced to improve the system.

Separately from the dispute settlement processes under the General Agreement, the various supplementary codes and agreements concluded during the Tokyo Round have their own procedures for the resolution of disputes arising from their operation. Most of the disputes have arisen under the Code on Subsidies and Countervailing Duties; many of them were resolved without bringing the panel process into operation, and some others remain unresolved. The two disputes that involved Canada dealt with complaints by the European Community about Canadian countervailing duties on boneless manufacturing beef and on pasta products.

Growth of GATT Membership

In the 1980s, membership in GATT steadily expanded, demonstrating a broadening of interest on the part of developing countries in participation in the international trade system. In 1980 eighty-five countries were members, two others had acceded provisionally and another thirty applied the General Agreement on a de facto basis. Membership has since grown to 101 contracting parties to include: the Philippines (1980), Colombia (1981), Zambia (1981), Thailand (1982), the Maldives (1983), Belize (1983), Hong Kong (1986), Mexico (1986), Antigua and Barbuda (1986), Morocco (1987), Lesotho (1988), Tunisia (1988), Costa Rica (1990) and Macau (1991). Another two countries have signed their protocols of accession, which will take effect 30 days after ratification by their respective legislative bodies: El Salvador (13 December 1990) and Guatemala (16 April 1991). In addition, six other countries are the process of negotiating membership: Algeria, Bulgaria, China, Honduras, Nepal and Paraguay. Vietnam and Mongolia are exploring the possibility of joining the GATT.[13]

Membership in the GATT for the People's Republic of China would be an event of special importance: China was a founding member of GATT; it occupies an important position in world trade; and China's resumption of membership is likely to contribute to significant changes in its economic and trade system. Another significant development is the granting of observer status, on 16 May 1990, to the Soviet Union. This represents a major economic and political development in the world trade system.

The GATT Secretariat in the 1980s

Arthur Dunkel of Switzerland, who was appointed in 1980 as Director General to succeed Olivier Long, was reappointed in 1986 for a further three year term. Mr. Dunkel was subsequently reappointed twice: in 1989 for a two year term ending 30 September 1991; and again, after the GATT Council recommended that his contract be extended for a final period to the end of 1992.

The pace of GATT activities in the 1980s is reflected in the growth of the budget, which amounted in 1980 to around 50 million Swiss Francs and in 1987 to 61 million Swiss Francs (about Cdn $55 million). Canada contributes around 5 per cent of the budget, an amount determined by Canada's share of world trade.

The GATT Secretariat in 1987 numbered around three hundred and fifty. GATT continues to be regarded as among the best managed and most efficient of the United Nations organizations. Its budget finances the International Trade Centre (ITC) jointly with the United Nations Conference on Trade and Development (UNCTAD). The ITC operates a program of seminars and other activities in support of the trade promotion efforts of developing countries.

Developments in GATT leading to the Uruguay Round and the progress of the negotiations are described in readily available publications by the Secretariat. These include the annual series *Basic Instrument and Selected Documents*; an annual review titled *GATT Activities*; and the periodic newsletter *GATT Focus*. A special series of press releases, *News of the Uruguay*

Round, describes the activities of the various groups that are carrying out negotiations on issues in the Uruguay Round. The Secretariat also publishes annually a series titled *International Trade* that contains a detailed analysis of world trends and issues in world trade by main product categories and geographic regions.

In 1983, the Secretariat introduced a new publication, *Review of Developments in the Trading System*, which summarizes developments in the trade policies and practices of member countries. Twelve series of the reviews were published until February 1989. The review was terminated, in part because at the mid-term review in Montreal a decision was made to establish a trade policy review mechanism (TPRM) in the GATT Secretariat.

All the above publications are available either free of charge or at various prices from the Secretariat, in English and French (some in Spanish).[14]

Preparations for the Uruguay Round

As noted earlier, the first half of the 1980s was a period of great stress and disorder within the multilateral trade system: the GATT was widely perceived to be incapable of preventing the drift into protectionism and restrictive bilateral agreements; the system itself appeared to be threatened and rudderless; and serious frictions developed among the main trading countries. The United States was preoccupied with budgetary and trade deficits and with trade conflicts with the European Community and Japan. The European Community was engaged in the enlargement of its membership to include Greece, Spain and Portugal, and was preoccupied with bilateral trade relations with Japan. For its part, Japan made little effort to assume a leadership role corresponding to its eminent position in world trade and finance. Canada was engaged first in a series of trade frictions with the United States and later with negotiations for a free trade agreement with its large neighbour. Many developing countries, heavily burdened by debt repayments, further tightened import restrictions. Scholars and other GATT-watchers published studies that expressed despair about the future of GATT.

The main trading countries, therefore, moved forward with hesitation and lack of enthusiasm towards a new round of negotiations. During 1984, the United States and Japan joined in calling for a new round. Canada supported the initiative but the European Community was disinterested, as were a number of developing countries. The subject was discussed, without coming to any decision, at a Quadrilateral meeting in Tokyo in early 1985 of trade ministers from the European Community, United States, Canada and Japan. In May 1985, at the G7 Summit in Bonn, the United States pressed unsuccessfully against the opposition of France for a decision on a date to open the negotiations. By July, a further meeting of the Quadrilateral group of trade ministers ended with agreement on holding a new round, with trade in services on the agenda. However, a number of developing countries continued to resist opening a new round of multilateral negotiations, partly because of their opposition to negotiations in the "new areas"—trade in services, and the trade-related aspects of intellectual property and foreign investment.

In an effort to force a decision, the United States called for a special session of the GATT Contracting Parties in September 1985. In a statement after the meeting, the parties announced that "a preparatory process on the proposed new round of multilateral trade negotiations has now been initiated." Later, the regular annual session of the Contracting Parties in November established a preparatory committee to "prepare by mid-July 1986 recommendations for the program of negotiations for adoption at a Ministerial Meeting to be held in September 1986."[15] This Ministerial meeting was held, as planned, in Punta del Este, Uruguay, under the chairmanship of the Uruguayan foreign minister.

The Punta del Este Declaration

The Punta del Este Declaration formally launched the Uruguay Round and set the agenda for multilateral negotiations. The agenda set by this Declaration is very ambitious. It covers virtually all of the unresolved issues in GATT, with agricultural trade issues high on the list. It is aimed at major new liberalization of world trade, involving the further removal of tariffs and non-tariff measures. It is designed to bring a large number of bilateral, restrictive trade arrangements within GATT disciplines. It proposes to enlarge substantially the area of GATT rules to cover "new issues"—trade in services, and the trade-related aspects of the protection of intellectual property and of barriers to foreign investment.

During the process of drafting the Declaration, coalitions of the middle sized and smaller member countries emerged that were anxious to have the negotiations launched without delay. In particular, Canada joined with Australia, New Zealand and the member countries of the European Free Trade Association (EFTA). This group was later enlarged to include some twenty like-minded developing countries, and then further enlarged to include the three larger economic powers, the United States, the European Community and Japan. Outside this grouping, a coalition of ten developing countries formed, led by India and Brazil, to resist the inclusion in the negotiations of the "new issues." These countries argued that negotiations should rather be aimed primarily at resolving outstanding issues in GATT surrounding trade in goods.

Agreement on the text of the Declaration at Punta del Este, therefore, represented a difficult process of consensus-building: compromises had to be made on the text of many sections of the Declaration; differences over the inclusion of "new issues" had to be managed; and agreement had to be reached on the structure and organization of the negotiations. As an example, one compromise involved dividing the negotiations on trade in services from the negotiations on trade in goods, but placing both sets of negotiations under the direction of a Trade Negotiations Committee, on which all participating countries are represented.

This process of consensus-building in particular issue-areas within coalitions of like-minded countries has continued throughout the Uruguay Round negotiations. The so-called "Cairns group" is one such coalition; it comprises fourteen members, including nine developing countries, in pursuit of reducing distortions and obstacles to world trade in agricultural products. Canada is a member of the Cairns group, which also includes Australia, New Zealand, Argentina, Thailand and other agricultural exporting countries, but not the United States, European Community or Japan.[16] Another coalition is the so-called "de la Paix group," which includes Canada and a number of middle sized and smaller member countries, including several developing countries, that are concerned with advancing the negotiations on tariff reductions as well as some other elements of the negotiations.

The emergence of these and other broadly based coalitions of like-minded countries in pursuit of common interests on particular issues is only one of the features of the Uruguay Round that distinguishes it from earlier rounds of GATT negotiations. Other distinguishing features include: the addition of "new issues" to the negotiations; the greater complexity of the negotiations due to uncertainty about the nature and scope of multilateral rules that might be adopted; the fundamental changes in the nature of GATT as an organization that may be required and the possible role of GATT in the monitoring and surveillance of the domestic policies of member countries that affect international trade; and a membership that is larger than ever before in a world economy that is becoming increasingly interdependent.[17]

Organization of the Negotiations

The broad and complex structure of the Uruguay Round negotiations can be summarized as follows:

- The negotiations are open to all GATT contracting parties, provisional members, countries applying GATT on a de facto basis, countries which have notified their intention to negotiate terms of membership, and developing countries that by 30 April 1987 initiated procedures for accession to GATT and for negotiating terms of accession during the Uruguay Round. As of April 1991, there are 101 contracting parties to the current GATT Round.

- Only GATT contracting parties can participate in negotiations relating to the amendment or application of GATT provisions, or the negotiation of new provisions.

- Participants agreed "not to take any trade restrictive or distorting measures" inconsistent with GATT or its supplementary codes; not to use GATT-permitted measures which go beyond "that which is necessary to remedy specific situations"; and not to take trade measures designed to improve negotiating positions. A "Surveillance Body" was set up later to oversee commitments to these standstill and rollback commitments.

- Trade restrictive measures that are inconsistent with GATT or GATT codes are to be "phased out or brought into conformity" by the end of the Uruguay Round.

- A Trade Negotiations Committee (TNC) was established, with membership of all participants. A "Group on Negotiations on Goods" (GNG) is carrying out the program of negotiations covering trade in goods. Arthur Dunkel, Director General of GATT, is chairman of both the TNC and the GNG at the officials level. Since the launching of the Uruguay Round, H.E. Ricardo Zerbina, and later H.E. Hector Gros Espiell, the Uruguay Foreign Minister, has held the post of Chairman of the TNC at the ministerial level. A "Group on Negotiations on Services" (GNS) is dealing with the negotiations in the services area; its chairman is Felipe Jaramillo of Colombia.

- The Group on Negotiations on Goods was authorized, among other things, to "designate the appropriate mechanism" for the surveillance of the commitments to standstill and roll back of trade restrictive measures; to establish negotiating groups as required; to decide on the inclusion of additional issues in the negotiations; and to coordinate the work of the various negotiating groups.

- The principle of "differential and more favourable treatment" for developing countries will apply to the negotiations. However, those countries at a higher stage of development are expected "to make contributions or negotiated concessions or take other mutually agreed action under the provisions and procedures of the General Agreement."

The "subjects for negotiations," apart from trade in services, as set out in the Declaration, were later assigned to fourteen negotiating groups:

- tariffs
- non-tariff measures
- natural resource-based products
- textiles and clothing
- agriculture
- tropical products

- GATT articles
- MTN agreements and arrangements
- safeguards
- subsidies and countervailing measures
- trade-related aspects of intellectual property rights, including trade in counterfeit goods (now known as TRIPS)
- dispute settlement
- trade-related investment measures (TRIMS)
- functioning of the GATT system (FOGS)

Mid-Term Ministerial Meeting in Montreal

The mid-term review of the Uruguay Round of Multilateral Trade Negotiations was held in Montreal on December 5-9, 1988. Agreement was reached on 11 of the 15 subjects covered by the negotiating agenda. However, in four key areas—agriculture, textiles, protection of intellectual property rights, and reforms of the safeguard systems—no agreement was reached. Specifically, negotiations foundered on the scale of the reform to be undertaken in the agricultural sector and on the procedures to eliminate all subsidies having a trade-distorting effect within a specified timeframe. The priority placed by a number of countries on an agreement on agriculture helped to weaken the pace of negotiations on the other three subjects that have not yet been settled.

On the positive side, agreement was reached on approximately U.S.$25 billion worth of concessions on tariffs and non-tariff measures related to tropical products. In the new area of services, there was an agreement on a framework to govern trade that included: transparency concerning existing laws, regulations and agreements; the principle of national treatment for foreign suppliers as an element of market access and non-discrimination among them; progressive liberalization of trade in services; and assurances for the growing participation of developing countries in the trade in services.

Some of the agreements relate to the ability of the GATT to act on economic concerns. For example, there was agreement that trade dispute settlement should be accelerated and made more effective. There was also a consensus that a regular review of trade policies of GATT members and their impact on the trading system should also be conducted. Ministers also recognized the need to take a broader view of issues, taking account of the increasing interdependence of economic, trade, financial and monetary policies. The holding of ministerial sessions of the contracting parties at least every two years will also provide the GATT with greater weight in national political circles and strengthen adherence by governments to the GATT system and its rules.

With respect to safeguard issues, the stumbling block has been longstanding arguments about "selectivity", "coverage", and "surveillance." During the first half of the Uruguay Round, negotiations focused on those elements which could form the basis of a safeguard agreement: transparency, temporary nature of safeguard actions, degressivity and structural adjustment, compensation and retaliation, product and geographic coverage, "grey-area" measures, multilateral surveillance and dispute settlement, special and different treatment for developing countries, and legal framework. Real movement, however, did not begin until the mid-term review, during which a procedural formula was largely accepted and an attempt was made to secure immediate agreement on certain principles: that safeguard actions should be of limited duration and non-discriminatory; and that "grey-area" measures, applied selectively, should be proscribed.

With respect to dispute settlement, agreement was reached at the mid-term review on a system, which was subsequently adopted by the GATT Council in April 1989, that would be implemented on a trial basis for the remainder of the Uruguay Round. The system's main features included:

- specific time limits on procedures for consultations;

- arbitration as an alternative to panel proceedings;

- dispute panels to be established at the first GATT Council meeting following the one at which the initial request for a panel was made;

- strict time limits for determining terms of reference and composition of panels as well as a time schedule for their work (normally a six months maximum);

- delays to the adoption of panel reports by the Council to be avoided;

- timeframe from initiating consultations to decision on report by Council not to exceed 15 months;

- legal advice for developing contracting parties involved in a dispute; and

- implementation of panel recommendations to be considered by Council no more than six months after adoption of the panel report.

Still, by the end of the mid-term review, it was clear that difficult political decisions still had to be made and that agricultural trade reform would further retard any progress in the other areas. Nevertheless, given the global nature of the negotiations, ministers decided that further efforts should be made to reach agreement and, consequently, they extended the deadline for the Trade Committee to the beginning of April. The effect of this was to put on hold the positive accomplishments reached during the mid-term review.[18]

Ministerial Meeting, 5-8 April 1989

The 5-8 April 1989 Geneva meeting of the Trade Negotiations Committee completed the mid-term review of the Uruguay Round. Participants at the senior official level adopted decisions in the four outstanding subject areas of the Montreal meeting: agriculture, textiles and clothing, safeguards, and trade-related aspects of intellectual property rights. These agreements, along with the decisions on twelve others (including on standstill and rollback) adopted at Montreal, constituted the mid-term review package of results. There was also the decision for the immediate implementation of the agreed-upon improvements to the dispute settlement procedures and two elements related to the functioning of the GATT system—the trade policy review mechanism and increased ministerial involvement in GATT.

Several trade policy reviews have since taken place. Under the new review mechanism, the GATT Secretariat and the country under review prepare separate reports. A special GATT Council meeting reviews the reports and questions the country under review. The objective is to promote close adherence to GATT principles through greater transparency and understanding of the contracting parties' respective trade policies and practices. A caveat to the influence of the review mechanism is that it should not be the basis for either the enforcement of specific GATT obligations or a substitute for dispute settlement procedures.

In December 1989, the United States, Australia and Morocco were the first countries to undergo a series of trade policy reviews. In 1990, reviews were undertaken of the trade policies of Sweden, Columbia, Canada, Hong Kong, Japan and New Zealand. For 1991, reviews are scheduled for the following countries: the EC as a unit, Hungary, Indonesia, Bangladesh, Chile, Thailand, Norway, Switzerland, Nigeria, Argentina, Austria, Finland, Ghana, Singapore and the United States.

Under the review mechanism, four members of the GATT—the United States, Japan, the EC and Canada—are to be examined every two years. The next 16 countries to be examined—the list for which is determined by their share of world trade—are to be analyzed every four years. The trade policies and practices of the remaining contracting parties are to be reviewed every six years.[19]

The Final Countdown

The momentum began to accelerate after the April meeting in Geneva. A three-phase plan was developed to organize the completion of the Uruguay Round. The objective of the first phase, between September and December 1989, was to provide participants with the opportunity to complete the development of their respective positions. Delegations were also invited to table compromise proposals. The objective of the second phase, January to August 1990, was to reach broad agreement in every group. The final phase, up to the December 1990 Ministerial meeting in Brussels, was devoted to polishing the agreements and preparing the necessary legal instruments for final adoption.[20] During these final phases, Canada tabled a proposal for a World Trade Organization, an offer for agricultural trade reform, and an initiative on services.

During the final countdown, some progress was achieved. In June 1989, a draft text was tabled on a comprehensive agreement on safeguards, based upon proposals by the contracting parties and the basic principles of the GATT. In the May meeting leading up to the tabling of this text, ministers stressed the importance of re-establishing multilateral control over safeguards by inter alia, eliminating measures which escape such control. There was also recognition that safeguard measures are by definition of limited duration.[21] Meetings up to the end of 1989 were largely devoted to a detailed examination of the draft agreement. The issue of selective safeguard measures continued to be rejected by most participants.

In early 1990, the EC submitted a proposal concerning a selective safeguard regime that would be applicable in special circumstances. The proposal, however, received little support and generated scepticism.[22]

Ministerial Meeting in Brussels, 3-7 December 1990

The ministers of the GATT contracting parties gathered in Brussels in December 1990 to conclude the Uruguay Round. However, a deadlock again surfaced between the United States and the EC on agricultural reform, which squandered the accomplishments in other areas up to that point. After the meeting, GATT Director-General Arthur Dunkel was given the mandate to reconvene the TNC "at the appropriate level to conclude the negotiations at the date he considers appropriate in the light of his consultations." His consultations would be based on the draft Final Act embodying the results of the Uruguay Round negotiations submitted to the ministerial TNC meeting in Brussels, and the considerable amount of work carried out during the Brussels meeting.[23]

Developing Countries in the Uruguay Round

For many years the effectiveness of the GATT system has been weakened by perceptions in many developing countries that the international system of trade and payments embodied in the GATT and the international financial institutions was irrelevant and even hostile to their interests. These perceptions were understandable. The developed, industrialized countries, while declaring their dedication to a liberal trade system, continued to maintain a variety of tariff and non-tariff barriers to exports from developing countries and have progressively imposed more restrictive controls on their imports of textiles, clothing and some other products from developing country sources.

In recent years, the divisions and confrontations between the groups of developed and developing countries have moderated, reflecting in part changes in patterns of world production and trade. Many developing countries are playing a more active, constructive role in GATT activities; there is a growing recognition that a liberal world trade and payments system based on internationally agreed rules serves the interests of all countries and has special advantages for smaller, weaker countries; and there is evidence of a growing recognition among developing countries of their responsibility for the maintenance of an orderly, rule oriented trade system.[24]

As noted earlier, many developing countries were active in the preparations for the Uruguay Round; they participated in the drafting of the Punta del Este Declaration of September 1986 which launched the Round; and they are active in the fifteen groups which have opened negotiations on particular issues in Geneva. The developing countries have a varied range of interests in the Round, reflecting their particular patterns of production and trade, but their participation in the negotiations has been uneven. The smaller, least developed countries in sub-Saharan Africa and elsewhere face particular problems in providing the personnel and other resources in Geneva and their capitals that are needed to follow and participate in the detailed negotiations.

As an overview of the international trade system, this book does not attempt to analyze the numerous and complex issues on the agenda of the Uruguay Round, nor to analyze the special interests of developing countries in regard to these issues. Nevertheless, the participating developing countries are particularly interested in the following issues:

- the implementation of commitments on the standstill and rollback of protectionist trade measures, especially those affecting the exports of developing countries;

- evidence of early progress in the removal of tariffs and other barriers by the main trading countries to exports of the least developed countries, including tariffs and other barriers to their exports of agricultural products, processed resource products and manufactured products;

- early progress in the removal by the main trading countries of tariffs and other barriers to the exports of tropical products, including the processed forms of tropical products;

- prospects for improvement of the GATT rules governing the use of "safeguard" import measures; for bringing so-called "grey area" measures under GATT disciplines; and for resisting proposals for the "selective" use of GATT safeguard measures against particular exporting countries;

- early agreement on a framework for the removal of distortions and trade restrictions in the agricultural sector, for the reduction of subsidies especially by the main trading countries, and for bringing agricultural trade more effectively under GATT rules and disciplines;

- progress towards agreement on the abandonment of the Multifibre Arrangement, for the phasing out of restrictive arrangements under the MFA, and for bringing trade in textiles and clothing back under the normal GATT rules;

- reducing most-favoured-nation tariffs especially on products of export interest to developing countries, and in sectors where preferential tariff rates have not been introduced for exports of developing countries;

- early agreement on strengthening the monitoring and surveillance functions of GATT, so as to bring to light and analyze the evolving trade policies and practices of all member countries; and introducing regular meetings at the Ministerial level for discussions of important issues in the world trade system;

- early progress towards more effective coordination between GATT, the International Monetary Fund, the World Bank and other international banks;

- proposals for strengthening the GATT dispute settlement provisions in ways that make the process more open for use by developing countries;

- progress in the liberalization of the trade regimes of the developing countries, in support of their own economic development and as a contribution to the achievement of a more liberal world trade system;

- progress towards the "graduation" of the more advanced developing countries, in ways which avoid increasing barriers to their exports but which involve acceptance by them of the normal rules of GATT;

- clarification of the issues surrounding proposals for extending GATT rules to cover trade in services, the trade related aspects of the protection of intellectual property and the trade related aspects of controls on foreign investment.[25]

The list of these issues indicates the large stake of developing countries in the Uruguay Round; it also indicates that the active participation of the developing countries in the negotiations is essential to a successful, balanced outcome. The Uruguay Round offers new opportunities for developing countries, individually and collectively, to redefine their role in the GATT system, to participate in shaping the agenda of the trade system over the next decade, and to pursue their separate and common objectives at the negotiating table, in cooperation with other GATT members with similar objectives. These countries stand to gain from the further liberalization of world trade in sectors of special interest to them; and their role in the system would be strengthened by the institutional reforms that are under discussion, such as for stronger monitoring and surveillance functions for GATT.

Notes

1. An account of developments during the Tokyo Round and the outcome of the negotiations is in GATT, Director-General, *The Tokyo Round of Multilateral Trade Negotiations* (1979) and *Supplementary Report* (1980), Geneva, the Secretariat.

2. Good accounts of strains in the GATT system in the early 1980s are in Miriam Camps and William Diebold, Jr., *The New Multilateralism: Can the World Trading System be Saved?*, New York, Council on Foreign Relations, 1983; and Amnuay Viravan and others, *Trade Routes to Sustained Economic Growth: Report for the United Nations by a Study Group of the Trade Policy Research Centre*, London, MacMillan, for the United Nations, 1987.

3. The GATT Work Program is set out in the Declaration adopted at the end of the November 1982 Ministerial Meeting, and is contained in GATT, *Basic Instruments and Selected Documents, Twenty-ninth Supplement*, Geneva, The Secretariat, 1983. Accounts of activities under the Work Program are contained in the Thirtieth Supplement (1984; the *Thirty-first Supplement* (1985); and the *Thirty-second Supplement* (1986).

4. *GATT Focus*, 76, November 1990, p. 6.

5. *Law and Practice Under the GATT*, p. 19.

6. The Leutwiler Report is in *Trade Policies for a Better Future: Proposals for Action*. Report to the GATT Director-General by a Group of Eminent Persons, Geneva, GATT Secretariat, 1985.

7. *GATT Activities*, 1988, pp. 101-03.

8. The relationship between the Canada-United States FTA and the GATT system is discussed in the following chapter. There is also a discussion of the deliberations leading up to the negotiations of a North American free trade agreement.

9. **Agreement on Technical Barriers to Trade**
Technical regulations and standards—adopted for safety, health, environmental protection or other reasons—can become unnecessary obstacles to trade. The revised text of this Agreement significantly improves and clarifies the key concept of "unnecessary obstacle" and introduces criteria for determining whether a measure is necessary. This clarification reduces the risk of disputes arising out of diverging interpretations and, when necessary, facilitates their settlement.
The disciplines of the Agreement are extended to requirements specified

in terms of processes and production methods which are of growing importance in international trade.

With respect to the standardizing activities of local government, non-government bodies as well as regional bodies of which parties are members, a Code of Good Practice lays down the principles with which they are expected to comply, and increase considerably the transparency of their activities.

Disciplines on Import Licensing

Negotiators in the Uruguay Round have provisionally agreed on a revised version of the Tokyo Round Agreement on Import Licensing procedures. The revised Agreement strengthens the disciplines on the users of import licensing systems and increases transparency and predictability for the trading community.

The Agreement aims at ensuring that licensing procedures do not act themselves as restrictions on imports; members commit themselves to having simple procedures and to administer them in a neutral and fair way.

Among revisions to the Agreement is a provision that non-automatic licensing procedures should be limited to what is absolutely necessary to administer the measures to which they apply. It sets criteria under which automatic licensing procedures are assumed not to have trade restrictive effects.

The revised Agreement will require parties to publish sufficient information for traders to know the basis for granting or allocating licenses. It provides for time limits for implementing new licenses in order to permit governments and traders to get acquainted with them and to permit other signatories to make comments.

Customs Valuation

Technical work has been completed on elaborating on an ad referendum basis, text addressing problems encountered by some of the developing countries in applying the Agreement on Customs Valuation or wishing to accede to it. It is expected that the final adoption of these texts would facilitate accession to the Agreement of a number of developing countries.

Based on Article VII of the General Agreement, the Customs Valuation Agreement sets a fair, uniform and neutral system for the valuation of goods for customs purposes. The Agreement prohibits the use of arbitrary or fictitious valuation.

One decision relates to cases where customs administrations have reasons to doubt the truth or accuracy of the declared value. It shifts the burden of proof from the customs administration to the importer, who can be asked to provide further evidence that the declared value represents the total amount actually paid or payable for the imported goods. If the customs administration maintains a reasonable doubt, it may be deemed that the customs value of the imported good cannot be determined by the declared value.

Source: *GATT Focus*, 75, October 1990, p. 5.

10. As of December 31, 1990, there were 40 participants in the Multifibre Arrangement (the EC counting as a single signatory): exporting countries—Argentina, Bangladesh, Brazil, China, Columbia, Costa Rica, Czechoslovakia, Dominican Republic, Egypt, El Salvador, Guatemala, Hong Kong, Pakistan, Peru, the Philippines, Poland, Romania, Singapore, Sri Lanka, Thailand, Turkey, Uruguay and

Yugoslavia; importing countries—Austria, Canada, the EC, Finland, Japan, Norway, Sweden, Switzerland, and the United States.

11. *GATT Press Release*, GATT/1509, 18 April 1991.

12. *GATT Activities 1988*, pp. 59-60.

13. *GATT Press Release*, 18 April 1991.

14. Orders for GATT publications can be placed with the Information Service of the General Agreement on Tariffs and Trade, Centre William Rappard, 154, rue de Lausanne, CH-1211 Geneva 21, Switzerland.

15. The Decision adopted by the GATT Contracting Parties at the Special Session in October 1985, and the Decision of the Contracting Parties at their Forty-first Session in November 1985 on the establishment of the preparatory committee are in *Basic Instruments and Selected Documents, Thirty-second Supplements*, Geneva: GATT Secretariat, 1986.

16. The full membership of the Cairns Group includes the following countries: Argentina, Australia, Brazil, Canada, Chile, Colombia, Fiji, Hungary, Indonesia, Malaysia, New Zealand, the Philippines, Thailand and Uruguay.

17. There are several good studies of issues in the Uruguay Round; these include Gary Clyde Hufbauer and Jeffrey J. Schott, *Trading for Growth: The Next Round of Trade Negotiations*, Institute for International Economics, Washington, D.C., 1985; and J. Michael Finger and Andrzej Olechowski, editors, *Multilateral Trade Negotiations*, World Bank. Washington, D.C., 1987.

18. *GATT Focus*, No. 59, January 1989.

19. *Law and Practice under the GATT*, Vol. II, p. 31.

20. *GATT Focus*, No. 64, November 1989.

21. *GATT Activities 1988*, pp. 46; *Law and Practices under the GATT*, p. 21.

22. *GATT Focus*, No. 69, March 1990, p. 4.

23. *GATT Focus*, No. 77, December 1990, p. 1.

24. There is a considerably body of recent literature on the participation of developing countries in GATT; these include Sidney Golt, *Developing Countries in the GATT System*, Trade Policy Research Centre, London, 1978; *Global Strategy for Growth*; a *Report on North South Issues*, by a study group under the chairmanship of Lord McFadzcan, Trade Policy Research Centre, London, 1981; T.N. Srinivasan, "Why Developing Countries Should Participate in the GATT System," in the *World Economy*, March 1981; and Robert E. Hudec, *Developing Countries in the GATT Legal System*, Trade Policy Research Centre, London, 1987.

25. A study by the Commonwealth Secretariat "The Uruguay Round of Multilateral Trade Negotiations"; London, 1987, covers many issues of special interest to developing countries. A "Statement on the Uruguay Round" by the South Commission, Geneva, 1988, contains an analysis of issues of special concern to developing countries, following a traditional "Group of 77" approach. The World Bank handbook *The Uruguay Round* contains several articles on issues of special interest to developing countries.

19

The Canada-United States Free Trade Agreement and the GATT

Beginning with the release of the elements of the Canada-United States Free Trade Agreement in October 1987 and reaching a climax during the 1988 Canadian federal election that culminated in the return to power of the Progressive Conservatives under Prime Minister Brian Mulroney, a fierce debate raged in Canada about the merits of a bilateral trade agreement with Canada's largest trading partner. During this debate, concerns were raised in both countries that such an agreement would conflict with and weaken the multilateral trade system that has been built during the postwar years around the General Agreement on Tariffs and Trade (GATT). In Canada, fears were also expressed that entering into a free trade agreement with the world's largest economic power would limit Canada's ability to play its traditional, leadership role in GATT, and limit Canada's independence in its trade relationships with other countries. These concerns must be taken seriously, and deserve continuing analysis and public debate. Since its inception, Canada and the United States have been among the more vigorous champions of the GATT. Any weakening of support by the two North American countries would have damaging consequences for the multilateral trade system. This issue is of particular importance in mid-1991 as Canada, the United States and Mexico negotiate a trilateral free trade agreement while the results of the Uruguay Round remain inconclusive.

The following is an analysis of the relationship of the Canada-United States Free Trade Agreement (FTA) with GATT, its compatibility with the GATT rules governing free trade areas, and the ability of members of free trade areas to participate independently in GATT and carry on their own, independent trade policies and relationships with the rest of the world.

Relationship of the Agreement with GATT

In 1935, thirteen years before the GATT came into being, Canada and the United States concluded a bilateral trade agreement—and extended it in 1938—that substantially lowered the very high tariffs on bilateral trade which were in place during most of the inter-war period. This agreement was suspended in 1947 when the two countries became members of the GATT.[1] Since that time, GATT has served as Canada's main trade agreement with the United States, as well as the main trade agreement of both countries with other GATT members. For both countries, GATT provides several benefits, including: a body of multilaterally agreed rules that govern their crossborder trade as well as their trade with other countries; a framework for the progressive reduction of tariffs and other barriers to crossborder trade along with barriers to world trade; and processes to resolve a number of bilateral trade disputes as well as individual disputes with other GATT members. Outside GATT, and until the present time, Canada and the United States have concluded only a few purely bilateral trade arrangements, notably the Automotive Agreement of 1965 that opened up the automotive sector to a nearly free trade environment.

Coming into force on 1 January 1989, the Canada-United States Free Trade Agreement (FTA) should be viewed neither as a replacement of GATT as the basic trade agreement between the two countries, nor as an alternative to GATT and its supplementary codes. The FTA leaves intact all of the GATT rights and obligations of each country vis-à-vis the other, while supplementing these with additional, bilateral rights and obligations. For example, GATT rules will continue to govern the countervailing and anti-dumping systems of the two countries—at least for 5-7 years while new joint rules governing the use of countervailing and anti-dumping duties are being drawn up.[2] The GATT processes also remain available to settle disputes arising from the many continuing commitments of the two countries under GATT.[3]

The Free Trade Agreement should thus be viewed as extending and elaborating the longstanding commitments of the two countries to each other under GATT. It completes the process of crossborder trade liberalization which has been underway under GATT and on a bilateral basis since the mid-1930s. The removal of tariffs on crossborder trade, which will take place in stages over 10 years, would be almost impossible to achieve through the process of multilateral negotiations under GATT. It would require the removal of Canadian and American tariffs on an MFN basis; this would involve, in effect, the agreement of most other GATT members to reciprocate by removing their import tariffs. This is an unlikely prospect in the foreseeable future, although it is hoped that existing world tariffs will be lowered substantially as an outcome of the current Uruguay Round of multilateral trade negotiations under GATT. In this regard, the liberalization achieved by Canada and the United States under the FTA will set a good example for further trade liberalization on a global scale.

The FTA reconfirms and extends GATT rules in a number of non-tariff areas. It contains special rules, beyond those in GATT, for the use of safeguard (escape clause) measures when these are used to limit surges in imports of particular products from each other and also when such measures are imposed on a global basis.[4] The Agreement will enlarge, beyond the opportunities opened by the GATT code on government procurement,[5] the volume of purchases by the two federal governments upon which firms from both countries can bid. The FTA goes beyond the GATT rules and prohibits the subsidization of crossborder exports of agricultural products.[6] The Agreement also clarifies and elaborates the GATT rules that are aimed at the avoidance of product standards that obstruct bilateral trade.[7] In some other non-tariff areas, the existing GATT rules will continue, as before, to apply to crossborder trade. As discussed above, the most notable of areas is GATT rules governing countervailing and anti-dumping duties.

The FTA also covers a number of areas that have not, so far, been covered by GATT rules, but where GATT rules might well be put in place as an outcome of the Uruguay Round. Some of these elements of the Agreement deal with longstanding or potential frictions between the two countries (e.g., controls on foreign investment, crossborder trade in certain services sectors, and trade in energy). The provisions of the FTA in these sectors could possibly set a useful example and precedent for the negotiations in the Uruguay Round. In some other areas that the FTA does not cover, such as the protection of intellectual property, efforts are being made in the Uruguay Round to draw up international rules and disciplines that might then be applied by Canada and the United States to each other.[8]

The GATT rules and procedures for the settlement of trade disputes will remain available for bilateral disputes between the two countries, especially those involving the extensive commitments to each other that will remain under GATT. However, the FTA also creates its own processes for the resolution of disputes arising from its operation. These are modelled on the GATT procedures but improve on them in several important ways. For example, upon the agreement by both countries, Chapter 18 of the FTA provides for recourse to "binding arbitration" involving the use of independent, joint panels. There is no corresponding provision for binding arbitration in GATT. Under the FTA, this arbitration process will be mandatory if one side complains about a "safeguard" measure on imports taken by the other. Moreover, under the Agreement, either party can compel a dispute to be referred to an independent binational panel for investigation and recommendations that are advisory in nature; under the GATT this process requires the agreement of both parties to a dispute.

There are separate provisions in Chapter 19 of the Agreement for creating binational panels to carry out "judicial reviews" of final determinations in either country for the use of countervailing and anti-dumping duties. These binational review panels replace judicial reviews of final determinations by domestic courts. Chapter 19 also prohibits either country from applying to the other changes in its anti-dumping or countervailing duty laws unless the other country is specifically named; any changes must be consistent with GATT rules as well as with "the objective and purpose" of the FTA. Moreover, either country may require a review by a binational panel of any changes in the other's anti-dumping or countervailing duty laws in the event of a dispute about these changes. These provisions, as noted earlier, apply over the first 5-7 years of the Agreement while new bilateral rules for countervailing and anti-dumping systems are being negotiated. They go well beyond any GATT rules, and are precedent-setting in subjecting decisions by domestic government agencies to an international court process.[9]

Since the implementation of the FTA, there has only been limited progress toward developing common rules on subsidy practices and trade remedy laws used to adjudicate disputes. Preparatory studies are being conducted, but both sides would prefer to wait for the outcome of the Uruguay Round before negotiating bilaterally. In its preparatory work, the Canadian side has a broad agenda, which includes research studies on U.S. subsidy practices and the development of a large data base of federal, state, provincial and municipal assistance programs.

Consistency of the FTA with GATT

GATT member countries have always had the right to form free trade areas (and customs unions) provided these conform to the rules that are set out in GATT Article XXIV; many such regional trade groups have been formed over the past few decades. When free trade areas do not conform with GATT rules, the countries concerned have had to obtain special "waivers" from their GATT obligations; these waivers require the approval of two-thirds of the GATT membership.

No such waiver was needed for the Canada-U.S. Free Trade Agreement, which is considered to be fully compatible with the Article XXIV rules of GATT. These rules call for the removal of "duties and other restrictive regulations of commerce with respect to substantially all the trade" between members of free trade areas either immediately or over a reasonable period of time. The FTA will achieve this result over the next 10 years. The FTA also accords with the GATT rule that prohibits member countries from using their arrangement to raise new barriers to trade with third countries.[10]

The GATT rules permit the continued maintenance of restrictions on agricultural trade between members of free trade areas where these are needed to protect supply management and similar farm support programs.[11] Canada's continued restrictions on imports of dairy products, eggs and poultry are thus in conformity with the rules of GATT. Although U.S. import restrictions on dairy products, sugar and some other agricultural products may not be similarly in accord with GATT rules, they are sheltered by a special waiver obtained by the United States in the mid-1950s.[12] The GATT rules also permit members of a free trade area to maintain restrictions on imports from each other that are imposed for environmental reasons (i.e., "to protect human, animal or plant life or health"), for national security reasons, and for some other specified reasons. They also allow members to impose restrictions on their exports of particular products to each other under conditions of "general or local short supply," provided such restrictions do not deny the importing country an "equitable share" of the restricted products.[13]

In effect, the GATT rules thus have established a large part of the framework within which the Canada-U.S. Free Trade Agreement, like many other regional trade groups, has been created. The Canada-U.S. Agreement is probably more in line with the GATT rules than most other free trade areas and customs unions that have been established among GATT member countries. The agreements that established the European Community and the European Free Trade Association, for example, contain features that are widely regarded as inconsistent with GATT, although the New Zealand-Australia and the U.S.-Israel free trade arrangements have encountered fewer objections in GATT.[14]

The actual approval of the GATT Contracting Parties was not required for Canada and the United States to proceed to implement the Free Trade Agreement. The European Community, the European Free Trade Association, and most other regional trade groups have neither been approved nor disapproved in Geneva but have nevertheless operated for many years. The GATT Contracting parties could have similarly withheld judgment on the Canada-U.S. Agreement without in any way blocking it. However, they can require the submission of periodic reports on its implementation and reserve the right to review its operation.

Trade Policy Independence

Members of free trade agreements, unlike members of customs unions, are able to maintain their own independent trade policies and relationships with third countries. They also retain, of course, their separate membership in GATT. This means that Canada, and also the United States, will be free to maintain different levels of tariffs and other barriers to trade with third countries. Similarly, the FTA does not restrict in any way the ability of each country to either negotiate separately in GATT and elsewhere with third countries to improve access to world markets or enter into its own, separate arrangements with third countries to achieve its particular objectives.

Canada and the United States will thus continue to participate separately and independently in GATT and in the Uruguay Round of multilateral trade negotiations. Both governments have stated their intention to play active, leadership roles in these negotiations, and the goals and objectives of Canada and the United States will not always be in harmony. However, there is nothing in the Agreement to prevent Canada from pursuing its own particular negotiating objectives and strategies. The Agreement does specifically call for bilateral co-operation in liberalizing and improving the rules governing world agricultural trade. The FTA also introduces some new concepts which will be useful in pursuing these common objectives, especially in regard to the measurement of the trade effects of domestic subsidy programs.[16] This undertaking, however, has not prevented Canada from pursuing objectives for agricultural trade in the Uruguay Round that are rather different from U.S. objectives.

Bilateralism vs. Multilateralism

As noted earlier, the Canada-U.S. Free Trade Agreement is not an alternative to GATT, but complements and extends GATT as between the two countries; and GATT will remain as a basic trade agreement between Canada and the United States. The two countries will, of course, extend tariff preferences to each other, which is an important element of the Agreement. Their MFN tariffs, where these apply, will be removed on each other's goods, but each country's separate tariffs will continue to be imposed on imports subject to duty from other countries, whether on an MFN basis, under special preferential schemes such as those for less developed countries, or otherwise. At the same time, exporters in both countries whose goods enjoy free and preferential access in the other market can be expected to exert pressure to retain their preferential access and to discourage the reduction of duties that apply on the other side of the border to similar goods from other sources. Canadian exporters may also tend to concentrate on the open, preferential U.S. market, and overlook broader international markets. In this way, pressures to maintain bilateral and preferential advantages and trade patterns in North America could work against trade liberalization on a global basis and weaken the multilateral trade system.

The Free Trade Agreement will likely give rise to balancing counterpressures. For example, Canadian producers of some goods are likely to press for reductions in Canada's tariffs on imports from third countries of machinery, components and other inputs in order to reduce their production costs and help them meet increased competition from the United States. Similar pressures could be exerted by U.S. producers for the reduction of U.S. tariffs on their imports of inputs from third countries. Consumer groups in both countries will doubtless continue to urge reductions in tariffs and other barriers to imports from third countries.

It may also be expected that other countries will be more amenable than in the past to the negotiation of reductions in their own tariffs to secure reductions in Canada and U.S. tariffs; this would reduce adverse effects of the preferential Canada-U.S. Agreement on their own export interests. In return, Canadian and U.S. policymakers may be more prepared to reduce tariffs against third countries if the FTA is seen as a way for domestic goods to become more competitive with imported goods.

So far, there has not been any groundswell of pressure to reduce tariffs on imports from third countries, although there is some support in academic circles for some form of common external tariffs. As provided for in the FTA, however, there has already been one round of bilateral negotiations on accelerating tariff reduction schedules, effective 30 April 1990, and a second round is expected to be completed by 1 July 1991. As a result of the first round, scheduled reductions on over 400 tariff line items were accelerated.

On balance, it is difficult to make a convincing case that the FTA will stand in the way of global tariff liberalization. There are precedents, as well as theoretical reasons, for expecting the opposite to happen. Following the formation of regional, preferential groups in Europe, the member countries proceeded in three successive rounds of negotiations in GATT to bargain substantial reductions in their tariffs and other barriers to trade with outside countries, including Canada and the United States, at least for non-agricultural products.

As for the non-tariff elements of the Free Trade Agreement, some of these, as noted earlier, may provide useful models and precedents for the negotiation of multilateral arrangements in the areas concerned. This would, of course, require other GATT countries to accept the same kind of rules and disciplines that Canada and the United States have accepted under the FTA. Also, the experience gained in the Canada-U.S. negotiations has doubtless better equipped negotiators on both sides of the border to play leadership roles during the Uruguay Round to develop new or improved rules and arrangements on a global basis in a range of non-tariff areas.

There is no evidence to date that the Free Trade Agreement has changed or undermined the positive approaches and positions of either government towards strengthening and improving the GATT system. The bilateral Agreement, indeed, could well lead to a strengthening of the GATT system rather than work against it. The liberalization of trade in North America on a preferential basis could provide new incentives for dismantling trade barriers on a global basis. Over the past several decades a vast preferential tariff-free commercial system has grown up in Western Europe surrounding the European Community. On both sides of the Atlantic, pressures could now emerge for the elimination or reduction of trade preferences. Moreover, the current Uruguay Round of multilateral trade negotiations offers a framework to initiate such a process, as well as to pursue broader efforts to liberalize trade in goods and services on a global basis. Optimistically, the eventual outcome could be the complete removal of tariffs and many other barriers to trade, at least with respect to industrial products for the developed countries.

It is significant, in this regard, that the motivation for the bilateral Agreement was to create a more open trade and economic system between the two countries, not to insulate them from outside competition or to create an exclusive North American trading bloc. While crossborder trade is of immense importance to both countries, especially for Canada, each has a large stake in its trade and economic relations with other countries—governed in large part by commitments under GATT and other multilateral organizations. Neither country can afford to damage either its trade and economic relationships with Western Europe, Pacific Rim countries and other trading partners, or the multilateral systems within which these relationships are maintained. The prospect of a Canada-U.S. free trade area has thus not caused serious misgivings by outside countries; indeed their reaction to such an arrangement has been generally positive. For example, while the legislatures on both sides of the border were debating the terms of the FTA prior to ratification, the Director-General of GATT, Arthur Dunkel, in an address in Toronto, gave his support to the Free Trade Agreement as a contribution to efforts to further liberalize world trade on a global basis.[17] In June 1988, the leaders of the seven economic summit countries, meeting in Toronto, similarly expressed support for the Canada-U.S. Free Trade Agreement.[18]

A North American Free Trade Agreement

On 12 June 1991 in Toronto negotiators from Canada, the United States and Mexico began talks on a possible trilateral free trade agreement among the three North American countries. The objective is to complete negotiations by year's end.

It is not possible at this stage to determine either the kind of arrangement that may develop from the negotiations or, indeed, whether a trilateral agreement can be reached. What is clear is that there is a political commitment on all three sides to find an arrangement that would more closely integrate these three economies representing approximately 350 million people.

The process towards the trilateral negotiations began in June 1990 when United States President George Bush and Mexican President Carlos Salinas de Gortari declared in a joint statement in Washington "that a comprehensive free trade agreement is the best vehicle for achieving sustained economic growth and open markets in trade and investment." This statement was followed by a letter from President Salinas to his American counterpart on August 21st, which requested formally that bilateral trade negotiations be undertaken.

At the same time the federal government was considering Canada's options. Several months of internal study culminated with a recommendation by the Department of External Affairs and International Trade to the federal Cabinet that Canada participate in the talks. On 24 September 1991, Minister of International Trade John Crosbie announced that Canada was entering preliminary negotiations with the United States and Mexico. The next day, President Bush formally notified the U.S. Congress of his intention to commence free trade negotiations with Mexico. The statement included a reference to Canadian interests in the negotiations:

> I am hereby notifying the (Committees) of trade negotiations with Mexico. I also want to inform you that the Government of Canada has recently expressed a desire to participate in the negotiations, with a view to negotiating an agreement or agreements among all three countries. I welcome the opportunity to work with our two neighbours towards this end.

Preliminary negotiations among senior trade officials from the three countries began on October 18th in Houston, Texas. On 23 May 1991, the U.S. Congress gave formal approval to the Administration's request for "fast-track" negotiating authority for trilateral negotiations.[19] That was the last hurdle before formal negotiations could begin.

Canada's chief negotiator is John Weekes, a career diplomat who returned from Geneva in his capacity as Canada's ambassador to the Uruguay Round of the GATT to head the Canadian team. Across the table from Mr. Weekes are Emilio Blanco on the Mexican side, and Julius Katz, who will be representing the United States.

Conclusions

The Canada-United States Free Trade Agreement will complement but will not replace GATT as a basic trade agreement between the two countries, and GATT rules will continue to govern important areas of bilateral trade, as in the past. The Free Trade Agreement conforms to the GATT rules that govern the formation and operation of free trade areas, although member countries can be expected to raise problems that may be created for their own particular trade interests.

Canada and the United States will continue to maintain their own separate and distinct trade policies and relationships with third countries, as well as their independent membership in GATT. Both countries can be expected to play active, leadership roles in the Uruguay Round of multilateral trade negotiations under GATT, where the objectives of the two countries may well differ. The bilateral Agreement could set useful examples and precedents for global trade liberalization and for the strengthening of the GATT system; and it could provide new incentives for efforts during the Uruguay Round to reduce preferences with the world trade system and remove tariffs and other barriers on a global basis.

The Canada-U.S. Agreement could thus, on balance, create pressures to strengthen the GATT system, and not to weaken it. There is no evidence to date that the Agreement has changed or weakened the positive approaches and positions of either country towards strengthening, enlarging and improving the GATT system. Indeed, failure of the Free Trade Agreement to come into force would have been widely regarded in other countries as well as in Canada and the United States as a setback to efforts in the Uruguay Round to liberalize world trade on a global basis, and to strengthen and extend the GATT multilateral trade system.

Notes

1. On 30 October 1947, when Canada and the United States signed the General Agreement on Tariffs and Trade, they also signed a supplementary bilateral agreement to the effect that the 1938 trade agreement would "remain inoperative" as long as the two countries remained members of the GATT. (*Canada Treaty Series*, 1947, No. 27).

2. Article 1902 of the FTA allows each country to continue to apply its anti-dumping and countervailing duty laws, within the framework of GATT rules, to goods imported from the other side; Article 1906 calls for the development over a period of 5-7 years of "a substitute system of rules" for anti-dumping and countervailing duties to be applied to bilateral trade. Meanwhile, the GATT rules in these areas are also the subject of negotiations in the Uruguay Round.

3. Article 1801 of the FTA provides that disputes arising both out of the Agreement and the GATT can be settled in either forum "according to the rules of that forum, at the discretion of the complaining party"; however, the two processes cannot be used at the same time to deal with a particular dispute. Use of the GATT processes to deal with bilateral disputes arising from the operation of the FTA would, of course, require the agreement of the GATT members. In 1949, the GATT Contracting Parties declared that the determination of rights and obligations between governments arising under a bilateral agreement "is not a matter within the competence of the Contracting Parties"; but they also declared that it was within their competence "to determine whether or not action under such a bilateral agreement would or would not conflict with the provisions of the General Agreement." See *GATT, Basic Instruments and Selected Documents, Volume II*, Geneva, May, 1952, p. 11.

4. GATT Article XIX permits a member country to impose a "safeguard measure"

(i.e., to increase the tariff or impose quantitative restrictions) on an imported product, under specified conditions, if a surge in imports is causing or threatening serious injury to domestic producers of the product. Chapter 11 of the FTA sets out special rules for the application of such safeguard measures to bilateral trade. Among other things, any such safeguard measures cannot increase the tariff on a particular product beyond the prevailing MFN rate; and a safeguard action cannot last more than three years or beyond the end of the 10-year transition period. A safeguard measure imposed on a global basis cannot be applied to exports from the other country unless such exports are an important cause of injury to producers in the importing country. A dispute regarding the imposition of a safeguard measure on bilateral trade must, on the request of either side, be referred to an independent panel for "binding arbitration."

5. Under a GATT code on government procurement, concluded in 1979 as an outcome of the Tokyo Round, the signatory countries opened up purchases by specified lists of their federal government agencies to competition from firms in other signatory countries. Chapter 13 of the FTA extends these GATT commitments as they apply to Canada-U.S. trade. Chapter 13 does not change the lists of Canadian and U.S. federal departments and agencies that are covered by the GATT procurement code, but it lowers the threshold of purchases covered by the GATT code from about Cdn $238,000 to about Cdn $33,000. Chapter 13 also strengthens the rules of the GATT code relating to the "transparency" of federal government procurement practices.

6. GATT Article XVI prohibits the use of export subsidies on manufactured and industrial products, but not on agricultural products. Article 701 of the FTA prohibits export subsidies as well "on any agricultural goods . . . that are exported directly or indirectly to the territory of the other party."

7. See Chapter 6 of the FTA, by which the two countries essentially reaffirm their commitments under the GATT code on technical barriers to trade, concluded in 1979. Under this code, the signatories undertook not to use product standards and other such regulations as disguised obstacles to trade, and to work towards the development of internationally accepted standards. Chapter 6 of the FTA contains additional undertakings regarding the "transparency" of the practices Canadian and U.S. federal governments for the development of their standards and for testing methods. It does not call for the harmonization of Canadian and U.S. standards, although it requires that each country "to the greatest extent possible . . . shall make compatible its standards—related measures and procedures for product approval with those of the other Party."

8. The Declaration adopted by trade Ministers in September 1986 at their meeting at Punta del Este, Uruguay, sets out the objectives for negotiations in the Uruguay Round on trade in services and on the trade-related aspects of foreign investment and intellectual property. Descriptions of the FTA provisions regarding services and foreign direct investment are contained in articles by Murray G. Smith and A.E. Safarian in John Crispo, editor, *Free Trade: The Real Story*, Gage, Toronto, 1988. For a discussion of progress made during Uruguay in these areas, see Chapter 18.

9. The dispute settlement provisions of FTA Chapters 18 and 19 are examined in articles by L.H. Legault, Robert E. Hudec, Julius Katz, Debra P. Steger, Shirley A. Coffield, Richard G. Dearden and Gary N. Horlick and Debra A. Valentine in Donald M. McRae and Debra P. Steger, editors, *Understanding the Free Trade*

Agreement, (Proceedings of a Conference held at the University of Ottawa on 22 January 1988), Institute for Research on Public Policy, Halifax, 1988. It may be noted here that the Chapter 19 provisions in the FTA for judicial review of final determinations of anti-dumping and countervailing duties do not preclude either country from challenging decisions taken in the other country under GATT procedures.

10. The following extracts from GATT Article XXIV contain the key rules regarding the formation of free trade areas:

> "The contracting parties recognize the desirability of increasing freedom of trade by the development, through voluntary agreements, of closer integration between the economies of the countries parties to such agreements. They also recognize that the purpose . . . of a free-trade area should be to facilitate trade between the constituent territories and not to raise barriers to the trade of other contracting parties with such territories.
>
> Accordingly, the provisions of this Agreement shall not prevent, as between the territories of contracting parties, the formation of a free-trade area of the adoption of an interim agreement necessary for the formation of . . . a free-trade area; Provided that:
>
> • with respect to a free-trade area, or an interim agreement leading to the formation of a free-trade area, the duties and other regulations of commerce maintained in each of the constituent territories and applicable at the formation of such free-trade area or the adoption of such interim agreement to the trade of contracting parties not included in such area or not parties to such agreement shall not be higher or more restrictive than the corresponding duties and other regulations of commerce existing in the same constituent territories prior to the formation of the free-trade area, or interim agreement, as the case may be.
>
> For the purposes of this Agreement:
>
> • A free-trade area shall be understood to mean a group of two or more customs territories in which the duties and other restrictive regulations of commerce (except, where necessary, those permitted under Articles XI, XII, XIII, XIV, XV and XX) are eliminated on substantially all the trade between the constituent territories in products originating in such territories."

11. Article XXIV permits members of free trade areas to maintain quantitative restrictions on agricultural products where, in accordance with Article XI, these are necessary to support "governmental measures which operate . . . to restrict the quantities of the like domestic product permitted to be marketed or produced . . ."

12. The text of the U.S. waiver is in GATT, *Basic Instruments and Selected Documents, Third Supplement,* Geneva, June 1955, pp. 32-37.

13. See GATT Article XX (b) and (j) and Article XXI. Members of free trade areas may maintain the restrictions covered by these provisions on trade between themselves.

14. In August 1988 New Zealand and Australia signed a protocol to their 1983 Closer Economic Relations - Trade Agreement, by which they undertook to remove by 1 July 1990 all remaining tariffs, quantitative import restrictions and protective

export controls on bilateral trade, as well as to implement a range of other measures to liberalize their bilateral trade in goods and services. The New Zealand-Australia arrangement thus appears to conform fully with the requirements of GATT Article XXIV regarding the formation of free trade areas.

15. The FTA incorporates "rules of origin" which define these goods entitled to "free trade area" treatment when exported from one country to the other. Chapter 3 of the FTA requires that automotive products must incorporate 50 per cent of the "direct production costs" in one or other country, or both. Under the previous rules of the Automotive Agreement, 50 per cent of the "invoice price" needed to be incurred in Canada and/or the United States. The new rule is the equivalent of a 70 per cent requirement on the old basis. (See FTA Chapter 10). It is unclear, however, whether rules of origin for free trade areas fall under GATT rules.

16. Article 705 of the FTA calls for the elimination of Canadian import licences for wheat, barley and oats and their products, when U.S. grain support prices become equal to Canadian grain support levels. Annex 705.4 sets out methods for calculating support levels.

17. The GATT Director General gave support to the FTA in an address on 19 April 1988 to the International Business Council in Toronto.

18. The following is an excerpt from the "Economic Declaration" issued by the Toronto Economic Summit on 21 June 1988: "We strongly welcome the Free Trade Agreement between Canada and the USA . . . It is our policy that (this) development(s) . . . should support the open, multilateral trading system and catalyze the liberalizing impact of the Uruguay Round".

19. Under the U.S. system, constitutional authority to ratify international treaties negotiated by the Executive Branch rests with the Congress. The Congress has the authority to delay, alter or amend any such treaty. Under U.S. trade law, however, the Congress can allow the president "fast track" negotiating authority, which stipulates that there can be no amendments. In this situation congressional debate is restricted and brought to a conclusion with a simple yes-or-no vote. This authority had been extended to the Executive Branch for the negotiation of the Canada-United States Free Trade Agreement.

20

Protection of the Environment and the Trade Rules

O ver recent years, a variety of measures have been put in place by national governments, at home and under international arrangements, aimed at controlling the use and transport of hazardous products, the safe disposal of toxic and other waste products, the protection of fresh water resources, the oceans and the atmosphere, the conservation of soil, forests and fisheries, the protection of endangered species, and for other environmental purposes. Many of these national and international measures involve direct or indirect restrictions on international trade; and in some cases, these environment-related trade restrictions have given rise to questions about their compatibility with the rules of the General Agreement on Tariffs and Trade (GATT), whose membership now exceeds 100, and several conflicts among GATT member countries have arisen from the use of environment-related trade restrictions.

Growing concern about environmental issues is likely to lead to an increase in domestic and international measures for environmental protection. These measures, in turn, will create a need for continued attention to the effects of such measures on world trade. The objectives of environmental protection and the liberal trade system embodied in GATT need not be in conflict. But it seems important that officials of national governments and the international institutions concerned with environmental protection should be aware of, and sensitive to, the GATT principles and rules for international trade. It will be equally important that governmental and international officials concerned with trade matters should be aware of, and sensitive to, the purposes and objectives of domestic and international measures for environmental protection.

There are three sections to this chapter. The first is a summary review of the GATT rules and principles as they relate to the trade effects of measures adopted by governments for health, safety, conservation and other environmental purposes. This section is followed by a list of international measures for environmental protection, some of which may have effects on international trade. The chapter concludes pointing to the need for continued attention to the interface between measures and arrangement for environmental protection and the rules and arrangements governing international trade.

The GATT Rules and Principles

In broad terms, the GATT rules and principles are designed to reduce barriers to world trade, to eliminate discrimination, to assist the resolution of trade disputes, and to encourage co-operation in trade matters among GATT member countries. The original articles of the General Agreement have been maintained virtually without change since they were drawn up in 1947, but have been elaborated and extended by means of ancillary codes and supplementary agreements, notably those which emerged from the Tokyo Round of multilateral negotiations in the mid-1970s. The current Uruguay Round of negotiations, launched in 1986 at a meeting of trade Ministers in Punta del Este, Uruguay, is designed to reduce further tariffs and non-tariff barriers to world trade, and to extend and elaborate further the rules of GATT, including extending these rules into the area of trade in services and the trade-related aspects of intellectual property and foreign investment. There are no items on the Uruguay Round agenda that explicitly relate to environmental issues, but the outcome of the negotiations, like the General Agreement itself, can have an impact on domestic and multilateral measures by governments to protect the environment.

It should be noted that the General Agreement represents contractual undertakings by member governments, in contrast to less binding arrangements and guidelines concluded, for example, in the Organization for Economic Cooperation and Development (OECD).

From an environmental perspective, there are a number of relevant GATT rules and principles. First, there is the prohibition of quantitative restrictions on imports or exports, as set out in Article XI. There are, however, a number of exceptions to this rule, notably those set out in Article XX. (Articles XI and XX are to be found in Annex 1). These exceptions, for example, permit restrictions on imports and exports which are "necessary to protect human, animal or plant life and health," as well as restrictions "relating to the conservation of exhaustible natural resources if such measures are made effective in conjunction with restrictions on domestic production or consumption." Further, such measures must not be disguised restrictions on international trade.

These provisions of Article XX can be invoked to justify a wide range of restrictions on trade in hazardous and toxic products, for the protection of endangered species, to conserve fisheries in territorial waters or the high seas, to conserve fresh water resources and for other environmental reasons. The Article serves to ensure that the GATT rules do not prevent governments from pursuing needed environmental, health and conservation policies.

Secondly, where trade restrictions are adopted, they must be on a non-discriminatory basis, as required by Article I, except where departures from this principle may be justified among members of free trade areas and customs unions, as provided for under Article XXIV. Moreover, under Article III, imported products must be accorded "national treatment," for example, in regard to domestic taxes and regulations. This rule does not require the importing country to accord them the same treatment as in the exporting country but only to treat them the same as domestic products in the importing country once they are imported. Finally, Article X requires that all trade measures by national governments be made public.

To date there has been little consideration in GATT of the links between environmental measures and the GATT rules. The only formal discussion of these links took place in 1971, when the GATT Contracting Parties established a "standby group" which could examine upon request "any specific matter relevant to the trade policy aspects of measures to control pollution and protect human environment especially with regard to the application of the provisions of the General Agreement, taking into account the particular problems of developing countries." It does not appear that any matters have been referred to GATT pursuant to this decision, nor does it appear that the standby group has ever met.

Recent Trade Disputes Involving Environmental Measures

Many GATT members have long restricted the importation from certain countries of meat, fish and other food products for health reasons; if these were challenged, the restrictions were justified as consistent with GATT Article XX. What is significant about recent trade disputes involving environment- and health-related trade measures is the fine line between legitimate health and environmental standards and new forms of non-tariff barriers. The following are case studies that illustrate the arguments that develop on both sides of this fine line.

(a) European Community Ban of Hormone-Fed Livestock

In 1987, the European Community banned the importation of meat treated with hormones, arguing that this measure to protect their citizens' health is in accord with the exceptions set out in GATT Article XX. The United States, however, countered, arguing that since there is a lack of scientific evidence on the effects of hormone-fed livestock on humans, the EC directive represented an unnecessary barrier to trade, particularly for U.S. beef exports. The EC refused the U.S. request to test its claim under the dispute settlement provisions of the Standards Code. The United States retaliated on 1 January 1989 by increasing unilaterally tariffs on certain EC goods. After several meetings, both sides agreed to consultations under the general disputes resolution provisions of Article XXIII.

(b) Canadian Fish Landing Requirements

In April 1986, the United States Trade Representative (USTR) initiated a Section 301 investigation into Canada's export ban on unprocessed Pacific salmon and herring. In March 1988, the GATT panel concluded that this practice was contrary to Article XI(1) of the GATT. Canada responded by replacing its export ban with a policy of a landing requirement.

In response to Canada's replacement measures, in early 1989 the USTR continued its 301 investigation. It concluded that Canadian regulations violated U.S. rights and threatened retaliatory action. Canada responded by claiming its landing requirements were in accord with Article XX(g) that allows for conservation measures for exhaustible natural resources; under this new rationale, Canada argued that its policy should remain in place.

The United States continued to disagree, arguing that the real rationale for Canadian regulations was the protection of jobs rather than resource management. The United States requested consultations under the Chapter 18 dispute panel procedures of the Canada-United States Free Trade Agreement (FTA) and suspended retaliatory action until after a panel decision.

In its report, the panel argued that a 100 per cent landing requirement was a restriction on Canada's obligations under GATT Article XI(1) and incompatible with Article 407 of the FTA. It then went further than normal GATT panels in providing an interpretation of GATT Article XX(g): that a 80-90 per cent landing requirement could be acceptable as a conservation measure.

Both governments claimed victory, although the interests most affected—fish processors on both sides of the border—each claimed defeat. Between September 1989, when the panel report was issued, and March 1990, negotiations proceeded to find an acceptable compromise. The final agreement allows U.S. fish packers access to 20 per cent of Canada's salmon and herring catch in 1990, and 25 per cent in each of the following three years, at the end of which the Commission will review the issue.

(c) Size of Canadian lobsters

Certain provisions in the U.S. Magnuson Fishery Conservation and Management Act restrict the inter-state sale and transport of lobsters below a certain size. There are more lenient size restrictions in Canada because the waters around Prince Edward Island are warmer than those off the coast of Maine, which results in lobsters that begin spawning at a much early stage of development. Amendments to the Magnuson Act in December 1989 banned the importation of the smaller-sized Canadian lobsters. Canada responded by requesting a Chapter 18 panel review of the consistency of the new law with Article 407 of the FTA, which incorporates GATT Article XI. If the panel determined that the U.S. measures violate the Article, the panel was asked to determine whether the measures could be considered as an exception under Article 1201 of the FTA, which incorporates GATT Article XX.

The panel failed to reach an unanimous decision. The majority ruled that the U.S. regulations were acceptable because the law applied to both imported and domestic lobsters; as such, they did not constitute a restrictive border measure. The majority opinion also contended that the issue should more appropriately be dealt with under Article III, but gave no ruling on this because this Article was not placed before the Commission. The minority report argued that the regulations conflicted with Article XI and violated Article XX(g) since they were intended primarily for conservation reasons.

Unlike the fish landing case, the panel did not suggest a compromise solution. The Commission decided not to adopt the panel findings, but rather attempt to reach a solution through consultation among industry representatives on both sides of the border. In July 1990, both industries agreed that the U.S. minimum size requirement could be applied to Canadian imports and that size increases planned for the next three years should be postponed. The effect is that Canadian lobsters of a certain size are not permitted into the United States, but are sold within Canada and in third markets.

(d) Softwood Lumber Case

In both 1983 and 1986, the U.S. International Trade Administration ruled countervail investigations into alleged government subsidies in the production of Canadian softwood lumber exported to the United States. In a preliminary determination, the United States concluded that provincial stumpage fees were considered to be lower than fair market value which, when combined with the supposed preferential treatment by the provincial government in the allocation of stumpage licenses, constituted a subsidy. The Canadian government responded to the allegations by arguing that the stumpage fees could not be considered as a subsidy under GATT Article XVI. Canada also argued that these fees were consistent with the management of the resources, as determined by Canadian governments, and that the lower cost of processing and harvesting Canadian softwood lumber reflected Canada's comparative advantage. To avoid countervail duties, Canada agreed to either allow provinces to raise stumpage fees or impose an export charge equivalent to the amount of subsidy as determined by the United States.

(e) U.S. Superfund Legislation

In 1986, the United States instituted the U.S. Superfund Amendments and Reauthorization Act, which sought to change revenue sources to finance government initiatives with respect to hazardous waste. Included in the Act were provisions to: increase taxes on petroleum; re-impose a tax on certain chemicals; and introduce a new tax on certain imported substances produced or manufactured with chemicals subject to the tax on certain chemicals.

Canada, the EC and Mexico responded to this initiative by requesting a GATT panel investigate the higher tax rate on petroleum imports relative to domestic products. The panel ruled that the tax on petroleum was inconsistent with Article III(2)—i.e., national treatment principles.[1]

(f) Export of Domestically-Prohibited Chemicals

Several developing countries have pressed for the adoption of GATT rules on the trade of products such as pesticides or herbicides, whose use is prohibited in the country of export. These countries argue they require these rules because: they lack knowledge about prohibitions or restrictions on the use of these products in the exporting countries; they face difficulties in enforcing controls at their borders; and they lack adequate domestic regulations to control the use of these products.

The Uruguay Round negotiations have attempted to deal with this issue by building on the 1982 Ministerial decision that GATT members endeavour to:

> to the maximum extent feasible, notify GATT of any goods produced
> and exported by them but banned by their national authorities for sale
> on their domestic markets on grounds of human health and safety.

The GATT Council established a working group in July 1989 to examine the need for new disciplines to regulate the exportation of domestically-prohibited goods and the trade-related aspects of the disposal of toxic waste. In Brussels in December 1990, the chairman of the group reported that a draft

Decision on Products Banned or Severely Restricted in the Domestic Market was being considered. The objective of the report was to ensure that at least one international organization was responsible for the trade of domestically-prohibited goods. Completion of the draft, however, was stalled by one member who reversed its position. Completion of the group's work was then extended until March 1991 and remains unresolved.

From the above, it is clear that GATT is already involved in a number of trade issues involving measures adopted by governments for environmental and health reasons. It seems likely that the adoption of such measures, nationally and internationally, will give rise to further debate and conflict among GATT member countries. It is worth noting, however, that many such measures have not been challenged, presumably because of general recognition that they were consistent with the exceptions set out in Article XX.

The Uruguay Round

As noted earlier, the Uruguay Round began with an agenda that did not include any issues that related directly and explicitly to environmental protection. However, at the February 1991 Council meeting, Austria, on behalf of the EFTA countries, announced that it had requested that the 1971 Working Party on Environmental Measures and International Trade be convened. Noting the variety in environmental policies among contracting parties, Austria suggested that the differences "could set the stage for trade disputes." Austria emphasized the need for greater understanding of the increasing linkages between environmental policies and trade disputes and suggested the GATT consider proposals to be submitted to the 1992 United Nations Conference on Environment and Development.

> Today, no one can say with any certainty exactly what the interlinks between environmental policies and trade are. A great deal of technical work needs to be done before we can say with any certainty that we have a reasonable appreciation of the problems that may arise from a trade policy point of view. Only then can we start discussing what conclusions to draw, to strike a balance between different interest in this area. Understandably, therefore, we feel that it is important to start studying the complex issues in the field of trade environment as soon as possible.

Members were divided on the appropriateness of the GATT getting involved in this area at this time. The EFTA proposal was supported by many delegations, including Canada, New Zealand, the European Community, Australia, Poland, Hungary, and Yugoslavia. Brazil agreed with the need for a greater understanding of the interlinks between environmental policies and trade, but suggested that consultations should precede any initiatives by the working group. The United States was more hesitant, arguing that more time was needed to study the proposal. Thailand, speaking for the ASEAN countries, agreed with the main thrust of the proposal but suggested that it would be inappropriate for GATT to address environmental problems as a general policy issue. India warned about the dangers of an over-extended GATT, particularly one dealing with non-trade issues such as health, education, and the environment. Chile stressed the importance of maintaining Article XX as an exception rather than its gradual evolution into a general rule. Others reserved judgment, questioning the appropriateness of the GATT as a forum for the consideration of such issues. This view was reinforced by the position of some that GATT should wait for the outcome of the 1992 UN Conference before proceeding further on this issue.

Regardless of any movement to reconvene the 1971 Working Party on Environmental Measures and International Trade, the further liberalization of world trade need not, in itself, have any adverse identifiable environmental effects. However, it could shift patterns of world production and consumption in ways which could affect the local and the global environment. For example, trade liberalization could shift certain industrial and agricultural production to countries that have a higher comparative advantage. This could lead to larger gains from international trade and raise living standards in both exporting and importing countries. This process would not imply any aggravation of the issues surrounding global sustainable development; indeed, it could lead to more efficient and rational use of the world's resources, and contribute to economic growth in developing countries.

The reduction of distortions and barriers in world agricultural trade, for example, would likely be beneficial from an environmental perspective. Among the results would be: a reduction of highly subsidized, uneconomic agricultural production in developed countries, which often makes intensive use of chemicals and pesticides; a more efficient, rational use of world agricultural resources; and a reduction in pressures for subsidized over-production on marginal agricultural land. The GATT negotiations also serve to facilitate the long-term harmonization of national sanitary and phytosanitary regulations and measures, on the basis of standards developed by relevant international organizations such as the International Plant Protection Convention.

Benefits could also arise from a reduction in barriers to trade in the growing sector of goods and services employed in pollution abatement and other environmental protection efforts. Reduction of barriers to trade in this sector could lead to a diffusion of technology and the reduction of costs involved in abating and controlling pollution on a global basis.

On the other hand, trade liberalization could shift production to "lower cost" regions, which may not have adequate measures to control adverse environmental effects, and could alter patterns of land use and also increase consumption of the products concerned. It is possible that these shifts in production and consumption patterns, unless accompanied by sound environmental practices, could, on balance, result in global environmental degradation.

The Uruguay Round agenda also includes negotiations on the trade-related aspects of intellectual property rights. The outcome of these negotiations is difficult to predict. The negotiations could lead to a broader adoption internationally of stronger standards and principles governing the protection of patents, trade marks, and copyrights. This outcome could also lead to a wider diffusion of advanced technology. From an environmental perspective, it seems important that the outcome not create new impediments to the production and use of goods, services and technology designed for the protection of health and for other environment-related purposes.

It is difficult to identify any potential environmental implications in the negotiations on the trade-related aspects of foreign investment, again assuming sound environmental practices in host countries. These negotiations are generally aimed at reducing barriers to the flow of international investment, and limiting controls by host countries that require foreign investors to engage in non-economic production and marketing. If successful, the outcome could promote more rational, efficient use of resources and an increase in the gains from trade for the countries concerned.

International Measures for Environmental Protection

Below is a list of multilateral environmental treaties, conventions and agreements, as of December 1990. Not all have evident effects on the pattern of world production, consumption or trade; but the list demonstrates the extent of environmental co-operation already in place among countries. The list will undoubtedly continue to grow in the light of increasing recognition of critical issues facing the global environment, and the need for co-operation among governments to deal with these issues. This is particularly the case as governments prepare for the 1992 United Nations Conference on Environment and Development in Brazil.

Selected Multilateral Environmental Treaties, Conventions and Agreements

- OECD Guiding Principles Concerning International Economic Aspects of Environmental Policies

- Global Convention on the Transboundary Movement of Hazardous Waste

- Convention Concerning the Protection of the World Cultural and Natural Heritage

- Convention on Wetlands of International Importance Especially as Waterfowl Habitat (Ramsar)

- International Plant Protection Convention

- International Tropical Timber Agreement

- Convention on International Trade in Endangered Species of Wild Fauna and Flora (CITES)

- International Agreement on the Conservation of Polar Bears and their Habitat

- Interim Convention on the Conservation of North Pacific Fur Seals

- International Convention for the High Seas Fisheries of the North Pacific

- Convention for the International Council for the Exploration of the Sea

- Convention on the Future Multilateral Co-operation in the Northwest Atlantic Fisheries

- Convention for the Conservation of Salmon in North Atlantic Ocean

- International Convention for the Conservation of Atlantic Tunas

- Convention for the Prevention of Pollution of the Sea by Oil (OILPOL)

- Convention for the Prevention of Marine Pollution by Dumping of Wastes and other Matter

- Convention on the Continental Shelf

- Convention for the Protection of the Ozone Layer

- Convention on Long-Range Transboundary Air Pollution (LRTAP)

- The Antarctic Treaty

- Convention on the Prohibition of Military or any other Hostile Use of Environmental Modification Techniques

- Convention on the Prohibition of the Development, Production and Stockpiling of Bacteriological (Biological) and Toxic Weapons and their Destruction

- Treaty on Principles Governing the Activities of States in the Exploration and Use of Outer Space including the Moon and other Celestial Bodies

- Convention on the International Liability for Damage Caused by Space Objects

- Treaty on the Prohibition of the Emplacement of Nuclear Weapons of Mass Destruction on the Sea-bed and the Ocean Floor and in the Subsoil Thereof

- Treaty on the Non-Proliferation of Nuclear Weapons

- Convention on the Physical Protection of Nuclear Material

- Treaty Banning Nuclear Weapons Tests in the Atmosphere, in Outer Space and Under Water (Limited Test Ban)

- Montreal Protocol on Substances that Deplete the Ozone Layer

Conclusions

In considering the relationships between environmental quality and international trade, it is important to distinguish trade itself from the international regime of trading rules under GATT. Trade is the exchange of goods and services internationally; GATT is an international agreement and institution aimed at trade liberalization and co-operation.

Trade and the liberalization of trade need not, in themselves, have any direct effects on the environment, but may have environmental consequences because of resultant shifts in the international distribution of production and consumption. Of course, there is also the issue of the transportation of certain goods, such as petroleum, which can present environmental hazards. To the extent that freer trade leads production of a commodity to shift from a nation with strict environmental controls to one with more lenient controls—whose leniency may be reflected in a lower price in international markets—freer trade could promote both an increase in global environmental degradation and a shift in where it occurs.

The environmental consequences of freer trade need not, however, be unfavourable. Trade liberalization can involve placing limits on certain national policies that both restrict trade and degrade the environment. An example would be the conclusion of trade agreements that reduce agricultural subsidies in the industrial nations, which promote over-cultivation and degradation of marginal farmland. Moreover, trade expansion brings about general increases in wealth, and wealthier people and nations have tended to be more attentive to environmental quality.

At the same time, freer trade promotes increased production and consumption generally. Environmentally, this effect cuts both ways. When the production of environmentally destructive products is increased, the environment suffers; when the production of new advanced technologies for the mitigation of pollution, the recycling of materials, and the more efficient use of materials and energy is increased, the environment benefits.

The effects of international trade on the environment, then, are complex and can go in several directions. Simple denunciations of international trade as intrinsically destructive of the environment—such as are implied by the common assertion that environmental sustainability requires "local self-reliance"—are simply not tenable. Nor are sanguine assertions that the environmental effects of trade are always benign. Different goods, traded in different markets, under different conditions, have different environmental effects. Some may require regulation or even prohibition; others should be promoted to the greatest extent possible. Specific analysis of the positive and negative effects of trade and its liberalization is needed for various sectors, goods and markets. Such analysis must be both exact and even-handed and must include the admittedly difficult procedures for internalizing the environmental costs of goods.

In considering the regulation or control of some kinds of international trade for environmental purposes, careful attention should be paid to the international distributive implications both of trade and of its control. Trade in goods whose production brings local environmental degradation (e.g., minerals that leave tailings or stripped land behind) tends to send the pollution to the countries with resource-extractive economies—mostly, but not all, less developed countries. Some argue that this has led to an international division of labour in which the poor countries, which need export earnings too urgently to exercise environmental controls, become "pollution havens," while the developed countries obtain the benefits of the production without degrading their own environments.

The same argument applies to the movement of hazardous wastes from rich to poor countries for disposal. Imposing restrictions on such trade would benefit the environments of the developing countries that receive the hazardous waste, but would also reduce their earnings of foreign exchange. It may be that the governments concerned would regard such restrictions on their trade as unacceptable interference in their internal affairs. For example, the Basel Convention on trade in hazardous waste, which includes compulsory reporting requirements, but does not forbid the trade, represents an attempt to compromise on this issue. At the same time, the industrialized nations should not try to force the international division of labour to the opposite extreme; poor nations cannot be compelled to maintain a state of rustic environmental purity in order to protect the global environment.

Some international trade involves environmental effects that are global, not local. Here, the distributional implications are more complex. The Convention on Trade in Endangered Species reflects the view that all of humanity has an interest in the preservation of the elephant and other endangered species, not just the countries where they live. However, the burden of enforcement, and of foregone export earnings, falls on only a few countries. For example, the provision of a small legal ivory market under CITES has not provided a large enough transfer to equalize this burden.

Other international trade sectors have strong connections to the global atmospheric issues of the greenhouse effect and stratospheric ozone depletion—principally CFCs, coal, and petroleum. The Montreal Protocol attempts to use trade restrictions against non-signatories in order to keep CFC production from simply shifting to non-participating nations. Attempts to tighten the Protocol, however, have since been stalled by the complaints of several large developing countries—notably China and India—that the costs of giving up CFCs fall disproportionately on them, and that the industrial countries must share the burden.

The situation with fossil fuels is more complicated still. While international co-operation to reduce use of fossil fuels is imperative, the focus is likely to be on reducing consumption. Nevertheless, the effects of a 20 to 50 per cent reduction in world fossil fuel use would be huge and unequally borne. Unlike the case of controlling consumption, production and trade to reduce local environmental damages, however, the costs of reducing the consumption and production of petroleum would fall on both rich and poor countries.

In summary,

- The relationships between international trade and the environment are complex and multi-directional. There are certain environmental goals that are effectively pursued through prohibitions, restrictions, or taxation of international trade—but these may impose particularly large burdens on poor nations, which would have legitimate grounds for claiming compensation.

- The design of arrangements to protect health and the environment should be sensitive to the implications for international trade. However, the place to consider international measures to protect health and the environment is not in the GATT, but rather in separate institutions and agreements such as UNEP, the OECD, the Montreal Protocol, the CITES, and the Basel Convention. The GATT is a specialized body focusing on trade and lacks the expertise necessary to make sound international environmental policy; it should not be overloaded with responsibility for measures to protect the environment. The place to develop environmentally-motivated controls on international trade will be in separate agreements and institutions such as UNEP, the Montreal Protocol, the CITES, and the Basel Convention; but if these arrangements involve trade sanctions, the arrangements should be reviewed by the contracting parties.

- At the same time, the relationship between the GATT trade rules and measures to protect health and the environment raise complex issues that need further consideration in GATT. National and international arrangements to protect the environment should not provide cover for unnecessary or disguised barriers to international trade. Further, those responsible for negotiations aimed at trade liberalization and strengthening the trade rules should be sensitive to and recognize the environmental implications of trade arrangements, and avoid placing obstacles in the way of national and international arrangements to protect health and the environment.

Note

1. For more information on the case, see "The Greening of the GATT: Trade and Environment," working paper prepared by Carol Nelder-Corvari, Department of Finance, Government of Canada.

Annex 1

Article XI*
General Elimination of Quantitative Restrictions

1. No prohibitions or restrictions other than duties, taxes or other charges, whether made effective through quotas, import or export licences or other measures, shall be instituted or maintained by any contracting party on the importation of any product of the territory of any other contracting party or on the exportation or sale for export of any product destined for the territory of any other contracting party.

2. The provisions of paragraph 1 of this Article shall not extend to the following:

(a) Export prohibitions or restrictions temporarily applied to prevent or relieve critical shortages of foodstuffs or other products essential to the exporting contracting party;

(b) Import and export prohibitions or restrictions necessary to the application of standards or regulations for the classification, grading or marketing of commodities in international trade;

(c) Import restrictions on any agricultural or fisheries product, imported in any form,* necessary to the enforcement of governmental measures which operate:

(i) to restrict the quantities of the like domestic product permitted to be marketed or produced, or, if there is no substantial domestic production of the like product, of a domestic product for which the imported product can be directly substituted; or

(ii) to remove a temporary surplus of the like domestic product, or, if there is no substantial domestic production of the like product, of a domestic product for which the imported product can be directly substituted, by making the surplus available to certain groups of domestic consumers free of charge or at prices below the current market level; or

(iii) to restrict the quantities permitted to be produced of any animal product the production of which is directly dependent, wholly or mainly, on the imported commodity, if the domestic production of that commodity is relatively negligible.

Any contracting party applying restrictions on the importation of any product pursuant to sub-paragraph (c) of this paragraph shall give public notice of the total quantity or value of the product permitted to be imported during a specified future period and of an change in such quantity or value. Moreover, any restrictions applied under (i) above shall not be such as will reduce the total of imports relative to the total of domestic production, as compared with the proportion which might reasonably be expected to rule between the two in the absence of the restrictions. In determining this proportion, the contracting party shall pay due regard to the proportion prevailing during a previous representative period and to any special factors* which may have affected or may be affecting the trade in the product concerned.

Ad *Articles XI, XII, XII, XIV* and *XVIII*

Throughout Articles XI, XII, XIII, XIV and XVIII, the terms "import restrictions" or "export restrictions" include restrictions made effective through state-trading operations.

Ad *Article XI*

Paragraph 2 (c)

The term "in any form" in this paragraph covers the same products when in an early stage of processing and still perishable, which compete directly with the fresh product and if freely imported would tend to make the restriction on the fresh product ineffective.

Paragraph 2, last sub-paragraph

The term "special factors" includes changes in relative productive efficiency as between domestic and foreign producers, or as between different foreign producers, but not changes artificially brought about by means not permitted under the Agreement.

Article XX
General Exceptions

Subject to the requirement that such measures are not applied in a manner which would constitute a means of arbitrary or unjustifiable discrimination between countries where the same conditions prevail, or a disguised restriction on international trade, nothing in this Agreement shall be construed to prevent the adoption or enforcement by any contracting party of measures:

(*a*) necessary to protect public morals;

(*b*) necessary to protect human, animal or plant life or health;

(*c*) relating to the importation or exportation of gold or silver;

(*d*) necessary to secure compliance with laws or regulations which are not inconsistent with the provisions of this Agreement, including those relating to customs enforcement, the enforcement of monopolies operated under paragraph 4 of Article II and Article XVII, the protection of patents, trade marks and copyrights, and the prevention of deceptive practices;

(*e*) relating to the products of prison labour;

(*f*) imposed for the protection of national treasures of artistic, historic or archaeological value;

(*g*) relating to the conservation of exhaustible natural resources if such measures are made effective in conjunction with restrictions on domestic production or consumption;

(*h*) undertaken in pursuance of obligations under any intergovernmental commodity agreement which conforms to criteria submitted to the CONTRACTING PARTIES and not disapproved by them or which is itself so submitted and not so disapproved;*

(*i*) involving restrictions on exports of domestic materials necessary to ensure essential quantities of such materials to a domestic processing industry during periods when the domestic price of such materials is held below the world price as part of a governmental stabilization plan; *Provided* that such restrictions shall not operate to increase the exports of or the protection afforded to such domestic industry, and shall not depart from the provisions of this Agreement relating to non-discrimination;

(*j*) essential to the acquisition or distribution of products in general or local short supply; *Provided* that any such measures shall be consistent with the principle that all contracting parties are entitled to an equitable share of the international supply of such products, and that any such measures, which are inconsistent with the other provisions of this Agreement shall be discontinued as soon as the conditions giving rise to them have ceased to exist. The CONTRACTING PARTIES shall review the need for this sub-paragraph not later than 30 June 1960.

Key to Acronyms

ACP	African, Caribbean and Pacific (Countries)
ASEAN	Association of South-East Asian Nations
BP	British Preference
CAP	Common Agricultural Policy (European Economic Community)
CARICOM	Caribbean Common Market
CICT	Committee on International Commodity Trade (UN)
CMEA (=COMECON)	Council for Mutual Economic Assistance
COCOM	Coordinating Committee for Multilateral Export Controls
DISC	Domestic International Sales Corporation (US)
EC	European Community
ECE	Economic Commission for Europe (UN)
ECOSOC	Economic and Social Council (UN)
ECOWAS	Economic Community of West African States
EFTA	European Free Trade Association
EPU	European Payments Union
FAO	Food and Agriculture Organization
FIRA	Foreign Investment Review Agency
GATT	General Agreement on Tariffs and Trade
GNP	gross national product
GPT	General Preferential Tariff

GSP	Generalized System of Preferences
ICCICA	Interim Co-ordinating Committee for International Commodity Arrangements (UN)
ICITO	Interim Commission for the International Trade Organization
IMF	International Monetary Fund
IPC	Integrated Program for Commodities (UNCTAD)
ITO	International Trade Organization
LAFTA	Latin-American Free Trade Association
LAIA	Latin American Integration Association
LTA	Long-Term Arrangements (for Cotton Textiles)
MFA	Multifibre Arrangement
MFN	most-favoured nation
MTN	multilateral trade negotiations
NIC	newly industrialized countries
NIEO	New International Economic Order
OECD	Organisation for Economic Co-operation and Development
OEEC	Organization for European Economic Cooperation
OPEC	Organization of Petroleum Exporting Countries
OTC	Organization for Trade Cooperation
TCB	Textile and Clothing Board (Canadian)
TSB	Textile Surveillance Body (GATT)
UDEAC	Central African Customs and Economic Union (Union douanière et économique de l'Afrique centrale)
UN	United Nations
UNCTAD	United Nations Conference on Trade and Development

Bibliography

Aho, C. Michael and Bayard, Thomas O. "The 1980s: Twilight of the Open Trading System?" *The World Economy* 5 (December 1982): 379-406.

Annett, Douglas Rudyard. *British Preference in Canadian Commercial Policy.* Toronto: Ryerson Press, 1948.

Aubrey, H.G. *Atlantic Economic Cooperation: the Case of the OECD.* New York: Praeger for Council on Foreign Relations, 1967.

Balassa, Bela. *The Tokyo Round and the Developing Countries.* World Bank Staff Working Paper No. 370. Washington, D.C.: International Bank for Reconstruction and Development, 1980.

Balassa, Bela. "World Trade and the International Economy: Trends, Prospects and Policies." In *World Trade: Constraints and Opportunities in the 1980s.* Paris: Atlantic Institute for International Affairs, 1979.

Bergsten, C. Fred and Cline, William R. *Trade Policy in the 1980s.* Washington, D.C.: Institute for International Economics, 1982.

Biggs, Margaret A. *The Challenge: Adjust or Protect?* Ottawa: North-South Institute, 1980.

Blackhurst, Richard; Marian, Nicolas; and Tumlir, Jan. *Trade Liberalization, Protectionism, and Interdependence.* Geneva: GATT, 1977.

Blake, Gordon. *Customs Administration in Canada: An Essay in Tariff Technology.* Toronto: University of Toronto Press, 1957.

Brewer, Thomas L. "International Regulation of Restrictive Business Practices." *Journal of World Trade Law* 16 (March/April 1982): 108-18.

Brown, Christopher P. *The Political and Social Economy of Commodity Control*. New York: Praeger, 1980.

Brown, William Adams, Jr. *The United States and the Restoration of World Trade*. Washington, D.C.: The Brookings Institution, 1950.

Camps, Miriam and Diebold, William. *The New Multilateralism: Can the World Trading System Be Saved?* New York: Council on Foreign Relations, 1983.

Canada. Canadian Trade and Tariffs Committee. *Review of Developments in the GATT Multilateral Trade Negotiations in Geneva*. Ottawa: The Committee, 1977.

Canada. Department of External Affairs. *Canadian Trade Policy for the 1980s: A Discussion Paper*. Ottawa: Minister of Supply and Services Canada, 1983.

Canada. Department of External Affairs. *Documents on Canadian External Relations, Vol. 12 (1946)*. Ottawa: Minister of Supply and Services, 1977.

Canada. Department of External Affairs. "Government Response to the Report of the Parliamentary Task Force on North-South Relations." Ottawa: The Department, 1981.

Canada. Department of External Affairs. *A Review of Canadian Trade Policy: A Background Document to Canadian Trade Policy for the 1980s*. Ottawa: Minister of Supply and Services Canada, 1983.

Canada. Department of External Affairs. *Statements and Speeches, No. 47/20*. Ottawa: The Department, 1947.

Canada. Department of External Affairs. *Summary of Canada's Bilateral Restraint Arrangements—Textiles and Clothing*. Ottawa: The Department, 1982.

Canada. Department of Finance. *Proposals on Import Policy: A Discussion Paper Proposing Changes to Canadian Import Legislation*. Ottawa: Minister of Supply and Services Canada, 1980.

Canada. Department of Industry, Trade and Commerce. *Canada's Trade Performance 1960–1977. Volume 1: General Developments*. Ottawa: Minister of Supply and Services Canada, 1978.

Canada. Office of the Coordinator for Multilateral Trade Negotiations. *Multilateral Trade Negotiations 1973–1979*. Ottawa: The Office, 1979.

Canada. Parliament. House of Commons. Standing Committee on Finance, Trade and Economic Affairs, Subcommittee on Import Policy. *Report on the Special Import Measures Act*. Ottawa: Minister of Supply and Services Canada, 1982.

Canada. Parliament. Senate. Standing Committee on Foreign Affairs. *Canada-United States Relations: Volume III, Canada's Trade Relations with the United States*. Ottawa: Minister of Supply and Services Canada, 1982.

Canada. Parliamentary Task Force on North-South Relations. *Report to the House of Commons on the Relations Between Developed and Developing Countries*. Ottawa: Minister of Supply and Services Canada, 1980.

Canada. Tariff Board. *A Report by the Tariff Board: Reference 161 Relating to the Re-instatement of the General Preferential Tariff on Imports of Rubber Footwear*. Ottawa: Minister of Supply and Services Canada, 1982.

Canada. Tariff Board. *A Report of an Inquiry by the Tariff Board Respecting the GATT Agreement on Customs Valuation. Part 1: Proposed Amendments to the Customs Act*. Ottawa: Minister of Supply and Services Canada, 1981.

Canada. Tariff Board. *A Report of an Inquiry by the Tariff Board Respecting the GATT*

Agreement on Customs Valuation. Part 2: Tariff Adjustments. Ottawa: Minister of Supply and Services Canada, 1983.

Canada. Textile and Clothing Board. *Clothing Inquiry: A Report to the Minister of Industry, Trade and Commerce.* Ottawa: The Board, 1977.

Canada. Textile and Clothing Board. *Textile and Clothing Inquiry: Report to the Minister of Industry, Trade and Commerce.* Vol. 1 and Vol. 2. Ottawa: Minister of Supply and Services Canada, 1980.

Caves, Richard E. and Jones, Ronald W. *World Trade and Payments: An Introduction.* 3d edition. Boston: Little, Brown, 1981.

Clark, M.G. "Canada-United States Trade Relations." *Canadian Business Review* 8 (Spring 1981): 48-52.

Coffey, Peter. *The External Economic Relations of the EEC.* London: Macmillan, 1976.

Cohn, Theodore. "Canada and the European Economic Community's Common Agricultural Policy: The Issue of Trade in Cheese." *Journal of European Integration* 1 (January 1978): 125-42.

Commonwealth Secretariat. *Protectionism: Threat to International Order. The Impact on Developing Countries.* London: The Secretariat, 1982.

Corbo, Vittorio and Havrylyshyn, Oli. *Canada's Trade Relations with Developing Countries: The Evolution of Export and Import Structures and Barriers to Trade in Canada.* Study prepared for the Economic Council of Canada. Ottawa: Minister of Supply and Services Canada, 1980.

Cuff, R.D. and Granatstein, J.L. *American Dollars—Canadian Prosperity: Canadian-American Economic Relations 1945–1950.* Toronto: Samuel-Stevens, 1978.

Curzon, Gerald. *Multilateral Commercial Diplomacy.* London: Michael Joseph, 1965.

Dam, Kenneth W. *The GATT: Law and International Economic Organization.* Chicago: University of Chicago Press, 1970.

Dauphin, Roma. *The Impact of Free Trade in Canada.* Study prepared for the Economic Council of Canada. Ottawa: Minister of Supply and Services Canada, 1978.

Diebold, William, Jr. *The End of the ITO.* Essays in International Finance No. 16. Princeton, N.J.: Princeton University Press, 1952.

Drummond, Ian M. *Canada's Trade with the Communist Countries of Eastern Europe.* Montreal: Private Planning Association of Canada, 1966.

Eastman, S. Mack. *Canada at Geneva: An Historical Survey and Its Lessons.* Toronto: Ryerson, 1946.

Economic Council of Canada. *For a Common Future: A Study of Canada's Relations with Developing Countries.* Ottawa: Minister of Supply and Services Canada, 1978.

Economic Council of Canada. *Looking Outward: A New Trade Strategy for Canada.* Ottawa: Minister of Supply and Services Canada, 1975.

Elliott, G.A. *Tariff Procedures and Trade Barriers: A Study of Indirect Protection in Canada and the United States.* Toronto: University of Toronto Press, 1955.

Ellis, L. Ethan. *Reciprocity, 1911: A Study in Canadian-American Relations.* New Haven, Conn.: Yale University Press, 1939.

Evans, John W. *The Kennedy Round in American Trade Policy: The Twilight of the GATT?* Cambridge, Mass.: Harvard University Press, 1971.

Finlayson, Jock A. and Zacher, Mark W. "The GATT and the Regulation of Trade

Barriers: Regime Dynamics and Functions." *International Organization* 35 (Autumn 1981): 561-602.

Finlayson, Jock A. and Zacher, Mark W. "International Trade Institutions and the North/South Dialogue." *International Journal* 36 (Autumn 1981): 732-65.

Fischer, Lewis A. "The Common Agricultural Policy of the EC: Its Impact on Canadian Agriculture." *Journal of European Integration* 3 (September 1979): 29-50.

Forbes, J.D.; Hughes, D.R.; and Warley, T.K. *Economic Intervention and Regulation in Canadian Agriculture.* Study prepared for the Economic Council of Canada and The Institute for Research on Public Policy. Ottawa: Minister of Supply and Services Canada, 1982.

Forrester, G.H. and Islam, M.S. "The Generalized System of Preferences and the Canadian General Preferential Tariff." Ottawa: Tariff Board, 1979.

Frank, Charles R., Jr. *Foreign Trade and Domestic Aid.* Washington, D.C.: The Brookings Institution, 1977.

Frank, Isaiah. "The 'Graduation' Issue for the LDCS." *Journal of World Trade Law* 13 (July-August 1979): 289-302.

Friesen, Connie M. *The Political Economy of East-West Trade.* New York: Praeger, 1976.

Gardner, Richard N. *Sterling-Dollar Diplomacy: The Origins and the Prospects of Our International Economic Order.* Expanded edition. New York: McGraw-Hill, 1969.

GATT. Analytical Index. 3d revision. Geneva: The Secretariat, 1970.

GATT. *Basic Instruments and Selected Documents, Volume 4.* Geneva: The Secretariat, 1969.

GATT. *GATT: What It Is, What It Does.* Geneva: The Secretariat, 1982.

GATT. *Trends in International Trade: Report by a Panel of Experts.* Geneva: GATT, 1958.

GATT. Director-General. *The Tokyo Round of Multilateral Trade Negotiations: Report* (1979) and *Supplementary Report* (1980). Geneva: The Secretariat.

Georgetown University Law Center. "Symposium on the Multilateral Trade Agreements." *Law and Policy in International Business* 11 (No. 4, 1979) and 12 (No. 1, 1980).

Golt, S. *The GATT Negotiations 1973–1975: A Guide to the Issues.* London: British-North America Committee, 1974.

Golt, S. *The GATT Negotiations 1973–1979: The Closing Stage. London: British-North America Committee, 1978.*

Gosovic, Branislav. *UNCTAD: Conflict and Compromise.* The Hague: A.W. Sijthoff-Leiden, 1971.

Granatstein, J.L. *A Man of Influence: Norman A. Robertson and Canadian Statecraft 1929–1968.* Ottawa: Deneau, 1981.

Grey, Rodney de C. *The Development of the Canadian Anti-dumping System.* Montreal: Private Planning Association of Canada, 1973.

Grey, Rodney de C. "The General Agreement After the Tokyo Round." In John Quinn and Philip Slayton, eds., *Non-Tariff Barriers After the Tokyo Round,* pp. 3-18. Montreal: The Institute for Research on Public Policy, 1982.

Grey, Rodney de C. *Trade Policy in the 1980s: An Agenda for Canadian-U.S. Relations.* Montreal: C.D. Howe Institute, 1981.

Grey, Rodney de C. *United States Trade Policy Legislation: A Canadian View.* Montreal: The Institute for Research on Public Policy, 1982.

Haviland, William E. *International Commodity Agreements.* Montreal: Private Planning Association of Canada, 1963.

Hawkins, Harry C. *Commercial Treaties and Agreements; Principles and Practice.* New York: Rinehart, 1951.

Hay, Keith A.J. and Lovatt, Masako Oashi. *Canadian Food for Japan.* A study prepared for the Canada-Japan Trade Council. Ottawa: Econolynx International, 1983.

Helleiner, G.K. *et al. Towards a New Bretton Woods: Challenges for the World Financial and Trading System.* London: Commonwealth Secretariat, 1983.

Henderson, Michael. "The OECD as an Instrument of National Policy." *International Journal* 36 (Autumn 1981): 793-814.

Hudek, Robert E. *The GATT Legal System and World Trade Diplomacy.* New York: Praeger, 1975.

Hufbauer, G.C.; Erb, J. Shelton; and Starr, H.P. "The GATT Codes and the Unconditional Most-Favored-Nation Principle." *Law and Policy in International Business* 12 (No. 1, 1980): 59-93.

Independent Commission on International Development Issues. Willy Brandt, Chairman. *North-South: A Programme for Survival.* London: Pan Books, 1980.

Jackson, John H. "The Crumbling Institutions of the Liberal Trading System." *Journal of World Trade Law* 12 (March-April 1978): 93-106.

Jackson, John H. *World Trade and the Law of GATT.* Indianapolis: Bobbs-Merrill, 1969.

Jenkins, Glenn P. *Costs and Consequences of the New Protectionism: The Case of the Canadian Clothing Industry.* Ottawa: North-South Institute, 1980.

Johnston, Charles R., Jr. "United States Trade Agreements Act of 1979: Introductory Note." *International Legal Materials* 18 (September 1979): 1256-58.

Kock, Karin. *International Trade Policy and the GATT 1947–1967.* Stockholm: Almqvist and Wiksell, 1969.

Kostecki, M.M. *East-West Trade and the GATT System.* London: St. Martin's Press for Trade Policy Research Centre, 1978.

Krauss, Melvyn B. *The New Protectionism: The Welfare State and International Trade.* New York: International Center for Economic Policy Studies, 1978.

Labib, H. and Ritter, A. "Stabilizing the International Copper Market: The Viability and Impacts of Alternate Market Management Arrangements." *Canadian Journal of Development Studies* 2 (1981): 70-115.

Law, Alton D. *International Commodity Agreements: Setting, Performance, and Prospects.* Lexington, Mass.: Lexington Books, 1975.

Lazar, Fred. *The New Protectionism: Non-Tariff Barriers and Their Effects on Canada.* Toronto: James Lorimer for Canadian Institute for Economic Policy, 1981.

League of Nations. *Commercial Policy in the Interwar Period: International Proposals and National Policies.* Geneva: The Secretariat, 1942.

League of Nations. *Commercial Policy in the Post-War World: Report of the Economic and Financial Committees.* Geneva: The Secretariat, 1945.

Letiche, John M. *Reciprocal Trade Agreements in the World Economy.* New York: King's Crown Press, 1948.

MacBean, Alasdair. *A Positive Approach to the International Economic Order. Part I: Trade and Structural Adjustment.* London: British-North American Committee, 1978.

Mackintosh, W.A. *The Economic Background of Dominion-Provincial Relations.* Study prepared for the Royal Commission on Dominion-Provincial Relations. Ottawa: King's Printer, 1939.

Masters, Donald C. *The Reciprocity Treaty of 1854.* Toronto: McClelland and Stewart, 1963.

McDiarmid, Orville John. *Commercial Policy in the Canadian Economy.* Cambridge, Mass.: Harvard University Press, 1946.

McMillan, Carl H. *Canada's Postwar Economic Relations with the U.S.S.R.: An Appraisal.* Ottawa: Carleton University, Institute of Soviet and East European Studies, 1980.

Moroz, A.R. and Back, K.J. "Prospects for a Canada-United States Bilateral Free Trade Agreement: The Other Side of the Fence." *International Journal* 36 (Autumn 1981): 827-50.

Myrdal, Gunnar. "Twenty Years of the United Nations Economic Commission for Europe." *International Organization* 22 (Summer 1968(L 617-28.

Nadeau, Bertrand. "L'entrée de la Grande-Bretagne dans le marché commun et les exportations agricoles du Canada à ce pays." Research essay prepared at The Norman Paterson School of International Affairs. Ottawa: Carleton University, 1983.

Nappi, Carmine. *Commodity Market Controls: A Historical Review.* Lexington, Mass.: D.C. Heath, 1979.

Nelson, Douglas R. *The Political Structure of the New Protectionism.* World Bank Staff Working Paper No. 471. Washington, D.C.: International Bank for Reconstruction and Development, 1981.

Nicol, Davidson; Echeverria, Luis; and Peccei, Aurelio, eds. *Regionalism and the New International Economic Order.* New York: Pergamon Press, 1981.

Nowzad, Barham. *The Rise in Protectionism.* IMF Pamphlet Series No. 24. Washington, D.C.: International Monetary Fund, 1978.

Office for Official Publications of the European Communities. *The Agricultural Policy of the European Community.* 2d edition. Luxembourg: The Office, 1979.

Organisation for Economic Co-operation and Development. *Activities of OECD: Annual Reports by the Secretary-General.* Paris: OECD.

Organisation for Economic Co-operation and Development. *Policy Perspectives for International Trade and Economic Relations.* Report of the High Level Group on Trade and Related Problems to the Secretary-General of OECD. Paris: OECD, 1972.

Organization for European Economic Cooperation. *A Decade of Co-operation: Achievements and Prospects.* Ninth Annual Report of the OEEC.

Patterson, Gardner. *Discrimination in International Trade: The Policy Issues 1945–1965.* Princeton, N.J.: Princeton University Press, 1966.

Pearson, Charles and Salembier, Gerry. *Trade, Employment and Adjustment.* Montreal: The Institute for Research on Public Policy, 1983.

Perez-Guerrero, Manuel. *UNCTAD's Contribution to a Just and Durable Peace.* Geneva: Graduate Institute of International Studies, 1970.

Perlow, Gary H. "The Multilateral Supervision of International Trade: Has the Textiles

Experiment Worked?" *American Journal of International Law* 75 (January 1981): 93-133.

Pestieau, Caroline. *The Canadian Textile Policy: A Sectoral Trade Adjustment Strategy?* Montreal: C.D. Howe Research Institute, 1976.

Pestieau, Caroline. *The Sector Approach to Trade Negotiations: Canadian and U.S. Interests.* Montreal: C.D. Howe Research Institute, 1976.

Plumptre, A.F.W. *Three Decades of Decision: Canada and the World Monetary System, 1944–75.* Toronto: McClelland and Stewart, 1977.

Plumptre, Wynne. "Exports to the United States." In J. Douglas Gibson, ed., *Canada's Economy in a Changing World*, pp. 208-43. Toronto: Macmillan, 1948.

Pomeranz, Morton. "Toward a New International Order in Government Procurement." *Law and Policy in International Business* 11 (1979): 1263-1300.

Preeg, Ernest. *Traders and Diplomats: An Analysis of the Kennedy Round of Negotiations Under the General Agreement on Tariffs and Trade.* Washington, D.C.: The Brookings Institution, 1970.

Protheroe, David R. *Imports and Politics: Trade Decision Making in Canada, 1968–1979.* Montreal: The Institute for Research on Public Policy, 1980.

Reuber, Grant L. *Canada's Interest in the Trade Problems of Less-Developed Countries.* Montreal: Private Planning Association of Canada, 1964.

Robertson, Charles L. "The Creation of UNCTAD." In Robert W. Cox, ed., *International Organization: World Politics*, pp. 258-74. London: Macmillan, 1969.

Rothstein, Robert L. *Global Bargaining: UNCTAD and the Quest for a New International Economic Order.* Princeton, N.J.: Princeton University Press, 1979.

Sharp, Mitchell. "Introduction." In Philip E. Uren, ed., *East-West Trade*, pp. xiii-xvi. Toronto: Canadian Institute of International Affairs, 1966.

Sharp, Walter R. *The United Nations Economic and Social Council.* New York: Columbia University Press, 1969.

Stanford, J.S. "The Application of the Sherman Act to Conduct Outside the United States: A View from Abroad." *Cornell International Law Journal* 11 (Summer 1978): 195-214.

Stegemann, Klaus. *Canadian Non-Tariff Barriers to Trade.* Montreal: Private Planning Association of Canada, 1973.

Swann, Dennis. *The Economics of the Common Market* 2d edition. London: Penguin, 1972.

Trade Policy Research Centre. Advisory Group. *Towards an Open World Economy.* London: Macmillan for the Centre, 1972.

UNCTAD. *Protectionism and Structural Adjustment in the World Economy: Report by the UNCTAD Secretariat.* (TD/B/881). Geneva, 1982.

UNCTAD. Secretary-General. *Assessment of the Results of the Multilateral Trade Negotiations.* Part I (TD/B/778(12 February 1980; Part II (TD/B/778/Addition 1). Geneva.

United Nations. *Three Decades of the United Nations Economic Commission for Europe.* New York: U.N., 1978.

van Meerhaeghe, Marcel A. *A Handbook of International Economic Institutions.* The Hague: Martinus Nijhoff, 1980.

Veatch, Richard. *Canada and the League of Nations.* Toronto: University of Toronto Press, 1975.

Warley, T.K. *Agriculture in an Interdependent World: U.S. and Canadian Perspectives.* Montreal: Canadian-American Committee, 1977.

Wilcox, Clair. *A Charter for World Trade.* New York: Macmillan, 1949.

Wilgress, Dana. *Memoirs.* Toronto: Ryerson Press, 1967.

Wilgress, L.D. *Canada's Approach to Trade Negotiations.* Montreal: Private Planning Association of Canada, 1963.

Wilkinson, B.W. *Canada in a Changing World Economy.* Montreal: C.D. Howe Research Institute, 1980.

Wilson, Charles F. *Grain Marketing in Canada.* Winnipeg: Canadian International Grains Institute, 1979.

Winham, Gilbert R. "Bureaucratic Politics and Canadian Trade Negotiation." *International Journal* 34 (Winter 1978-1979): 64:90.

Wolf, Martin. *Adjustment Policies and Problems in Developed Countries.* World Bank Staff Working Paper No. 349. Washington, D.C.: International Bank for Reconstruction and Development, 1979.

Wonnacott, Ronald J. *Canada's Trade Options.* Study prepared for the Economic Council of Canada. Ottawa: Information Canada, 1975.

Young, John H. *Canadian Commercial Policy.* Study prepared for the Royal Commission on Canada's Economic Prospects. Ottawa: Queen's Printer, 1957.